RELIGIOUS MOVEMENTS IN MEDIEVAL INDIA

RELIGIOUS MOVEMENTS IN MEDIEVAL INDIA

Bhakti Creation of Alternative Spaces

REKHA PANDE

GYAN PUBLISHING HOUSE

NEW DELHI-110002

Religious Movements in Medieval India

ISBN: 81-212-0875-0

Published in 2005 in India by
Gyan Publishing House
5, Ansari Road, Darya Ganj, New Delhi-110002
Phones : 23282060, 23261060
Fax : (011) 23285914
E-mail : gyanbook@vsnl.com
Website : www.gyanbooks.com

Laser Typesetting at : Master Computers, Delhi
Printed at : Salasar Imaging System, Delhi

Dedicated to my Father
Major M.D. Tewari
for his humanism, honesty, integrity and idealism
and If I am able to pass even some of this to my children-
my elder son Sankalp
and my twins-Tarun and Varun,
I will consider my life a well lived one

Contents

Preface

Through out the long course of Indian history there have been a large number of religious movements which have sprung from time to time with varying degrees of impact. Historically the religious beliefs and practices of the Hindus were too divergent to constitute a coherent, monolith religious system that has been a part of the imagined image of Hinduism in modern times. This fundamental mismatch between the sacred literature and their modern readings set me off on this endeavour on a path of tracing the history of the Bhakti movement on its own terms. A historical gaze at Hinduism clearly points out, that to view this as a single religious system is not correct and a distortion of the heterogeneous religious practices which has become well entrenched in the academia and our mindset. This exercise has also spurred a school of revivalists who have adopted equally narrow readings by imputing categories into medieval India to present a purely spiritual past obscuring the diversities. Thus the exercise of finding the diversities of language, region, caste, gender and religion and their narratives in the Bhakti was a logical starting point.

Through out history alternate spaces have been created and Bhakti was one such effective medium. It was only in the 19th century that a monolith definition of Hinduism was given basing on textual constructions. The British perception of Hinduism was from the point of view of Christianity. In the divide between the Colonizer and the Colonized it was the western standards and Christianity which became the basis to evaluate Hinduism. There was an inability to view Hinduism on its own terms and conditions. Efforts were made to find notions of Christianity like monotheism, a salvation and notions of after life in Hinduism. Hinduism to the Colonial administration became an imagined religion of a vast majority of the population. This was a concept that never existed in the consciousness of the Indian people them selves. In the rise and flowering of the Bhakti Movement we glean a revealing luminosity on the heterogenous religious practices of the Indian people.

Hinduism can never be viewed as one monolith tradition or a unitary practice. Through out history there have been various independent reform movements which questioned the authority of the Vedas and created an alternative religious space through different modes and means and we find a great representative in the Bhakti movement. India witnessed significant socio-economic changes during the Medieval period giving rise to the emergence of new social groups which could not fit into traditional hierarchy. The Law books were ossified as they did not anticipate these changes which were engendered by large scale socio-economic transformations at a macro-level. The newly emerging social groups attempted to redefine their position and status with in the given traditional hierarchy and spearheaded a movement articulating their demands for restructuring the existing order. By declaring that God dwells in each individual and one could attain God through faith and devotion these saints brought religion to the downtrodden and henceforth marginalized sections of society. Religious movements acquire greater significance as they have a far reaching impact on society as a whole by penetrating even its ideological as well as pragmatic base.

Bhakti as a concept literally means devotion and surrender. For the common person the term is understood in terms of religious devotion only, devotion to a personal God, a God who is conceived as a supreme God for salvation.

The earliest form of devotion was characterized with different kinds of rituals and sacrifices in which Vedic mantras played a significant role. The Brahmans were in the forefront and they initiated all kinds of ceremonies. But gradually the aspect of ritualistic religion began to be overtaken by the concept of Upasana or Bhajana in which *Sraddha* (devotion or genuine regard) had a fundamental place. The importance of this spirit of *Sraddha* bhakti or respectful dependence upon God was considered as the first step in the scheme of bhakti cult. It is interesting to see that even in the Vedic times *Sraddha* bhakti made its influence felt in many directions. Under its wholesome impetus, the Vedic religion progressed from Polytheism to Monotheism, for bhakti essentially stands for broad comprehensive faith in one who is adored.

Though this doctrine is traced to the Brahmanical tradition, in the religious scripture of Gita, it was in the south between the seventh and tenth centuries; this movement became broad based and acquired a huge social support. The great bhakti tradition that began in South India had its origins from the Sangam period. Bhakti or devotion appears for the first time in the literary accounts like *paripadal* and *Tirumurukarappadai* as the central concept which was to be later developed more fully by the Alvars and Nayanars and elaborated in the Vaishnava and Saiva canonical texts of medieval times. It was the Acharyas who provided a philosophical basis for this movement.

Of the four ways of attaining God, Bhakti is considered easy and simple since it makes one, more accessible to God directly. It creates a space which gives way to personal kind of relationship with the Almighty or the Creator eliminating any intermediaries. This aspect of bhakti attracted large number of people who began to follow these paths to attain salvation and hence, this became popular among the masses from all social backgrounds. The doctrine of bhakti as well as its practice can be traced to remote antiquity and infact medieval thinkers constantly appealed to these sources to give a long historical past. Therefore historically Bhakti manifested itself as early as Vedic hymns, but gradually developed through the time till medieval period when it reached its climax. A new wave of emotionalism spurred by a longing for a personal god who was addressed in the vernaculars is one of the main features of medieval Bhakti and this appears as a response to the existing situation. Emerging from the southern regions, we find this movement spreading in North and thence to Bengal, Mahrashtra, Kashmir, Gujarat and Assam.

The Bhakti movement is a very good example of unity in diversity in Indian culture and a vibrant living tradition that is very much a part of our plural identity and rich cultural heritage. It is one of the strengths of Indian civilization to accommodate a wide variety of voices which to the outsider may seem contradictory, confounding, disorganised and illogical. It is in this rich tapestry of creativity that the many voices interact over time to produce many hybrid forms which keep the vibrancy of Indian civilization alive as they are responses to a wide variety of situations from the homestead, village to the regional and universal. Today our myopic readings of the past using singular frames of references has brought about rigidity in public life leading to communalism that are based on watertight compartmentalization of identities, rather than as a fluid view of the past which stands as a negation of all that the Bhakti saints stood for. Though this movement occurred in many parts of India over the centuries, there were many regional variations. Sustaining this vibrancy over a vast spatial and temporal canvas was a common thread running through out this movement exemplified in the ways of questioning the existing religious system and promoting socio-religious egalitarianism. The Bhakti saints wanted the religious space to open up and provide alternative spaces to the existing one.

The historical works on Hinduism written prior to the nineteenth century by western scholars did not mention the term bhakti. From the second half of the nineteenth century different theories were propounded on the character of the movement and its origins. H.H. Wilson first used the term Bhakti to denote Krishna bhakti of the Vaisnavas of Bengal. It was George Grierson who developed the idea of bhakti as a religion, a cult and a doctrine. Orientalists like William Jones, H.T. Colebrook, closely related to the, "Asiatic Society of India" looked back at the glory of the past and covered a wide range of themes in Sanskrit literature, on philosophy and Hindu religion in general. Theorization about Bhakti really started with the Orientalists who conjured up images of an exotic opulence and the othering of India commenced. European constructions of the varied images of Asia started within the context of imperialism as a binary opposite to demarcate the progressive and the backward. It was a period that saw a discourse of power which characterised a particular set of social, economic and political relations between Europe and its colonies. Many of the ideological texts transformed the ideals and normative values of ancient Indians as standard and this led to distortions of reality as there is a fundamental disconnectedness between the text and the context. The Orientalists created Hinduism in their own image. Most of their theoretical formulations were based on contemporary Christian reaction in Europe against explaining God in abstract and personal terms.

In many modern day writings also, the bhakti movement is treated as literary or at best an ideological phenomena which had religion at the basis of its inspiration and more works have been written about this movement by Literateurs than historians. This has mainly happened due to the lack of emphasis on social history and also the lack of analytical tools in history writing till the 1950's and hence the socio-economic factors that have been responsible for bringing in a change have been ignored. Since most of these saints were from marginalized groups and were composing and writing in the vernacular literature in an oral tradition which was passed down from generations, there is a major problem of sources for the historian as these text presupposed an oral consciousness that is improperly translated when we print the same and is only now being recognized with the interest in consciousness studies. There is very little historical information on these saints and they were not patronized by any kings or court biographers and therefore were outside the established system. Nor is any religious hagiography available about them from the time they deemed to have inhabited. Much of their history has been reconstructed much later by writers and biographers arising from the emerging anglicized middle class. Yet most of these saints are very much alive in the popular culture and the day to day life of India in different regions and are the most important link to the continuities between past and present in Indian culture.

Over the centuries, the transformation of the oral tradition into a textual one saw many accretions and these interpolations served to marginalize, domesticate or valourise certain events and personalties using a plethora of devices but it is still possible for a historian to arrive at the essence of the texts by deconstructing the meanings using an array of methodological tools borrowed from different disciplines. The text is therefore seen in its historical context against the background of larger questions that conditioned the socio-economic and politico-cultural context rather than probing into the literary nuances and niceties since the focus is on broad socio-religious patterns.

There are multiple dynamics of any movement seen in the constant interplay of opposition and co-option and a gendered reading offers us such glimpses where we see alternating phases of radicalism and domestication. We see that bhakti created an alternative space for women by stressing that all were equal in the eyes of God and everyone could realize God. Thus, we had a large number of women who practiced Bhakti. There is a palpable tension that finally comes out in the divergent views of the women who were very outspoken and wanted to lead life on their own terms and conditions and the men who were not willing to provide this space to them, implying that they wanted reform to end at a certain point. While the women wanted to lead life as they pleased, the forces of reaction set in as it would deprive the men of their domestic dominance and these contradictory features manifested to reinforce and reiterate the already existing notions of women, family and their roles.

Doubts have been raised about this movement being a mass movement and if at all the label of movement can be applied to this vastly different streams and practices as they emerged in different parts of India. No doubt there were wide differences regarding the attitude of these saints to scriptures and their agendas of social reform and many of them especially the sagun Bhaktas never challenged the living conditions of the people and the over all aim of the movement was individual salvation and mystical union with God, through the help of a guru, yet it cannot be denied that they did question the existing hierarchies in their own way and were critical of many of the structures and institutions. Regional flavours and complexities only added to finding newer solutions to what was essentially a same problem and thus we find the substance of the Bhakti saints having a remarkable similarity.

A rationale for such a study is too obvious to need any justification for there are many conventional explanations that do not lead us to a holistic understanding of the Bhakti movement. Religion has always played a major role in the establishment of a cultural identity, which is firmly rooted in history. The abiding image of India today as a modern day nation ready to move on to the 21st century and yet rooted in tradition is primarily due to the presence of both old and new in multiple combinations. Socio-cultural continuitics and discontinuties resonate in India from the past to the present especially in the arena of religion and culture. The need to see the complex linkages between the large scale socio-economic changes in the Indian subcontinent and the contingent expression of religiosity as intertwined aspects without demarcating them into separate blocs was another need. There is also a need to read the sources in their context otherwise we would end up reading history backwards with an idea of fixed religious boundaries that are commonplace nowadays where as in the medieval period, socio-religious boundaries were being constantly redrawn. One only hopes that through this endeavour, it would be possible to bring out a vibrant tradition in all its complexities giving space to all facets and themes in history.

Rekha Pande

Acknowledgements

As a Feminist historian, interested in issues of religion and culture, the Bhakti Movement has always interested me as a very good example of India's unity in diversity and the continuities in Indian culture and civilization between the past and the present. While growing up I had always heard the Bhajans of Kabir and Mira, Surdas and other saint poets being played and sung at home. Even then and at present the songs of Mira, Surdas and Kabir sung by Neela Bhagvat and Subbalakshmi continue to stir and motivate me and bring about a soothing effect in the day to day life. Never did I imagine as a student that this could be an area of study. Today, I experience a fundamental disconnect between the Bhakti that we were schooled in and practiced at home to the anachronistic political readings of religion in contemporary India, which motivated me at some point or the other to embark on this exercise. This is a humble attempt to set the historical record straight by rehabilitating the vibrant traditions of Bhakti as practiced in different parts of the country in a language accessible to the lay person avoiding the hyperboles of jargonisation and excessive word play.

During the days of my graduation, I was slowly drawn and eventually became interested in Religious and Cultural history especially the Bhakti movement. For this I cannot find words to thank my teachers in the University of Allahabad, Prof. Rekha Joshi, Prof. C.B. Tripathi, Prof. Radhey Shyam, Prof. Chandra Pant and Prof. Farooqi who inculcated a deep love for medieval history. Sitting in those class rooms one was transported back to the medieval times when this history was being made. The love inculcated for history from those days has always been a major source of inspiration. I recollect with fond remembrance the class lectures by Prof. Tripathi on the Bhakti movement. The various discussions which we had related to Bhakti movement always remained fresh in my mind including the recital of many of these songs sung by the saint poets. I was very much influenced by the fact that here was a movement which arose from the lower sections of society and could challenge a religious system which was well established. That it provided a little space to women was an added attraction of this movement. I am deeply indebted to all my teachers in the University of Allahabad for opening my eyes to such a fascinating movement.

As I joined the University of Hyderabad and taught courses related to Religion, Culture and society of India this interest continued to grow. Recently when I started teaching a course on Religion, Society and Cultural heritage of India to the students of International Institute of Information Technology (IIIT), the pointed questions I had in class and the various discussions which followed emphasized on how this movement can be of relevance today in the modern day scenario when religious spaces were getting restricted. This book is an effort to answer some of the questions with which I am attempting to grapple as a historian interested in Women's issues for the last three decades. I am highly indebted to my students, all of whom I cannot name in the University of Hyderabad and the International Institute of Information Technology (IIIT), for keeping my interest alive in this theme.

I like to thank my students, Dr. A. Padma and Dr. B. Lavanya for helping me with the Telugu translations. I also acknowledge the assistance provided by P.S. Harish. They are all very enthusiastic about their work and I sincerely hope all of them will carry forward this love of history in their future works. I owe a lot of debt to my various friends, working in different disciplines and in the Department with whom I can always discuss and share many thoughts.

I extend my thanks to Prof. Jaganathan, a renowned Prof. of chemistry, who is well versed with Shri Vaishnavism, his second love, its philosophy and literature and shared his knowledge with me. I would also like to thank Dr. Suruchi, from the Department of Sociology, and Marsha Henry from the College of Social work, University of Bristol, U.K. who had the patience to sit with me for hours discussing the various nuances of the movement and making me see things differently.

I would like to thank Prof. Gopeshwar Singh from the Department of Hindi, Delhi University for spending a lot of time with me and explaining the Bhakti literature. To him I owe a lot of gratitude for sharing many of his books of Hindi literature. I also would like to acknowledge the help received from a young research scholar, who not only shares my interest and passion for Bhakti literature but also shares my name, Rekha Pandey, for introducing me to the books of Hindi literature and giving insight into the poetry of the saints.

I, especially like to thank Dr. M.N.Rajesh from the Department of History, University of Hyderabad, for helping with all the computer know how and always being willing to find time for my work inspite of his busy schedule. He made me familiar with the literature in Tamil and has often translated a lot of this for my benefit. I am highly indebted to him for going through the rough draft of my book and suggesting valuable inputs.

I would also like to thank Mr. B.P. Garg of Gyan Publishers for bringing out this book in its present form.

I also like to acknowledge with gratitude the help given by Shaheen, who took care of my daily household chores and thus gave me enough time to concentrate on my academic work. But for her help in seeing that the house ran smoothly, I am not sure how far I would have been successful in carrying out my academic work.

Last but not least I like to thank my husband Dr. Suresh Pande, Principal Scientist, ICRISAT for his continuous support in all my activities. He has been the rock that has always stood firm behind all my achievements and efforts and I can always rely on his unflinching support. But for his efficient and programmed managing of the house and the children in my absence, my field trips could not have taken place. I would also like to mention my children Sankalp who assists me a lot with all the computer work and the twins, Tarun and Varun who managed well in my absence and never complained that I was out for too long and busy with my reading and writing. They have learnt to manage things and this has been a big comfort. They provided me the much needed diversion when things became too hectic.

Rekha Pande

1

Introduction

Beginning from the 7th century A.D. to the 18th century, Medieval India saw a phenomenal outpouring of religiosity in the vernacular oral traditions on themes ranging from dilemmas of every day life to the mysteries of the Universe. To the unlettered masses these were set in tune to produce soul stirring medley of melodies reflecting separation from the beloved, release from feudal and caste hierarchy and an imagined utopia that could be attained by devotion or Bhakti. The later centuries enshrined these words into texts which were a reflection of large scale social upheavals on the field, reflective of tensions in the society. These centuries saw a phenomenal increase in the production of religious literature and this ran parallel to the oral tradition. Scholars have focused on the analysis of the texts, philosophical constructs or the societal aspects enlightening us with many readings. While any one cannot be reduced to another, the study of Bhakti therefore demands a holistic and integrated approach drawing analytical tools from many disciplines.

The 19th century saw a rediscovery of many sacred texts that contributed to the construction of Hinduism as a monolith. The process of reducing orality to textuality saw the wholesale standardization of very vibrant, dynamic and diverse religious practices. In the confrontation between the Colonizer and the Colonized it was the western standards and Christianity which became the basis to evaluate Hinduism from a standpoint influenced by the print revolution which had swept contemporary Europe and did not take into account the consciousness of oral traditions of pre-Colonial India. There was an inability to view Hinduism on its own terms and conditions. Attempts were made to find notions of monotheism, a salvation and notions of after life of Christianity in Hinduism. Hinduism to the Colonial administration became an imagined religion of a vast majority of the population. This was something which never existed in the consciousness of the Indian people themselves but now has become internalized and the past is viewed using the category of Hinduism as a monolithic entity.

The transition from the Company's commercial activities to direct rule in the late 18th century also marked a period of colonial self questioning, with in the British society. It was in this long process that it made various political and ideological adjustments to justify its rescue of India. Many of the texts of this period represented India as a site of eastern decadence and despotism breeding corruption. It was also during this time that the first generation of British Civil servants of India like Sir William Jones and H.T. Colebrooke discovered an Indian classical past as a Hindu golden age or a pristine Aryan society which had fallen into decline and decadence. The goals of both these visions of India were to lead the way to the 19th century civilizing mission as the corner stone of British Empire (Singh, 1996, 53). The originator of this grand Imperial project was Warren Hastings, who himself represented a complex transition from merchant to ill starred empire builder like Robert Clive before him. When Hastings founded the Asiatic society, in 1784, the knowledge of Indian languages inaugurated a way to reading of the texts and literature of the orient. These scholars went at great length to show that the religion practiced by the Hindus was highly evolved and questioned the colonial assumption that all cultures outside the Christian pale were primitive, tribalistic and animistic. Many of these scholars did not try to understand what Hinduism meant to millions of Indians. They invariably made a distinction between the popular Hinduism which they did not deem worthy of study and the philosophical Hinduism which they tried to define as a set of hard and fast doctrinal propositions and to place in current theories about the nature of history of religions. In the process they created Hinduism in their own image (Marshall, 1970, 43). These scholars brought in a new concept of the Hindu golden age as a legacy for the rising Indian intelligentsia (Knopf, 1969, 31). This was quite in keeping with the evolution of a new historical consciousness among Indian's for recovering their forgotten past. (Kejariwal, 1988, 232). This western attribution of unity to Hinduism strategically helped the anti colonial Indians create a national identity in religion. For the Indian intellectuals intent on purifying Hinduism of its popular, idolatrous association, a newly defined religion could give them an identity compatible with modernity they craved, while retaining their roots in indigenous traditions (Visvanathan, 2003, 35, 36).

The work of integrating a vast collection of myths, beliefs, rituals and laws into a coherent religion and of shaping amorphous heritage into a rational faith known as, Hinduism" were endeavours initiated by Orientalists (Knopf, 1980, 495). The study of Hinduism by the west is a very good example of Orientalism, a term popularized by Said in a different context but meaning the western domination and exploitation of the east, the west viewing the east as an alien as" the other" and by extension as the decadent 'other'. Using Foucault's notion of 'discourse', as a system of possibilities, Said suggests that the effect of Orientalist discourse is, "to formulate the Orient, to give it shape, identity, definition with full recognition of its place in memory, its importance to imperial strategy, and its natural role as an appendage to Europe (Said, 1978, 86). Though many think that the choice of Orientalism is unfortunate on several counts and should not be limited to the west alone. It has been pointed out that if Orientalism can be defined as a manipulative historical gaze based on a crude separation between us and other and which denies the representation of this other any intrinsic voice, then there is little in the Muslim discourse about Hindu India which was less orientalist than what contemporary Europeans perceived and wrote (Rubies, 2002, 286).

Deriving largely from the Orientalist construction of Hinduism, the emergent national consciousness appropriated this definition of Hinduism and the heritage of Hindu culture. Hindu identity was defined by those who were part of this national consciousness primarily from the Brahmanical upper caste and thus Hinduism had a primary upper caste, Brahmin dominated identity and all the other different kinds of other religious identities did not find space in this reconstruction. The evolution of Hinduism is not a linear progression from a founder through an organizational system, with sects branching off. It is rather the mosaic of distinct cults, deities, sects, ideas and the adjusting, juxtaposing or distancing of these to the existing ones, the placement drawing not only on beliefs and ideas but also on the socio-economic reality (Thapar, 2004, 340-341).

The very term Hindu from which Hinduism is derived and which was taken over by the western administrators, scholars and merchants was the Persian variant of the Sanskrit Sindhu, the Indus River, a word applied already in the Avesta both to the river and the country through which the Indus flows. In the plural it denoted the population living in that region, the Indus people. In the 17th and 18th century the designation for the Hindus was Bania, though the dominant word in this period was, "Gentoo" (heathen) (Stietencron, 1991, 13). Over a period of time the term Hinduism were applied to all, high culture and religion in India, especially to that which was of Aryan, Brahmanical or Vedic origin (Frykenberg, 1991, 31). Such a view ignores what has now often been referred to as either "popular Hinduism", "temple Hinduism", "Bhakti Hinduism", "Village Hinduism", Tribal Hinduism" and other localist forms of Indian culture and religion (Frykenberg, 1991, 32). Even the use of the word 'sect' in the Indian context appears problematic as the word sect indicates a splittist tendency, whereas the word 'movements' may do fuller justice to the religious phenomena that we are discussing above.

Hinduism can never be viewed as one monolith tradition. Hinduism is polytheistic, monotheistic and monastic. Many Gods and Goddesses are worshipped, some of them in forms that are at a considerable distance from Sanskritic textual depictions. Visnu, Shiva and Devi are the principal deities but they have many forms and there are many more deities (Smith, 2003, 34). Through out history there have been various independent reform movements which questioned the authority of the Vedas and created an alternative religious space through various means. The Bhakti movement was one such movement in Medieval India. India witnessed significant socio-economic changes during the thirteenth century giving rise to new social groups which could not fit into traditional hierarchy. The newly emerging social groups, attempted to redefine their position and status with in the given traditional hierarchy and spearheaded a movement articulating their demands for restructuring the existing order. By declaring that God dwells in each individual and one could attain God through faith these saints brought religion to the downtrodden and henceforth marginalized sections of society. This movement is referred to as the Bhakti movement.

The word bhakti means devotion, participation, reverence or adoration and can be used in many contexts like a mother child relationship, wife and husband relationship and nation and individual relationship. For the common person the term is understood in terms of religious devotion only. The historical works on Hinduism written prior to the nineteenth century by western scholars did not mention this term. From the second half of the nineteenth century different theories were propounded on the movement and its origins. The word was first used by H.H. Wilson to denote Krishna bhakti of the Vaisnavas of Bengal. It was

George Grierson who developed the idea that bhakti is a religion, a cult and a doctrine. His authoritative first voice also led to the classification of languages.

Medieval period saw both Nigun (worship of a formless God) as well as Sagun (worship of a form) worship.

Earlier the bhakti movement was treated as literary or at best an ideological phenomena which has religion at the basis of its inspiration. This has mainly happened due to the lack of emphasis on social history and hence the socio-economic factors that have been responsible for bringing in a change have been ignored. History writing in India took a social turn in the 1960's that brought about a fresh understanding of bhakti not only as a religious movement but also as a social protest movement under the rubric of religion, since religion was one of the sanctioned ways of protest. This view has thus rehabilitated the bhakti saints and has broadened our vision of seeing them as men and women with a larger social consciousness than we had imagined and not purely as spiritual beings as was the earlier trend.

Far from being a literary or religious movement, bhakti was solely rooted to the ground and was a reflection of the aspirations of the newly emerging agrarian and artisanal groups whose economic position improved on account of the large scale material changes, namely agrarian expansion and craft diversification. But, this did little to alter their ritual ranking in society and therefore this movement by newly emerging social groups was an attempt to get a new ranking. What followed then was only logical and we see that one of the main agendas of the bhakti movement is the creation of an alternative space. This movement by newly emerging social groups attempted to redefine their position and status with in the given traditional hierarchy and spearheaded a movement articulating their demands for restructuring the existing order. By declaring that God dwells in each individual and one could attain God through faith these saints brought religion to the downtrodden and henceforth marginalized sections of society. This movement also created space for women and we had a large number of women who actively practiced Bhakti. While the women were very outspoken and wanted their own little space the men continued to have a very traditional view of them and their roles. On the contrary the movement tended to reinforce and reiterate the already existing notions of women, family and their roles.

The Bhagavat Gita offers three paths to one who seeks salvation. The path of knowledge or *Gyan,* the path of action, *Karma* and the path of devotion, Bhakti. Bhakti as a concept means devotion and surrender. But generally, it is understood in religious term only meaning surrender or devotion to a personal God, a God who is conceived as a supreme God for salvation. Though this doctrine is traced to the early Brahmanical tradition, in the religious scripture of Bhagvat Gita, it was in the south that between the seventh and tenth centuries that this movement became broad based and acquired a huge social support. This was primarily due to the efforts of the Alwars and Nayyanars, the two sects in south India. The Alwars were people who had intuitive knowledge of God. They seem to have sprung from the Dravidian population and were intensely personal in their altitude to God and deeply emotional in their worship. For them caste did not count and of the recognized saints of the Alwars some were Sudras and some out caste and one was a woman also. The language they used was not Sanskrit but Tamil. This distinguished them from the other non Vedic sects like the Smartas whose sacred books were the Sanskrit *smrtis. The* movement probably started outside the Brahmanical fold but like many of the other subsequent movements that sought to do away with caste it was soon reabsorbed into the caste system. After them it was the Acharyas who provided a philosophical basis for this movement. A parallel movement along similar lines developed among the worshippers of Shiva. These saints called the Nayanars who spread the teachings that salvation could only be won by total self surrender to Siva. By the end of the eleventh century the hymns of these saints were collected together and given the title of *Devaram* and this together with the *Tiruvacakam* or sacred utterances, of Manika Vasagar and ancillary writings came to be known as the Tamil Veda. We again have a reemergence of this movement with the worship of a personal god in emotional terms from 13th century in the Indo Gangetic plains and it also has its impact in Punjab, Rajasthan, Gujarat, Bengal and Assam.

The Bhakti movement is a very good example of unity in diversity in Indian culture because though this movement occurred in many parts of India and there was much regional difference among the various movements. Yet there was a common thread running through out this movement because all the saints in their own ways questioning the existing system of religion and promoted religious egalitarianism. The Bhakti saints wanted the religious space to open up and provide an alternative space to the existing one that was rigid. This task was carried forward by the Acharyas in South India and they provided a philosophical base to the doctrine of Bhakti. Ramanuja was the first of the Acharyas who widened the social base of the movement. Ramananda and Vallabhacharya also widened the base of the Bhakti movement.

It has been pointed out that though Bhakti as a concept was very ancient in India it could not take roots in Northern India earlier because prior to the Turkish conquest in India the socio-religious milieu was dominated by the Rajput Brahmin alliance which was hostile to any heterodox movement. The Turkish conquest brought this supremacy to an end and paved the way for the rise of a large number of heterodox movements (Shobha, 1983, 11). The Turks deprived the Brahmins of their temple wealth and state patronage. The prestige and influence commanded by the Brahmins received a severe setback with the coming of Islam. The Brahmins had presented the images worshipped by the indigenous people not as symbols of God but as if the images themselves were God who could be commanded by the Brahmins, and would reward the faithful and cast down those who doubted their power and potency. These images were broken and trampled under foot by the heathen Turks and the Brahmins and other survivors of the temple killed or dispersed. Yet no harm befell the Turks. Materially also the Brahmins suffered, losing the wealth and properties commanded by many of the temples (Shobha, 1983, 11).

There are a large number of scholars, like Tarachand, Yusuf Hussain, who believe that this movement came about as a result of the Islamic influence on Indian religion and culture. Scholars have tried to point out the similarities between the Bhakti movement and Islam, especially with both their focus being on Universal brotherhood and making religion very simple. Though saints like Kabir were influenced by Islam and did borrow a lot of concepts from Islam especially faith in one personal God and equality of all human beings and attacked the caste system but he was equally equivocal in denouncing the orthodox Islam also. However this cannot be regarded as true for sagun Bhakti because sagun Bhakti did not denounce idolatry, nor the caste system. The impact of Bhakti movement and Sufism seems to have been mutual because the Sufi concept of Pir, mystic union with the beloved Fana, coincided with many of the concepts of Bhakti. Though this movement originated in South India it became popular in North India during the medieval period. We also find this movement spreading into Assam, Bengal, Maharashtra, Kashmir and Gujarat.

A thorough re-reading of the original sources and the subsequent historiography of India from the 19th century would lead us to certain conclusions beginning with the notion that earlier historiography of India, inaugurated by the colonial writers has presented a Unitarian and monolitihic picture of Hinduism as a religion based on Christian parallels of the 19th century which were themselves deeply affected by the impact of the enlightenment tradition and the print revolution. This view was further internalised by the Indian scholars and writers who faithfully reproduced the same there by leaving many gaps in history on account of the reliance of scriptures. Thus the bhakti movement was one such example, which was put in the forefront of research in the 1960's, thereby bringing back to the centre stage, a series of defining movements in Indian history. These movements, collectively called the bhakti movement in their regional and local settings ranging from the 7th to the 18th century had a wide geographical range from the tamil country in the deep south, to the Deccan, Central India, eastern India and the plains of northern India, Punjab and also the hills creating many alternative spaces.

A study of this kind has various problems arising out of a very large temporal and spatial context from where we get the sources. The problems become more intensified when we are looking at interconnected phenomena, coming primarily from the various lower sections embedded in diverse historical traditions which, also are encoded in the folk traditions and performing arts like the pilgrimage to Pandhrapur and the local jatras (car festival) or the aruvathu moovar festival of the nayanars where the statues of all the 63 nayanar saints are taken out in ritual procession in Mylapore. Historians are only now beginning to recover these facets and in the process many historical personalities are being rehabilitated.

Since the sources are multivocal and speak in different voices we see a strand of dominance, overtaking the element of protest and in course of time, muting the protest by relegating them. This is seen clearly when we locate production of texts situating around Kings and Courts, who were the main patrons and hence the royal input emerges pre-eminent in the medieval period. This phenomenon is hard to realise as the reading of the texts requires a nuanced reading since the royal influence is not very direct but layered. Looking back into history one does find that many separate factors interact at many levels to give rise to a complete pattern which is also complex. A holistic understanding of the development is necessary in order to understand the structure and its dynamics like the relationship between ideology and material cultures.

Sweeping winds of religiosity that straddled all over India, generally refer to by historians as a phenomenon called Bhakti movement. Large scale changes in production patterns and societal organization during the medieval period (which had its basis in the ancient period) created multiple spaces for different religious groups and castes to extrapolate on issues of religion. We can go beyond reading the Bhakti texts as pure religious texts and locate them at the intersections of production and ideology and explaining the regional variations as expressions of different time spans and production patterns. Interaction between this cannot be wholly comprehensible in chronological terms or geographical terms as there are significant overlaps of other factors like issues of gender relations, technology, and influence of Islam. A simple chronological approach is too limited to account for a complicated process that are in the realm of culture and economy and cannot be fitted into neat time spans. The approach has to be multidimensional borrowing tools of analysis from different disciplines like philosophy, history of religions, literary theory, gender studies and anthropology. To maintain a consistent narrative, I have attempted to translate some of the writings of the saint poets into my own language and used other translations where ever they are available. The above exercise is limited to the content of the songs and not the form and therefore does not delve into questions of stylistics and interpolation. It is through this dialogic process of reading a text and proceeding to read the meanings in their historical context, that I hope to reconstruct the total milieu of the medieval period where these changes were occurring. Borrowing from the interdisciplinary analytical tools and placing them in their historical context has helped to put voices into areas of silences that recur as patterns in medieval Indian history, thereby helping us to find more meanings than was assumed previously. Digressing from the central theme, other areas of investigation have revolved around the issue of gender. Here we posit that, the Bhakti movement did not translate to women, though there were a large number of women who were part and parcel of this movement there was a duality to the whole character of the movement. At one level there was talk of freedom and to do as one wishes, where as at another level we see features of co-option and contestation that ultimately reveals facets of progress and conservatism.

This book is divided into nine chapters drawing from regional and thematic divisions to present a comprehensive picture of Medieval Indian bhakti. This books start with an introduction that prepares the ground for launching such a project. Bhakti is a very good example of unity in diversity in Indian culture because, though this movement occurred in many parts of India and there was much regional variation among these, yet there was a common thread running through out this movement as all the saints in their own ways questioned the existing system of religion and promoted religious egalitarianism. On the agenda, the Bhakti saints wanted the religious space to open up and provide an alternative space to the existing one that was rigid.

Chapter II, discusses the origin and historiography of the movement and see how there was a sudden interest of the western scholars in this movement. History of religions as an area of academic enquiry was inaugurated by the colonial writers who constructed a Unitarian and monolitihic picture of Hinduism as a religion based on Christian parallels of the 19th century which were themselves deeply affected by the impact of the enlightenment tradition and the print revolution. We find that, this view was further internalised by the Indian scholars and writers who faithfully reproduced the same there by leaving many gaps in history on account of the reliance of scriptures.

In chapter III, we attempt to analyse the material base of this movement in the background of a set of interrelated and widespread changes in the production patterns that affected the social, cultural, political arenas which were then reflected through the religious sphere. It was a society where a number of far reaching changes like agrarian expansion, large scale craft specialization were taking place amidst the political background of emerging regional kingdoms in all parts of India. The coming of the Turks saw feudal oppression being intensified much more because now there was a clear mechanism to extract the surplus and pass it on to the ruling elite through the Iqta system. Though the Turkish ruling class lived in the towns the extraction of the surplus from the rural areas brought in enormous resources in their hands. This along with a spread of feelings of regionalism prepared the base for the Bhakti movement.

Chapter IV analyses the development and growth of the movement in Southern regions starting from the early medieval period. By and large the Bhakti movement has been studied as a pan-Indian movement using concepts and categories that translate to all parts of the country. While this approach no doubt helps us in providing a theoretical framework it does not answer various questions that are specific to the region of south India and one ends up looking at bhakti through a northern centre view. Spatial and temporal differences have seen different historical forces at play in southern India on an already existing base which was markedly different from that of northern or eastern India, two of which may be mentioned at the outset, the relative lesser to almost negligible Muslim influence in many southern regions and the predominance of the temple as an overarching social and religious institution. Hence we have to look at south India in order to understand the different aspects of this movement. Beginning with the Alwars and Nayanars and the growth of the different sects associated with it and the rise of the Acharyas, the Vir Vaisnavism and Vir Saivism.

Chapter V looks at the Bhakti Movement in Northern Regions, the area where there was the largest ferment of devotion in terms of numbers. When bhakti entered north

India, it was already centuries old and did not have to spend all the energies in evolving but could replicate many of the features that were already a part of the southern bhakti. The similarity cannot be extended further and we see that north India of the medieval period was fundamentally different from south India in at least two respects viz, the Turkish rule and also the clear demarcation of the varnas, whereas in south India the varna was just a theoretical concept while the jati reflected the local realities. Further, in north India one can see this movement in two streams, the nirgun, monotheistic movement and the sagun, Vaisnava movement. Kabir was a follower of Ramananda, who was a disciple of Ramanuja and hence one can see an ideological and philosophical connection between south and North India. The 14th century was a period of regeneration, marked by features like expansion of the agrarian base, increase in trade and commerce, growth of urbanization and an increase in commodity production. Under the Khiljis and Tughluqs, the narrow Turkish domination was replaced by a ruling class which had a broader social base among the Muslims. We discuss the rise of Nirgun Bhakti with its two branches of *Gyan Margi* and *Prem Margi* streams and Sagun Bhakti with Krishna bhakti and Ram Bhakti.

Chapter VI looks at the Bhakti Movement in Western, Eastern and North Eastern Regions. Bhakti movement in Gujarat begins from the fifteenth century and there are two major streams here. One is of sagun Bhakti around Krishna beginning with Narasinh Mehta and Mira and developed further under the Vallabha sect and the Swami Narayana sect of Sahajanand Swami. The Bhakti movement in Maharashtra has to be viewed against the background of the lack of an indigenous mercantile community and the traditional base of its chiefly agrarian economy in a variant of the Jajmani system, known as *balutedari,* which was made for a largely self sufficient village economy. In Bengal it was the Vaishnava Bhakti tradition which had a lot of impact. It centered on Bhagvata Purana with its emphasis on Krishna Lila and Sahatiya Buddhist tradition on one hand and the

Nathpanthi tradition on the other. Shankardeva's Neo-Vaishnavite movement was the first organized attempt in Assam at breaking down the age old bondage to the restrictions of caste, superstitions, ignorance, poverty and uncleanliness through the medium of Bhakti. Known as the land of Kirta-Mlecchas, the society of North East consisted of various tribes who were all regarded as outcastes. In the neighbouring foot hills areas inhabited the tribes such as Nagas, Khasis, Garos, Bhutiyas, Miris and others who were at a primitive stage of development but who had frequent contact with the plains. It was in this environment that Neo-Vaisnavism with ideals of humanism and non violence and simplification of heterogenous religious beliefs called for injunction against blood sacrifices.

Chapter VIII discusses the attitude of the Bhaktas towards women in general. Though many of the Bhakti saints were clamouring for change and questioned the existing hierarchies and injustices, women were not a party to this change. They could not rise above the age old prejudice of regarding women as a barrier to the path of salvation. The dominant discourse of the Bhakti movement was articulated by men and what emerges is that this protest against the prevalent social injustices did not address itself to women. It is interesting to note that, while the majority of the Bhakti saints especially, Nirgun are very critical of all institutions and revolted against idolatry, tyranny of castes' and creeds along with temples and rituals, in the change which they sought, women were not included. Though clamouring for a change and protesting vocally against the prevalent injustices in society, they conveniently left out the women, relegating her to the domestic sphere and only that women became an ideal who was an obedient wife, a *Pativrata* or a *Sati-Savitri*. She had no place in the change that was being sought. It was a change that was being defined by male parameters. Since the change was being sought with in a given structure it did not attempt at changing the power structure of society vis a vis man and women. The Bhakti saints were but depicting a reality of their times. The saints were living in a patriarchal society and holding patriarchal values, which consider a man superior and a woman subordinate. They could not rise from the traditional view of looking upon woman as Maya and an impediment to the path of Bhakti. A women's status was defined in terms of her role in the family Vis a Vis her husband and she had no worth outside the institution of marriage through which she must serve her husband. Though this attitude is by and large prevalent among both the Sagun and the Nirgun sants, it is more predominant among the Nirgun sants, who were related to the upcoming non agrarian sectors and being associated with tanning, weaving, trading and tailoring where women were slowly being marginalized and the old prejudice against them still continued. Women had no place in the change that was being sought.

Chapter VII discusses how the Bhakti movement created an alternative space for women. Through the centuries of patriarchal control, women have negotiated many layers and levels of existence working out forms of resistance that are often unnoticed and subtle, though subliminally and powerfully effective. This is done by creating their own space. Women's need to speak in their own ways, define their own truth in voices that revision society, polity, relationships and religion by creating their own space. It was the Bhakti movement which gives these women the moral courage to stand against patriarchal political authority and create an alternate space for themselves. They defy patriarchal norms of marriage and walk out (except in the case of Bahina bai). At this time many of the women saints led non-traditional, non-conformist lives and talked of individual freedom. While from the male bhaktas point of view there was every attempt at marginalising the women and pushing them back into the domestic sphere and only that women became an ideal who was an obedient wife, a *Pativrata* or *a Sati-Savitri*, the women Bhakta negotiated patriarchy and created an alternative space for themselves.

Chapter IX, has a conclusion that encapsulates the main arguments viz the construction of Hinduism and its readings have proceed from an orientalist view point, therefore a reading of religion has to deconstruct this view and we find the following. Bhakti originated in the southern regions and moved to the north. It spread in other regions of India. The Bhakti movement is a very good example of unity in diversity in Indian culture because though this movement occurred in many parts of India and there was much regional difference among the various movements. Yet there was a common thread running through out this movement because all the saints in their own ways questioning the existing system of religion and promoted religious egalitarianism. Though clamouring for change and a revision of existing relationships, the Bhakti movement did not translate to women, despite the fact that there were a large number of women who were part and parcel of this movement. There was a duality to the whole character of the movement. At one level there was talk of freedom and to do as one wishes, whereas at another level we see features of co-option and contestation that ultimately reveals facets of progress and conservatism.

The book ends with Appendices where we try to chart some of the saints and temples in different regions.

References

Frykenberg, Robert, E, 1991, "The emergence of modern Hinduism as a concept and as an institution-A reappraisal with special reference to South India" in Sontheimer, Gunther D. and Kulke, Hermann (ed), *Hinduism Reconsidered*, Manohar Publications, New Delhi.

Kejariwal, O.P. 1988, *The Asiatic society of Bengal and the discovery of India's past* 1784-1838, Oxford University Press, Delhi.

Kopf, David, 1969, *British Orientalism and the Bengal Renaissance:* The dynamics of Indian modernization, 1773-1835, University of California Press, Berkeley.

Kopf, David, 1980, "Henumeutics versus history", *Journal of Asian Studies*, 39, 3, pp. 495-505.

Marshall, P.J. (ed), 1970, *The British discovery of Hinduism in the eighteenth century*, Cambridge University press, London.

Rubies, Joan Pau, 2002, *Travel and Ethnology in the Renaissance: South India through European eyes*, 1250-1625, Cambridge University Press, London.

Said, Edward, W. 1978, *Orientalism*, Routledge and Kegan Paul, London.

Singh, Jyotsna, G. 1996, *Cultural Dialogues-Colonial Narratives :* Discovery of India in the language of Colonialism, Routledge, New York,

Shobha, Savitri Chandra, 1983, *Social life and concepts in Medieval Hindi Bhakti poetry*-A socio-cultural study, Chandrayan Publications, New Delhi.

Smith, David, 2003, Hinduism and Modernity, Blackwell Publishing, Oxford, U.K.

Stietencron, Heinrich, Von, 1991, "Hinduism on the proper use of a deceptive term", in Sontheimer, Gunther D. and Kulke, Hermann (ed), *Hinduism Reconsidered*, Manohar Publications, New Delhi.

Thapar, Romila, 2004, "Imagined religious communities-Ancient history and the modern search for a Hindu identity" in Lorenzen, N.David (ed), *Religious Movements in South Asia* 600-1800, Oxford, U.K.

Visvanathan, Gauri, 2003, "Colonialism and Construction of Hinduism, in Gavin Flood (ed), *The Blackwell Companion to Hinduism*, Blackwell, New York.

2

Origins and Historiography of the Movement

Indian culture and civilization has wielded an immense assimilative power and the Greeks, Sakas, Hunas were easily absorbed within the fold of her population. Initially they were designated as fallen kshatriyas and eventually absorbed as full members on performing certain rituals like the *garbagriha* ceremony after which they were, for want of a better term Hinduised or Indianised. Eventually they were completely integrated into the Indian society and became one of the main bulwarks of Hinduism which bears the creative imprint of all the groups and their practices. This however did not happen with the Turko-Afghan invaders who maintained their distinct identity. Therefore the advent of Islam in India had profound effects on its political, religious and socio-cultural life leading to a structural change where the earlier system that could accommodate many groups was constantly altered but the core ideas of varna-jati continued in changed forms. The history of medieval India is one of confrontation to co-operation followed by interaction and synthesis at various levels revealing patterns of accommodation, appropriation and assimilation as revealed in the practices of the people. This interaction and synthesis is very interesting. Face to face with the egalitarian social ideal of Islam, where all were equal in the eyes of God, the social rigidity of the Hindus was not relaxed and caste distinctions continued to exist. On the other hand, the lofty ideals of toleration of various religious sects and creeds of Hinduism were not accepted by Islam. These realities coupled with various socio-economic changes were the pre-conditions for the Bhakti movement. Bhakti as a concept however was found in the early period and does not emerge in medieval times.

Growth of the Bhakti Cult in Ancient Period

Bhakti as a concept is very ancient in Indian religion dating back to the Vedic period. The Bhagvat Gita also mentions that one should give up all religious path and take refuge in God alone, and it discusses ways to know God fully and practice Yoga and take refuge in God (Gita, Sivananda, 2003, 156-157). The word Bhakti is derived from root *bhaj*, meaning 'to adore'. The word bhakti occurs for the first time in Upanishads. In the *Svetasvatara* Upanishad we come across the doctrine of 'self-surrender' and 'grace'. In *Katha* Upanishad too there are traces of bhakti.

To one who has the highest devotion (bhakti) for God.

And for his spiritual teacher (guru) even as for God.

To him these matters which have been declared

become manifest (if he be) a great soul.

Yea, become manifest (if he be) a great soul.

It has been repeatedly told in the Epics that to achieve liberation one must transcend all the opposites, including good and evil. The goal of the path of knowledge and the path of action thus becomes the same-the realization of the eternal dimension in one self. The Yoga Sutras introduce a new element that concentration on the idea of God as being an eternal exemplar of the liberated soul but God actively helps the soul to liberation by the exercise of his grace.

It is in the Bhagavad Gita that this activity becomes more pronounced. The Gita tries to expound bhakti in a systematic manner. It is true that Gita synthesizes the three paths of Karma, Knowledge and Bhakti and this is the main idea contained in the bhakti cult. The *Ekant-ka Dharma*, the religion addresses itself to a single God in the Bhagvat Gita, is but the first exposition of the doctrine of bhakti. The Bhagavad Gita, is composed in the form of a mystical poem. It describes the encounter that takes place between the Divine and the human deep within every human person. The transpersonal divine mystery reveals itself as the personal Lord, inviting total surrender from the human seeker. In this encounter there is a process from the initial phase of spiritual life to a stage of integration along the threefold path of *jnana, bhakti,* and *karma.* The divine master liberates the human seeker from the grips of greed and leads him or her to the freedom of a worldview based on dharma.

The Gita has reached us as part of the great epic Mahabharatha. It is written in the form of a dialogue between Arjuna, the chief commander of the Pandavas, and Krishna, his charioteer, on the battlefield at a crucial moment of the story. However, this image of the chariot is found in the Katha Upanishad, which was written prior to the Gita. The Gita describes this mystical process in a dramatic way. The battlefield of Kurukshetra is only a symbol of the battlefield of life, on which the war is constantly being waged between greed *(kama)* and integration *(dharma).* Arjuna and Krishna are only actors on this battlefield of life. Hence, in order to grasp the perennial mystical message of the Gita, one has to detach it from the militant context of the epic. The real battlefield is within each of us. With the image of the physical battlefield Gita makes the ongoing spiritual battle of life clear to us and introduces us to the concept of Bhakti-devotion and divine grace.

During the ancient period, Vedic mantras and rituals played an important role as the mode of devotion. People desirous of health, wealth and prosperity were to please the powers of nature by performing holy rites and sacrifices and to the devoted worshippers the deities granted boons. If a person had to get something he or she had to appease the Gods. Later the aspect of ritualistic religion began to be overtaken by the concept of *Upasana* or *Bhajana* expressed in *namaskara, vandana, seva, archana* etc. Fundamentally it was *Sraddha* (devotion or geniune regard) which disclosed a geniune spirit of worship in the sacrificer (Goswami, 1924, 3). The importance of this spirit of *Sraddha* bhakti or respectful dependence upon God which is undoubtedly the first step in a scheme of Bhakti cult or the doctrine of bhakti was not lost upon. It is interesting to see that Vedic texts itself gave *sraddha* a high place in religious scheme. It says the following...

a. It is *sraddha* or faith, which brings on realization of truth.

b. It is *sraddha* or faith that is a most vital part of the rituals.

c. *Sraddha* is like mother of the whole world of rites as *mantra* is the father.

d. *Sraddha* lits the fire, pours out the oblation and

e. It is the *sraddha* that the God takes cognizance of in our prayers (Goswami, 1924, 3).

Even in Vedic age *sraddha* bhakti made its influence felt in many directions. Under its wholesome impetus, the Vedic religion progressed from polytheism to monotheism, for bhakti essentially stands for a broad comprehensive faith in one who is adored. The concept of one supreme God manifested in many and the idea of this God, known by different names began to take shape slowly.

Of the six philosophical schools of ancient India, *samkhya* system propounded *jnanayoga* and the Yoga system had the principles of *karma* yoga. In all the Smriti literature the doctrine of *Karma* and *Gyana* going hand in hand is emphasized. In the conception of the supreme principle of consciousness it was argued that impersonal knowledge is inconceivable, undemonstrable. Since in the actual experience it is a person, a rational being who is credited with knowledge, so how this personality, could be denied in the case of the ultimate principle. Knowledge could never be divorced from a person endowed with knowledge. The Bhagvat neatly sums this up, "The Vedas aim at him; knowledge aims at him, the Gods of life aim at him, the Yogas aim at him, asceticism aims at him, religion aims at him, the God's of life aim at him (Bhagvat, Goswami, 1924, 88). The conception of the highest principle as a personal God led to the emergence of the Bhakti concept.

Emergence of Bhakti in South India

In south India bhakti tradition can be seen from the sangam period onwards. *Paripadal,* a sangam classic that is one of the eight anthologies or *Ettutogai* introduces to the new milieu of religion and worship, namely the temple, which was to become one of the major traditions in south India. Bhakti or devotion appears here for the first time as the central concept that was later developed by the *Alvars* and *Nayanars* and elaborated in the Vaishnava and Saiva cannonical texts of medieval times (Pillai, 1956, 23).

The bhakti or hymnal literature comprising of hymns which is considered as a new form of poetry shows the evidence of synthesis of vedic, upanishadic and puranic influence as shown admirably by Friedhelm Hardy's study of emotional Krishna bhakti. Here it reveals the meeting point of northern sanskrtic devotional themes with the *agam* (interior\love) as well as *puram* (exterior\war) themes of Sangam literature. It marks a new synthesis and leads to the intensely powerful emotional bhakti in *Alvar* poetry, which derives its principle motives from the *mal* (visnu) hymns of the *Paripadal.*

Bhakti as a concept can be traced in another sangam text *Tirumurukarrupatai* (guide to Muruga or Karthikeya). It is surprising to see that Siva, one of the central deities of the puranic religion receives only marginal attention, as he was not one of the *Tinai* deities during Sangam times.

Both the *Paripadal* and Tirumurukarrupatai would seem to represent the transition from the worship of tribal or folk deities of the anthologies to the evolution of formal religious systems which under the Pallavas and Pandyas of 7th and 9th centuries became crystallized as the Puranic Vaishnava and Saiva religions. It was a new regional synthesis of puranic forms in which, the northern Sanskrit elements assumes a dominant position. The idea of temple as a focus of this devotional cult emerge in the two sangam works, but there did exist centres of worship during this period as there are references to *koyil, nakar* and *kantu* (pillar). The temple in many of the writings is not just a geographical but also a spiritual locale where the Early Alvars life takes place (Hardy, 1983, 288). What was absent was the institutionalization of such centres for the promotion of formal religious system.

Bhakti arose as a sophisticated expression, i.e., in singing the praise of God as an emotional seeking of the union with the absolute, symbolised by the temple image. This concept is traceable through various stages in *alvar* poetry dominated by emotional *Krsna* bhakti. The early three *alvars* from 5th to 7th centuries express a simple intellectual aspect of bhakti. (Nilakanta Sastry 1963, 45,) The early *alvar* bhakti has also been characterized as a special form of theistic yoga derived from Bhagvat Gita relatively calm expression of adoration, service, loyalty, a personal experience of intimacy and dependency on God. (Hardy, 1983, 282).

The development of Bhakti reaches its culmination in *Nammalvar* (seventh century), in whose hymns the intensely powerful emotional bhakti supersedes all other religious attitudes and methods. Here one finds the beginnings of the notion of complete trust and surrender though the concept is fully developed and used by the saints in the 12th and 13th century (Jagadeesan, 1977, Chapter III). In the hymns of Andal, the only lady saint among the *alvars*, the eroticism of Krishna bhakti attains a new intensity in her love for Lord Krishna and her marriage to God Ranganatha of Srirangam is expressed in *Tiruppavai*. The concept of the temple cult and pilgrimage slowly evolves now possible to ease the emotional tensions (Hardy, 1983, 400). It is Vittucittan another Brahmin Alwar who makes a reference to the Brahmin temple service, "My father and his father.... For seven generations in succession have performed the temple service" and his Bhakti has at its locale the hereditary and professional performance of the temple ritual; (Hardy, 1983, 403). The bhakti of Saiva *nayanars* is equally emotional like Krishna bhakti. The *Tevaram* of *nayanars* also represents a new synthesis of northern brahmanical traditions with regional tamil traditions (Indira Peterson, 1991, 5)

Bhakti as a concept first evolved in the southern regions with the hymns of Vaisnava Alwars and those of the Saiva Nayanars and became a major movement against existing Brahmanical domination moving to northern regions and spreading to western, eastern and north eastern regions also. Among the devices adopted by the bhakti saints, there arose a sophisticated expression i.e.. Singing the praise of God and seeking of union with the absolute, symbolized by the temple image, through emotional singing. There are elements of protest and dissent in the Alwar and Nayanar poetry representing an attempt to provide avenues of social acceptance and even mobility to less privileged castes and economic groups.

The bhakti hymns are featured by three themes...

a. Foremost is the idea of devotion to personal God i.e., bhakti

b. Protest against Orthodox Vedic Brahmanism and the exclusiveness of Brahmans in their access to Divine grace and salvation.

c. Vehment denunciation of the Jainas and Buddhists as non-believers, heretics and hence heterodox in nature (Champaklakshmi, 2004, 55)

In the medieval period from the 12th to 18th centuries, certain trends can be noticed which transformed the original character of Bhakti and it was shaped by the nature of the crystallized society. Attempts were made to give fresh lease of life to the decadent religion by reviving the past and attempting to interpret it in the light of the new socio-economic forces, giving rise to new ideas, more in keeping with the times.

The poets and saints of medieval bhakti appeared throughout India. Although all have their individual genius, the bhakti lyricists share a number of common features whatever their language. The Sanskrit education needed for authors of Sanskrit texts limited them largely to the Brahman class and thus put a definite stamp on them. Because bhakti poets could use any language, they might come from different class. They brought to their poetry a familiarity with folk religion unknown or ignored in the Sanskrit texts. The use of the spoken language, even though it was formalized, made possible the immediate expression of an unmediated vision that needed no further context; thus the lyrics are short, intensely personal, and precise. These works illustrate the localistic and reformist tendency evidenced throughout India in the vernacular literatures, especially in Tamil, Bengali, and Hindi.

The origin of these new forms of Hinduism, dominated by Bhakti has been attributed to the influence of Islam, but the proposition that the rise of popular emotional bhakti was a response to Islam is impossible, for the practice of singing ecstatic hymns in the current local language was well-known in South India even before Prophet Muhammad. All the features of this form of bhakti are found in the Bhagavata-Purana and in the commentaries of Ramanuja. The earliest bhakti literature in a living Indo-Aryan language is from Maharashtra and was composed before Muslims occupied the area. Thus, passionate bhakti existed long before the Muslim conquest. However, the presence of rulers of alien faith and the withdrawal of royal patronage from the temples and Brahmanic colleges may have encouraged the spread of new, more popular forms of Hinduism. The psychological effect of the Muslim conquest may also have predisposed the people to accept the powerful teachings of the poets, but Islam was only a contributory factor in the spread of the new movements.

Historiography

In Europe the post renaissance interests initiated an intensive study of the ancient world and these concerns are reflected in the historiography of India also. The interpretation of Indian history, which started from 18th century onwards, related closely to the world view of European renaissance historiographical writing with its emphasis on historical biographies and chronicles was largely ignored and European writings on India attempted to create a new historical tradition in accordance to their own world view (Thapar, 1973).

Investigations into India's past began with the work of the Orientalist scholars who had made India and particularly Indian languages their area of study. The scholars were European, the audiences were European and the Indian figured as inert object of knowledge (Thapar, 1973). Orientalist textual and institutional practices created the spiritual and sensuous India as opposed to the materialistic and rational British and offered them as justifications for the British conquest. It would not be out of place to quote Frits Staal here, who says that "India was discovered by the Europeans during the Romantic period and hence there was no science, where as China was discovered by them during the enlightenment age," which explains the characterisations of both the 'oriental' civilizations by the west in different brackets. The Orientalists had reconstructed the glory of

Indian civilization in the ancient past. This was done in part as a result of the romantic search for a distant ideal world, a utopia to escape the bewildering changes taking place in the 19th century. The orientalist was a typical product of the 18th century Enlightenment, a rationalist and universalist who sought to explain cultural unity through common origins (Kopf, 1969, 38).

In 1784, when Warren Hastings founded the Asiatic society the knowledge of Indian languages opened the way for professional advancement as well to the literary treasures of Oriental civilizations. There was a practical motive to this patronage. Hastings believed that even if the Company accepted full responsibility for the Government of Bengal and place some of its European servants in most important administrative posts, it should still govern in accordance with Indian traditions and it must find out what these traditions were (Marshall, 1970, 13). Hastings collected Indian paintings and manuscripts and also established College of Oriental learning. He felt that to rule effectively one must love India, to love India one must communicate with her people, and to communicate with her people one must learn her language (Kopf, 1969, 21).

William Jones, civil servant and first president of the Asiatic society till his death in 1794, discovered the links between Sanskrit and the European language family, thus reanimating a resplendent Hindu past and identifying it as a source of Western Civilization (Singh, 1996, 66). What the Orientalists were discovering was not only an ancient and different India but also the lost heritage of the Europeans. The work of the Orientalists was founded on a paradox, because on the one hand many of these orientalists as civil servants of the British shared a standard colonial belief in the superiority of western knowledge and institutions. On the other hand these indologists re-discovered a glorious India by identifying certain resemblances between East and West in a shared ancient past. What these different efforts at colonial reform had in common was a vision of eighteenth century India as a decadent and fallen East in need of a western civilization. (Singh, 1996, 71). Orientalists like William Jones, H.T. Colebrook, closely related to the, "Asiatic Society of India" looked back at the glory of the past and covered a wide range of themes in Sankrit literature, on philosophy and Hindu religion in general. It was these scholars who propounded a theory on the movement and its origins.

The assessment of the Bhakti Movement in Indian historical studies has not emerged from the discipline of history itself. It was not shaped by the historian but by the Indologist (Sharma, 2004, 316). Thus theorization about Bhakti really started with the Orientalists who conjured up images of an exotic opulence. The European construction of the varied images of Asia started within the context of imperialism. This period saw a discourse of power that characterized a particular set of social, economic and political relations between Europe and its colonies. Many of the ideological texts transformed thoughts and actions of ancient Indians to distortions of reality. According to these writings, Indian actions were attributed to social group caste, village, joint families, linguistic regions, for they felt that there were no individuals in India and individualism was attributed to bad motives. The meaning of non-violence was extended in such a way so as to see the Hindu as one who always lives in fear of killing even an insect, a characteristic which made them run away from danger-a phenomenon not witnessed in any part of the globe.

The Orientalists created Hinduism in their own image which clearly reveals the bewildering anxieties of industrialism and the rapid changes in contemporary Europe. Most of their theorctical formulations were based on Christian reaction in Europe against explaining God in abstract and personal terms. This was seen as a serious threat to Christianity and could be counteracted only through a reiteration of faith in the Biblical God, who was more personal in nature and different from the Gods of the philosophers.

The scholars who elaborated on the Bhakti theme first identified Bhakti with Krishna Bhakti and Vaishnavism as a whole. They associated religion and Hindu theism with the worship of personal deities. H.H. Wilson, Sketches of the religious sects of the Hindus (1846) writing on the Vaishnavism in Bengal noted that their religion could be summed up in one word, Bhakti (Wilson, 1846, 100).

In all the works that followed, Bhakti became a religion often identified with Krishna Bhakti or Vaishnavism in general. Albrecht Weber made an in-depth study of Krishna cult and established a link between Krishna Bhakti and Bhakti religion (Weber, Barth, 1906, 220-221). Referring to it as a meditative piety, and adorned with grace and love of God, he spoke of Christian influence on Bhakti. L Monier Williams also identified Bhakti religion with Vaishnavism. According to him the multi dimensional Hindu religious tradition can be divided under two broad divisions-Brahmanism, which was of the higher, cultured and thoughtful classes and Hinduism, of the lower, uncultured and unthinking masses. He categorized the Upanishads under the former and the cults of the personal deities under the latter (Williams, 1891, 96). He defined this as monotheism, whereas the former was Upanishadic and the Vedantic content was monism.

George A Grierson, based on the above definition constructed a historical account of Vaishnavism and called it the, "ancient monotheistic religion of India". He traced the antecedents of this religion to the Bhagavat Gita and the Mahabharata (Grierson, 1909, 8). He was the first one to link the medieval Hindi poets with the ancient religion of Bhakti and speak of their collective expression and their resurgence as, "Bhakti Movement". All these scholars made an artificial distinction between philosophical Hinduism which they thought was highly evolved and the popular Hinduism as practiced by the people.

In response to Orientalists and indologists writing on Bhakti, there were works of R.G. Bhandarkar (Bhandarkar,

1913) and R.C. Zaehner (Zaehner, 1960), who questioned the Christian influence and tried to show that the movement was indigenous in character. R.G. Bhandarkar brought forth literary and epigraphical evidences to show the antiquity of Krishna worship and Vaishnavism. R.C. Zaehner spoke of the Dravidian origin of Bhakti. Dr. S. Radhakrishnan traced the origin of Bhakti to Bhagvat Gita. He claims that Bhakti is in the Gita and is sustained by knowledge, but it is not knowledge itself. It involves no reference to Yoga techniques or longing for speculative knowledge of the Divine. Utter humility, meekness, prostration of self are other essential elements of Bhakti per se, apart from love and devotion. Devotion forces us from sin and brings us closer to the Almighty. Gita says in the Sixth discourse, "He who sees me every where and sees every thing in me, he never becomes separated from me, nor do I become separated from him" (Shivananda, 2003, 145). Bhakti also emphasises humility, obedience, readiness to serve, as the devotee longs to surrender himself, renounce self will and experience passivity, surrender of soul to God. Bhakti requires faith and emphasises the simple and austere purity of the relationship of surrender in a humble and direct attitude of trust. It perceives genuine piety in the competence of the surrender rather than in the intensity of the Bhakti disciplines (Radhakrishnan, 1970, 61). This cosmic force cannot be seen by the Vedas, or by austerity, or by gift, nor by sacrifice but only by single minded devotion can it be seen in reality (Shivananda, 2003, 292-93).

As the ascent of Islam in India coincided with the flowering of the Bhakti movement, the other historians argue that the Bhakti movement was largely inspired by Islamic ideology. The above argument is based on the egalitarian message of bhakti and an attempt to equate the idea of personal god with monotheism.

Barthwal claims that the Bhakti movement arose among the lower castes of Hindu society as a result of being caught between the devil and the deep sea. On the one hand was the oppression of the new Islamic rulers bearing a harsh Islamic religion and by high caste Hindus who imposed a caste based economic and social inequalities. Caught between the two, saints like Kabir and others brought forth a movement with religious message and practices from the oppression of both (Barthwal, 1978) To Tarachand, the 'principle of universal brotherhood and human equality which the Bhakti saints advocated had its parallel in Sufi thought (Tarachand, 1936, 120-121). Yusuf Hussain looks upon the Bhakti movement as one which can easily be divided into two distinct periods. The first from the time of the Bhagwata Gita to the 13th century, when Bhakti was only an individual sentiment and, the second period from 13th to 16th centuries, when as a result of the contact with Islam, it got transformed into a doctrine and a cult (Hussain, 1976, 5). He refers to this movement as reformation of Hinduism, where the concept of a personalized God and simplicity of faith of Islam had a special appeal (Hussain, 1976,26).

To many others, the whole Bhakti movement becomes one of dissent, protest and reform. Peaceful co-existence and self-respect for the individual has always been the cry for generations. Reform movements have often gained grounds depending upon the existing circumstances and have reflected the aspirations and desires of the common man. The Bhakti movement brought forth the existing resentment against the social order then existing and gave vent to the feeling of new classes and castes that were emerging by that time (Malik, 1977). M.S.A. Rao talking about the ideology of the protest movements shows how the ideology of the Protest movements in pre-British India were largely characterised by their concern with religious beliefs and practices, as these constituted the chief areas of relative deprivation. Brahmanical Hinduism had established a monopoly over paths of salvation and denied the common man access to them. The path of devotion provided the double edged ideology of establishing equality of all men in relation to God on one hand and attacking the monopoly and supremacy of certain sections of Brahmans over Vedic, knowledge and action on the other (Rao, 1977, 59-60). According to J.R. Kamble, the main aim of this movement was to establish an egalitarian society (Kamble, 1985, 108). It postulated and fostered equality only in religious sphere and not in secular life, because it failed to foster an organisation which would lead people towards the ideals enshrined in the Bhakti preachings (Kamble, 1985, 109). Socio-religious movements, even movements with political overtones are equally vociferous and at times may not be, overtly political, but are socially and religiously geared toward changing a system with requisite institutional and political changes. Individuals affected by such external influences to bring about changes in society and its institutions in order to ensure, greater happiness of the masses. Similarly the Bhakti Movement represents a revolt against feudal oppression. It also helped in the development of a composite Indian culture embracing different linguistic and religious communities expressing itself in the cultural field, as a national renaissance (Damodaran, 1959, 315).

The Bhakti movement in general shows that they tend to get organised and function within the existing socio-cultural order. While they do take a critical attitude towards this order, their activity seldom transcends beyond a mere negative position. In historical retrospect, their function appears to have been to reinforce the existing order by channelling discontent into a negative form, rather than bring about a structural change. It served as a safety value containing a variety of potential challenges. For example, it vaguely castigated caste as an iniquitous system and, in practice provided for some extraordinary escape from its crippling regime but it tended to blunt the consciousness of its victim through religious mystification. Thus a lot of individual dissent spills over into protests which is some what organised and eventually results in reform movements which more or less operate within the frame work of established socio cultural norms (Kinsley, 1980).

K. Ishwaran looks upon Lingayatism as an illustration of how the Bhakti tradition contributes to modernization (Ishwaran, 1980). Ishwaran refers to models of modernisation in relation to Bhakti. He identifies two transitory phases of ethnocentrism and realism in modernization theory and hopes for the emergence of a third phase of more lasting models. He offers Lingayatism as one such model, because according to him it rests on universal values of freedom, equality and rationality, to be pursued within a corresponding community (Iswaran, 1980). In this context, he analyses Basavanna's philosophy and shows how these values were either explicitly propagated or implicitly practiced. This he regards as a unique movement in the ongoing dynamics of Indian tradition. He concludes that while Bhakti movements merely upheld the old order and made it palatable, Basava's organised revolt produced a lasting model for universal emulation.

David Kinsley finds that in many devotional movements, the theoretical harmony between doing one's duty, (dharma) and loving the lord, (bhakti) is called into question. There seems to be a tension between the two. The tension is particularly clear in the lives of several women saints who found it difficult and ultimately impossible to reconcile their traditional marriages with their inherent urge to love the Lord. He gives examples of Mahadevi Akka from Karnataka, Lalleswari from Kashmir, Mirabai from Rajasthan and the whole of Krishna mythology with Radha as its central mode of devotion to show how in the lives of these women, devotion to God becomes an alternative to marriage. Crushed and confined to difficult domestic situations these women found an alternative possibility in their devotion. Renouncing marriage and life in the world generally, they directed their passions to heavenly consorts (Kinsley, 1980).

By stating that all are equal in the eyes of god and one does not have to look for God outside in the temple or rituals but with in one self, Bhakti also opened the doors to women and many women came out and practiced Bhakti and took stand against patriarchal political control. However the male bhaktas while clamouring for change and protesting vocally against the prevalent injustices in society, conveniently left out the women, relegating her to the background and the home. She had no place in the change that was being sought. It was a change that was being defined by male parameters. Since the change was being sought with in a given structure it did not attempt at changing the power structure of society vis a vis man and woman. The perception of change and the need to come to terms with it were not seen as synonymous with a radical ideology in favour of a 'total change'. There were no attempts at reorganization of social relationship with in the family. Women by and large were excluded from this, in fact there is every attempt at marginalizing women, pushing her into the domestic sphere and reinforce patriarchal ideology (Pande, 1991, 66).

It will not be out of place here to point out that Max Weber, remarks that the influence of women only tended to intensify those aspects of religion that were emotional or hysterical. Such was the case in India (Weber, 1922, reprint 1963, 106). He feels that the lower Hindu classes clung on to their caste duties with greatest tenacity as a prerequisite for their rebirth into a better position. To him the Bhakti movement led to the Brahmins, whose power had decayed in medieval times in the wake of the Islamic foreign domination to join with the masses. He also links this to the rise of the Guru, which permitted this to grow to grotesque heights (Weber, 1958, reprint, 1967, 312-317).

The Marxist historians have looked upon the Bhakti movement within the socio-economic context. To them the Bhakti ideology is one of submission as well as dissent. D.D. Kosambi was the first scholar to establish the link between Bhakti and feudalism. Writing on the Bhagvat Gita he interpreted the doctrine of Bhakti as, unflinching loyalty to God similar to the loyalty that linked together, "in a powerful chain the serf and the retainer to the feudal lord (Kosambi, 1970, 208). This according to him suited the feudal ideology perfectly. Though Bhakti was the basic need in a feudal ideology, its fruits were not enjoyed equally by all. By the 12th century, feudal taxation had begun to weight heavily upon the peasantry, who paid not only for the luxurious palace but also its counterpart the equally rich and even more ornate temple. (Kosambi, 1962, reprint, 1998, 32). This idea has been further elaborated upon by Dr. R.S. Sharma. Like other features such as feudal state organisation, reversion to closed economy, proliferation of castes, regional identity in arts, script and language he traces puja, bhakti and tantra to 6th and 7th centuries. To him Bhakti now with its being interlinked to puja doctrine, reflected the complete dependence of the tenant or the semi-serf on the landowners in medieval times (Sharma, 1974).

Irfan Habib speaks of the, "ties of caste and religious communities", in the peasant uprising and speaks of Kabir, Dadu, Haridas and Nanak as leaders of a movement that led to the formation of new religious' communities during the medieval period (Habib, 1963, 332). Elaborating further he states that the Turks in medieval India created an economic organisation that was definitely superior to the previous one. By the beginning of the 14th century one can see a considerable growth in towns and expansion in craft production and commerce due to the improvement in technology. Therefore he concludes that there was an expansion of the artisan class. Newer and greater demand for certain goods by the ruling class had led to the creation of new skills and crafts and the adoption of new professions by the members of the indigenous population. The lower castes readily took to these, for that could give them a new dignity in the caste hierarchy. Since this meant the breaking of caste rules. The anti-caste religious movements of Kabir and Nanak found greater following amongst the growing class of these artisans in Northern India.

Irfan Habib's view on the Bhakti movement as an expansion of the artisan class after the Muslim conquest was borrowed from Muhammad Habib. He had used the argument to explain the causes of the easy political success of the Muslim invaders in India. According to him their success was due to the appeal of the new egalitarian ideology of Islam' and the growing class of artisans in urban areas who were keen to get their freedom from the shackles of the caste system (Habib, 1967).

Marx believed that the forces of production determine the character of a society, as the "production relations determine the mode of production as well. Relations which human beings enter into during the process of social life possess a specific historical and transitory character. The distribution of' relations essentially coincides with the production relations (Marx, 1959, 878).

Hiren Gohain has also conferred that during the Bhakti movement in the 15th and 16th century, modes of production and its corresponding social relations undoubtedly underwent significant changes. Barter system was replaced by money transactions thus helping to improve the economic situation of the artisan class, which had emerged due to mercantile economy. The village artisan in such areas ceased to be a mere servant of the village community and began to cater to a wider clientele through the market specialization and division of labour which characterised the economy (Gohain, 1987, 2).

The Marxist views main lacuna is its failure in distinguishing between Sagun and Nirgun forms of bhakti and while their analysis can hold true for the Nirgun Bhakti, it does not apply to the sagun Bhakti. Chaitanya, Tulsidas and Surdas were all Brahmins and so were the four acharyas, Ramanuja, Nimbarka, Madhava and Vallabhacharya.

Krishna Sharma has questioned the treating of the Bhakti movement as a monolith. She thinks that accepting a unitary approach to the Bhakti Movement is not viable. She finds a lot of disparity in this movement. The ideological positions adopted by medieval Bhaktas, the religious modes, and organizational aspects of the sect and the origin of the sect show a wide range of variations. According to her, the Bhakti movement covers a number of religious movements each with its own distinctive features and ethos. Some of these were even anti-thetical to one another notwithstanding their common denominator Bhakti (Sharma, 1987).

Susmita Pande cautions that in the description and interpretation of medieval Indian religious movements, it is necessary to avoid the indiscriminate use of terminology drawn from other ages and types of thought. Thus the criticism of caste system should not be confused with social egalitarianism. The notion of social equality is hardly relevant according to her in pre-modern societies, in which inequalities of wealth, power and recognition were not only in built but rarely questioned. Thus slavery, aristocracy and priesthood were accepted features of ancient and medieval world. She finds the criticism of caste in Sramana tradition of Buddhism and Jainism. The criticism denied that birth could be the basis of cast distinctions; it attacked the privileged position of Brahmanas and ultimately denied the relevance of caste to spiritual life. But it did not propose the abolition of all socio-economic privileges nor the equalization of political or economic right. The only right proclaimed as universal was spiritual liberation. The criticism of caste in medieval Bhakti literature is to be understood as a continuation of the sramana tradition of caste transcendence and anti Brahmanism rather than in terms of modern notion of individual right or classlessness (Pande, 1989, 98).

In most of the studies so far, the Bhakti movement has been seen from a very north centric point of view, and it is assumed that the same theoretical postulations can be assumed for the South also. However the movement in the South developed very differently from the north (Pande, 1990). The Bhakti movement in the north developed along two streams of Nirgun and Sagun, and since the major dynasties ruling at that time were Islamic, they did not get any royal patronage. The region of Deccan, on the other hand, particularly the region south of river Krishna was comparatively peaceful and free from Muslim contact. So the movement here was not so much in reaction to Islam, as to eradicate the influence of Jainism and Buddhism. The movement received royal patronage from most of the kings- The Pallavas were Vaishnavites, The Cholas_ were Shaivites, Kakatiyas_ were also Shaivities and Vijaynagar kings patronised Sri Vaishnavism. A cursory look at the sacred geography of the Saivaite centres in the tamil country would give us an easy pointer to the links between royal patronage and religion as we see that of the 275 sacred sites of the saivaites mentioned in the Tevaram round 90% are located in the Kaveri valley, which was the core of the Chola dominions, whereas the important vaishnava centres are all found beyond this region since the Cholas consciously patronized Saivism Whereas in Northern India the dominant discourse is against Brahmanism, in South India they were in liaison with royalty and controlled temple rituals and were often employed in State services (Pande, 2000, 57). Temples emerged as powerful institutions, in spite of the opposition of Vir Saivism to temples. Therefore while it, cannot be denied that in the study of a movement like that of the Bhakti, the holistic perspective should not be lost, yet we cannot ignore the complexities and specificities of localities and regions.

References

Barthwal, P.D., 1978, *Traditions of Indian Mysticism based upon Nargun School of Hindi Poetry*, Delhi.

Bhandarkar, R.G, 1913, reprint, 1982, *Vaishnavism, Saivism and Minor religious system*, K.J. Trubnea, Strass burg (1913), Bhandarkar Oriental Research Institute, Poona, (1982).

Bhagavad Gita, 2003, tr. Swami Sivananda, Divine Life Society, Tihiri Garhwal, Uttranchal.

Champaklaxmi, R, 2004, "From devotion and Dissent to Dominance-The Bhakti of the Tamil Alvars and

Nayanars" in Lorenzen, David N. (ed), *Religious Movements in South Asia* 600-1800, Oxford University Press, New York.

Damodaran, K. 1959, *Indian thought*-A critical survey, Bombay.

Goswami, Bhagabat Kumar, 1924, *The Bhakti cult in Ancient India*, Calcutta University Post graduate Council, Calcutta.

George A. Grierson, 1909, *Narayana and the Bhagavatas*, Bombay.

Gohain, Hiren, 1987, "The labyrinth of Bhakti-on some questions in medieval history", *Economic and Political Weekly*, November 14th.

Hardy, Friedhelm, 1983, *Virah Bhakti*-The early history of Krsna devotion in South India, Oxford University Press, New York.

Habib, Irfan, 1963, *Agrarian system in Mughal India*, New Delhi.

Habib, Muhammad, 1967, "Introduction", in Elliot and Dowson, *History of India as told by its own historians*, Vol. II, Aligarh.

Hussain, Yusuf, 1976, 'Islam and the cult of Bhakti', in *Glimpses of Medieval Indian History and Culture*, Bombay.

Ishwaran, K. 1980, "Bhakti tradition and modernization, the case of Lingayatism", in *Journal of Asian and African Studies*, Vol. XV, No. 1-2.

Jagadeesan, N. 1977, *History of Sri Vaishnavism in Tamil Country* (Post Ramanuja), Koodal Publishers, Madurai.

Kamble, 1985, *In pursuit of Equality in Indian History*, National Publishing House, New Delhi.

Kinsley, David, 1980, Devoton as an alternative to marriage in the lives of some Hindu women devotees, *Journal of Asian and African Studies*, Vol. XV, No. 1-2.

Kopf, David, 1969, *British Orientalism and the Bengal Renaissance:* The dynamics of Indian modernization, 1773-1835, University of California Press, Berkeley.

Kosambi, Damodar Dharmanand, 1970, *The culture and civilization of ancient India*, Delhi.

Kosambi, Damodar Dharmanand, 1962, reprint, 1998, *Myth and reality*, Popular Prakashan, Mumbai.

Marshall, P.J. (ed), 1970, *The British discovery of Hinduism in the eighteenth century*, Cambridge University press, London.

Malik S.C. (ed) 1977, *Dissent, Protest and Reform in Indian Civilization*, Simla.

Marx, Karl, 1959, *Capitalism*-a critique of Political Economy, Vol. III, Moscow.

Pande, Sushmita, 1989, *Medieval Bhakti Movement*, Kusumanjali Prakashan, Meerut.

Pande, Rekha, 1990, "The Bhakti Movement in Medieval Andhra - Problems and Perspectives" *Proceedings A.P. History Congress*, Guntur, 1990, pp. 266 - 269.

Pande Rekha, 1991, The bhakti movement and the status of women in 14th and 15th century, in J.P.Mishra (Ed) *Aspects of Indian history*, New Delhi.

Pande, Rekha, 2000, The Bhakti Movement-A historiographical Critique, *Journal of Historical Research*, Vol. X.

Peterson, Indira, Viswanathan, 1991, *Poems to Siva:* The Hymns of the Tamil Saints, Delhi.

Pillai, Vaiyapuri, S. 1956, *History of Tamil Language and Literature*, Madras.

Radhakrishna, S., 1970, *Bhagvad Gita*-Introductory Essay, 1st edition, 1948, Bombay,

Rao, M.S.A. 1977, "Themes in the ideology of Protest movements", in S.C. Malik, (ed) *Dissent, Protest and Reform in Indian Civilization*, Simla.

Sastri, Nilkanth, K.A. 1963, *Development of religion in South India*, Madras.

Singh, Jyotsna, G. 1996, *Cultural Dialogues-Colonial Narratives :* Discovery of India in the language of Colonialism, Routledge, New York,

Sharma, Krishna, 1987, *Bhakti and the Bhakti Movement*, Munshiram Manohar Lal, New Delhi.

Sharma, Krishna, 2004, "Towards a new perspective", in Lorenzen, David N. (ed), *Religious Movements in South Asia* 600-1800, Oxford University Press, New York.

Sharma, R.S. 1974, "Problems of transition from ancient to medieval in Indian history", *Indian Historical Review*, Vol. 1, No. 1, March.

Sivanand Swami, 2003, *The Bhagvat Gita*-The word to word meaning, translation and commentary, Divine Life society, Uttranchal, Himalayas.

Thapar, Romila, 1973, *The Past and Prejudice*, Publication division, Government of India.

Tarachand, 1936, *Influence of Islam on Indian Culture*, Allahabad.

Wilson, H.H. 1846, *Sketch of the religious sects of the Hindus*, Bishop Cotton Press, Calcutta.

Weber, Albrecht, 1906, as quoted in Auguste Barth, *The religions of India*, Kegan Paul, London.

Weber, Max, 1922, reprint, 1963, "Religion of the non-privileged classes", *The Sociology of Religion*, Beacon Press, Boston.

Weber, Max, 1958, reprint, 1967, *The Religion of India*-The sociology of Hinduism and Buddhism, The Free Press, Macmillan Press, New York.

Williams, Monier, 1891, *Brahmanism and Hinduism*, John Murray, London.

Zaehner, R.C. 1960, *Hindu and Muslim mysticism*, Athlone Press, London.

3

Socio-Economic Background of the Movement

The socio-economic preconditions for the rise of the Bhakti movement can be located as a set of interrelated and widespread changes in the production patterns that affected the social, cultural, political arenas which were then reflected through the religious sphere. It was a society where a number of far reaching changes like agrarian expansion, large scale craft specialization were taking place amidst the political background of emerging regional kingdoms in all parts of India. Many scholars view this movement representing the sentiments of the common people against feudal oppression. Some scholars view this movement as an Indian counterpart to the Protestant reformation in Europe. Though many Nirgun saints especially in north India were very critical of the orthodox brahmanical religion they did not call for the overthrow of the state or the ruling classes. Hence for this reason the Bhakti movement cannot be regarded as the Indian variant of the European Protestant reformation movement which was much wider in scope and related to the decline in feudalism and the emergence of Capitalism.

In order to get a clear picture of this movement we have to first understand the material base of this movement. The coming of the Turks saw feudal oppression being intensified much more because now there was a clear mechanism to extract the surplus and pass it on to the ruling elite through the Iqta system. Though the Turkish ruling class lived in the towns the extraction of the surplus from the rural areas brought in enormous resources in their hands. This along with a spread of feelings of regionalism prepared the base for the Bhakti movement.

The medieval period is characterised by the rise of a large number of regional states. The period between thirteenth to sixteenth centuries was that of the decline of an all powerful state and the rise of a number of provincial and regional states (Bharatiya Vidya Bhawan, 1980, pp. 155-286). By the beginning of 16th century there were a number of feudal states like Bengal, Khandesh, Jaunpur, Malwa, Bihar, Kashmir and Sindh in the North and Golconda, Bijapur, Bidar, Gulburga, Ahmadnagar, Berar in the south.

In north India the dominant features of the period between 7th to 12th centuries have been identified as the growing weakness of the state, the growth of the power of the local landed elites and their decentralizing authority by acquiring greater administrative, economic and political roles, the decline of towns, the setback to trade, especially long distance trade and allocation of land to the Brahmins in larger proportion than before (Sharma, 1965, 263-73). This was also a period in Northern India of the rise of Rajputs. The Rajputs accepted the support of the Brahmins and accepted their claims to superiority by a tacit alliance with those who controlled land and possessed political authority. In fact the Rajputs paid the price of their elevation from barbarianism to civilization by accepting and confirming their claims of superiority (Tarachand, 1936, 131). A large number of land grants were also given for the building and maintenance of temples. The growth of magnificent temples all over India is an index not only of a resurgence of Hinduism but even more of the newly acquired power and wealth of the Brahmins. The Brahmins enjoyed many other powers and privileges. They were appointed as Raj-Purohits and often asked to advice on various matters of dharma and polity (Shobha, 1983, 7).

This period is also remarkable for the spread of Tantrism and Shakti worship, though much widely prevalent in eastern parts of India. Another off shoot of this the Nathpanthi movement originated in eastern U.P and slowly spread to Bihar, Northern and western parts of India. There was hinduization of many tribes and consequent growth of mixed castes (Sharma, 1969). Hence at the grass root one could see the rise of a number of dissident or heterodox movements.

The advent of Islam in north India and the overthrow of the powerful Rajput states by the Turks towards the end of 12th century paved the way for the growth of Bhakti as a popular movement, for the end of Rajput Brahmin alliance removed a big obstacle in the growth of popular heterodox movements. The economic forces unleashed through this change gave a further impetus to this movement.

On the economic front the Delhi Sultanate witnessed a number of changes. This period saw an economic organization which was considerably superior to the earlier one. The first phase of the Delhi Sultanate was a period of great turmoil and insecurity. There were frequent wars of succession and this told upon reducing the resources of the empire. In the absence of a law of succession, intrigues, civil wars and violence became the order of the day. In the post Illutmish period it was the nobles who rose to great prominence and deposed monarchs according to their will and played the role of kingmakers with considerable skill (Pande, 1991, 65). Yet in spit of the political turmoil on the economic front the Delhi Sultanate had released forces that led to the expansion of towns and alternations in agrarian conditions. As a result by the 14th century there was a considerable growth of these towns and expansion in craft production and commerce. All this had occurred due to a number of changes in the various crafts due to improvement in technology. This can be seen in Seri culture, carpet weaving on the verticle loom, introduction of the spinning wheel (charkha) in the cotton textile sector, the Persian wheel in irrigation, the introduction of paper, the appearance of magnetic compass as an aid to navigation and the invention of accurate time keeping devices for the regulation of economic activity (Habib, 1969). The generation of surplus in craft production was not only the result of political innovation but certain technological changes that were also occurring. The araghata made it possible to drive the Persian wheel by animal power. The spinning wheel and weaving loom furnished with treadles increased efficiency. These innovations in technology and increase in craft production released social forces that led to an expansion of towns and the altering of agrarian relations (Habib, 1983, 12-13). The iqta system which combined military commands with revenue assignments channellised the surplus from the rural country side to the urban areas. This surplus was also transported into towns by way of commerce (Moreland, 1929, 216-228). The increase in commerce can be seen in the increase of coinage as a result of the transfer of stored silver and gold into minted money (Habib, 1978, pp. 289-91). There is also seen an increase in the slave market, to provide artisans conversant with the new techniques and cheap labour for the various crafts (Habib, 1978, p. 291). However much of the surplus generated was appropriated by the ruling classes through taxation.

It was in the interest of the Sultanate's ruling class that the number of artisans should increase and there is no evidence to suggest that the Sultanate imposed any restrictions on inter professional mobility. Though doubts have been raised about craft production being predominantly based on free labour obtained in the form of both immigration and native artisans (Siddiqui, 1980, 244). Indeed slave labour after manumission must have swelled the ranks of the free craft labour (Habib, 1980, 14). The new artisan and mercantile groups that emerged were drawn from outside the hereditary, custom bound caste groups. For these groups the newly acquired wealth did not enable them to assimilate into the prevailing hierarchy or increase their status. A similar phenomena can be observed in an earlier historical period when the city had generated its own social stratification with the artisans and merchant enjoying pride of place but enjoying no social status with in the brahmanical order (Thapar, 1978, 43-45). It is in this context that we see dissident religions such as Buddhism and Jainism developing as alternatives to Brahmanism. When the rise of Buddhism and Jainism had taken place and the city had produced its own stratification where the artisans or merchants were more powerful, yet the Brahmanical literature did not include the trader and artisan among the superior groups (Thapar, 1978, pp. 43-45).

Society was becoming more ritualistic. In order to maintain their status quo, complex rites and rituals were practiced by the Brahmins and those that did not fit into the traditional four castes were termed outcastes or chandalas (Sachau, 1983, Chapter 1). The outcastes were denied any social prestige and all the privileges of a brahmin such as recitation of the Vedas, offering of sacrifices to the fire. If a Sudra or a Vaisya was proved to have recited the Vedas and he was accused by the Brahmin before the ruler the latter would order his tongue to be cut off (Sachau, 1983, p.136). This was a period when Jainism and Buddhism had practically disappeared and it was the orthodox Brahmins that had reigned supreme. They alone understood Sanskrit in which the ancient religious texts were produced and this made the performance of various rites and rituals their monopoly.

Even among the Muslims when it came to prayers and worship, the caste and class differences were ignored and the poor and the rich worshipped side by side but caste was recognized in social relations. The Muslims were clearly divided into *Sharif Zats* or high castes and *Ajlaf Zats* or low castes. The conversion to Islam had certainly not made an individual change his old environment which was deeply influenced by caste distinctions and a general social exclusiveness. The different classes of Muslims communities also began to live aloof from one another, even in separate quarters in the same city (Ashraf, 1959, reprint, 1970, 78).

The Bhakti movement was a product of this period when a number of changes were taking place on the political, economic, social and religious front, and its ideology served a purpose. Its saints were not idle philosophers. They mostly came from lower sections of society and worked for their living. They preached in vernaculars and tried to make religion easily accessible to one and all. Here we had the movement develop along two streams-the Nirgun stream which was opposed to the worship of a form and the sagun stream which was further divided into Krishna Bhakti and Ram Bhakti.

One can see a similar kind of material base in the Deccan also which gave an impetus to the Bhakti movement. The Deccan region is an amalgam of many eco zones, from the arid rocky plateau of the Rayalseema to the bountiful coastal plains flanked by the eastern and western Ghats to the vast hinterlands with agricultural Plains and forests such as Coorg and Dandakarnya with its varied social formations, agrarian, pastoral, hunting-gathering, artisans and other forms of production make up the amazing mosaic on which many great dynasties essayed their contributions. This region in the medieval period witnessed many transformations in the politico-economic and socio-cultural spheres. Politically, the state gradually transformed into a multi-centered power structure, fragmented and segmented at different levels, owing to the extensive growth of socio-religious, philanthropic and service tenures, which operated with in the matrix of tax-tribute–plunder. The dharmic kingship of ancient times transcended into ritual kingship, further legitimized by the performance of *Dana*, *dakshina*, *titha*, *darshana* etc. Deforestation and land reclamation during the Kakatiyan (1000-1323 AD) and Vijaynagara times (1327-1600 AD) contributed to the growth of brahmanical institutions, *brahmadeyas* and *devabhogas* on the one hand and the growth of industries and agricultural expansion on the other. This resulted in the consolidation of the peasant and non-peasant groups like the merchants and artisans into guilds; the caste cum professional organizations, but also the temple as an institution that controlled the power structure of state and society.

From the middle of 6th century onwards to a period of nearly 300 years South India was virtually ruled by three great Hindu dynasties-the Chalukya of Badami, the Pallavas of Kanchi and the Pandayas of Madurai. The present Maharashtra, the entire Andhra Pradesh and a good portion of the Mysore State constituted the Chalukya Empire. A large portion of the present Tamilnadu, plus a portion of Mysore State was under the suzerainty of the Pallavas. While the present Kerala State plus Tamilnadu down below Madura formed the state of the Pandayas. Of the three the Chalukya were the biggest state and one could safely call them the masters of the Deccan plateau which later on in the 14th century became the Bahmani state (Sinha, 1964, 1).

The last quarter of the 10th century was in some respects a period of marked transition in the political history of the Deccan. Old powers, which had held sway, were crumbling giving place to new. The basis for the union of Eastern Chalukya dynasty with the Cholas was laid down when Raja Raja Chola married his daughter to Vimaladitya (Appadorai, 1936, 61).

A relatively small State at the time of Raja Raja's accession, hardly recovering from the effects of the Rashtrakuta invasion the Chola kingdom grew under him under into an extensive and well knit empire. It was efficiently organized and administered, rich in resources and in possession of a powerful standing army and navy, well tried and equal to the greatest enterprise (Sinha, 1964, 24). He destroyed the Pandayas and conquered the entire Kerala, annexed the whole of the present day Mysore and made Ceylon a feudatory. He also humbled the western Chalukyas.

In this period it was the two strong powers that stood out above all the rest and these were the Chalukya of Kalyani in the north and the Cholas in the south.

In the history of the Western Chalukya there is a short interregnum, during which Kalachuris usurped the Kalyani throne in about 1156 A.D. and ruled till 1183 A.D. This usurpation was carried by Bijjala the Kalachuri ruler. It was during this time that Vir saivism propounded by Bijjala's minister Basava became very popular in Karnataka and spread to nearby regions.

The close of the 12th century forms a convenient halting point where we can observe another shift in the political power of South India. The Chalukya power had declined and their territories were shared by two powerful feudatory families-the Yadavas in the North and Hoyasalas in the South. It was Allaudin Khilji's invasion that obliterated the Yadava kingdom from the map of Deccan.

After the downfall of the Chalukyas it was the Kaktiyas who became supreme in the south of Deccan, the present Andhra Pradesh. Saivism became the prominent faith here. The Kaktiya period can be divided into two for convenience. From 1000-1158 A.D. they acted as feudatories to both Eastern and Western Chalukayas. From 1159 to 1261 A.D. they made Warangal as their center of activity and conquered the whole of Andhra region and became its undisputed masters. Now the political turmoil of the earlier period vanished and there was stability.

During the period of the fusion of the Chalukya Cholas in Andhra Desa the Sudra community gained some prominence in society. During the reign of Kulottunga I several land grants were given to the generals and to the loyal officers belonging to the Sudra community (Kumari, 1985, 246). These generals became very popular in due course of time and adopted royal insignias. They often claimed to be descendants of solar and lunar race (Vaidehi, 1978, 36-37). These subordinate chiefs did not hesitate in declaring their independence whenever they got an opportunity. The Kaktiyas were no exception.

In society, though the laws and codes of Manusmriti, Yagnavalkya smriti and Narada Smriti of Varnashram dharma had come into being and there was a lot of proliferation with in the four castes. Each caste was divided into a number of subcastes and communities. Each of these subcastes had their own distinctive character and status in the social hierarchy depending on the creed, profession, birth or locality to which they belonged. (Kumari, 1985, 206). Though the system of Varnashram dharma was well rooted in the social structure the division with in the caste and the tensions that subsequently followed were mainly due to the identity crisis of certain groups and castes in the existing order. It was in this process of struggle that some of the Brahmin communities lost their original status and started entering into administrative positions of the state.

The Sudra community too craving for social and ritual concessions must have faced certain problems with these nonprofessional communities. In the process many from the Sudra community who were well settled both economically and politically (particularly having gained political authority) started moving up the social ladder. The struggle for existence and survival of the fittest exemplifies the fact that while some of the communities attained Kshatriya status others just remained sudras serving the dominant communities. Several mandalikas in Andhra belonging to the Sudra communities such as Velanati Chodas, Kondapadumatis, Kotas and Parichhedis became rulers of the time (Bhandarkar, 1983, 170).

Even with in the Vaisya community we notice a lot of social mobility. The merchant classes also made superior claims equal to that of privileged classes by inventing a mythical origin to celestial beings and adopting several social honours. They had their own elaborate prasastis (Rao, 1973, 279). They also bore gotras like the Brahmins, though these did not originate from the sages like the Brahmin gotras. The epigraph of the period mention gotras like Nabela gotra, Puchhokola gotra, Yerraselti gotra (Rao, 1973, 279).

The Vyasas who were termed as Komatis, Chettis and Sreshtins, were involvement in both internal and external trade. They had organized themselves into a corporate community with their principal seat at Penugonda, on the West Godavari district in the case of Andhra region (Nirmala, 1989, 369). The art of business, following dharma, protecting the cows, obtaining expertise in examining precious stones like diamonds are said to be the chief characteristics of this community (Gupta, 1955, 51). As result of their new formed wealth, a number of Vyasas attempted to gain political power and questioned the authority of the kshatriyas.

Though the Vyasyas respected Brahmins and offered them gifts and grants it seems that the Vyasyas were denied the Vedic ritual like Aswamedha, Gomedha and Jayesthabhaga, along with reforms like widow marriage and intercaste marriage (Nirmala, 1989, 369). Instead of the Vedavidhi they followed the Puranaktavidhi. However their non Vedic ideology did not turn them against Brahmins. Many of them stated themselves as srotriyas. Infact during this period there is a lot of upward mobility among the various castes.

The Telikas were oil mongers. They aspired for a higher status and wanted to be classed among the Vaisyas. They claimed their descent from Manu. They formed themselves into an association with their principal seat at Bejawada (Parvathamma, 1972, 7). Viswakarmas another subcaste, who were metal workers, traced their descent from Viswakarma, the son of brahma. They also claimed a high status in the society and wanted to be considered as Brahmins. The Vishwakarmas of south India donned the scared thread and called them as Brahmins by the 18th century and were now known as the acari. Sects like Kamma and Telaga had their origin in the territorial division of the country. These terms were associated with those people who were in charge of a grama or village. The term Reddy, Rattadi or Kapu means he, who protects, safeguarded and looked after the revenue affairs and law and order in the place of his appointment. In due course of time they enhanced their power and held all the key posts in the administrative services. During the 14th century some of the Reddy communities attained Kshatriya status and became the rulers of Andhra Desa with Kondaveedu as their capital.

Epigraphic and literary references of the period reveal the existence of the community of Chandalas also. The Chandalas were considered untouchables (*Antyajati* or *Panchamas)* and were kept away from the towns. The place of their residence was termed Malvada, Madigavada or Velipalem. Vir saivism attracted these sects a lot because the Virsaiva teachers preached that spiritual salvation is available to all classes including the Chandalas. They preached that if a person is an ardent follower of Virsaivism he should be respected even if he happens to be a chandala or untouchable by birth thereby giving them dignity.

In theory the Brahmins continued to occupy the highest position in the social hierarchy. The learned Brahmins were respected and patronized by the rulers by giving them brahmadeya land grants. These land grants gave them a special position to exercise their religious powers as well as to become politically powerful. Many of these agraharas were primarily tax-free lands, the revenue of which went directly to the Brahmins. The emergence of sects and subsects with in the Varna system also affected the Brahmin community. We also have evidence of the Brahmins taking to various professions during the period like the state and military services, trades and agriculture and others as administrators, commanders and ambassadors. These Brahmins who entered the administrative machinery were called Niyogis.

All those Brahmins who were well versed in the Vedic knowledge performed rituals and confined themselves to the traditional brahmanical way of life became Vaidicas. (Vaidehi, 1978, 27). These people followed the Principle of Vaidica Karma and broke the traditional Brahmin monopoly over Vedic Knowledge. Those who did not believe in dual system of Siva and Vishnu became Samarthas and the Saivites worshipped Siva and the Vaishnavites worshipped Vishnu. In Andhra region one of the subsects of Virsaivites, namely Aradhya, started by Mallikarjuna Panditaradhya became prominent.

The large-scale migrations during this period resulted in further proliferation of this community. These migrant groups with their sect names also joined the main stream Brahmin community. A group of Brahmins hailing from a particular nadu or Vishya were named after them. Jinavallabha the brother of Pampa describes himself as a Brahmin born in the Kammanati Brahmin community (Suryanarayana, 1986, 244). Therefore we had three categories of Brahmins. These included the Vaidicas who were confined to performing Vedic karma and temple rituals, the Niyogis who entered the administrative services and the immigrant Brahmins who settled in the coastal regions in the agraharas granted by the kings.

As far as the Kashatriya community was concerned, the Kshatriya status was not confined to any one particular community or group but was kept open to all the communities. We do not come across the term Kshatriya in medieval Andhra Desa and they are referred to as Rajas. (Suryanarayana, 1986, 244) Most of these Rajas took up military, administrative service under various dynasties. In fact many mandalikas belonging to Sudra community such as Velanatin Chodas, Kondapadumatis, Kotas, and Parichhedis became rulers at this time and claimed Kshatriya status. They maintained matrimonial relations with both Brahmins and the Kshatriyas of this period (Vaidehi, 1978, 37).

In South India there is a lot of proliferation of castes. Nannaya in his Mahabharata cities the story of Yayati a

Kshatriya who falls in love with Devyani the daughter of Sukra, a Brahmin and decides to marry her. Referring to the decision of Yayati, Janamejeya Maharaja says that the marriage if it takes place would lead to Varna Samskara (mixed caste system) which is not a healthy sign for the society. He further states that Yayati being a Kshatriya should not go against dharma as he is supposed to be a custodian of Varnashramdharma. Surprisingly the original Mahabharata of Vyasa though mentions the Varna attaches no particular importance to it. The change takes place in Nannayas period because by this time the laws and codes of Manusmriti, Yagnavalkya smriti and Narada Smriti etc. of Varnashramdharma had come into being (Ramchandra Rao, 1985, 45).

Hence during the medieval period though at the ideological level the four fold Varna system existed, in reality among all these Varna there was a proliferation of sub castes. The change in the political sphere, and the establishment of peace, had an impact on the society and economy of the period. This phase of rule was marked by a general rise in civilization bringing about a taste and refinement in dress, decoration, manners and other fields of social activity (Sundaram, 1968, 10).

A large number of Brahmin migrants had already come from the Tamil region and settled in Andhra. They were known as Dravidulu. These were subdivided into various sub groups such as Velanati brahmins, Kammanati brahmins, Palanati brahmins depending on the changes in their habitats (Surya Narayana, 1986, 244).

The Brahmins were the chief beneficiaries of the agraharas or land tenures and endowments made to the temples. The endowments were made to provide income for the temple maintenance, for festivals, for honouring the deities and for food offerings. (Stein, 1984, 162). If the donation was made tax free it was an additional advantage for they would get the produce from land and were under no obligation to pay the taxes which were hitherto paid by the owners. In the village community, the Brahmin thus played a major role as a dominant social group as well as proprietors of land. Encountering no disturbance or trouble from the kings and their officers these brahmins spent a peaceful life in their agraharas by imparting spiritual knowledge to the students and participating in rituals (Surya Narayana, 1986, 245). Some Brahmins also took to other professions such as state service, military service, trade and agriculture. The descendants of the family of Nanduri Gundaya Mantri a Brahmin served as ministers for the Velanati chiefs (Kumari, 1985, 117). The Brahmins who took to arms formed a separate community called, Brahma Kshatriyas. Some are also referred to as Brahma Kshatriya Kula (South Indian Inscriptions, Vol. VI, No. 156, dt. 1154 A.D.)

Most of the ruling dynasties of the period belonged to the fourth caste and as their social status went up they started making claims of belonging to Kshatriya clans and descendants of the solar and lunar race for ritual purpose. They strengthened their power by marriage alliances with the original Kshatriya families on one hand and making donations to the temple and Brahmins on the other. The daughter of Velanati Gonka II, Mailadevi, belonged to the Sudra caste but was married to the Haihaya Kshatriya prince of Palanadu, Anguraju (Kumari, 1985, 190).

From the 11th century there is a marked change in the development of trade and commerce. Various industries like metal, oil, carpentry, masonry, textiles of the period increased the demand for luxury goods. Diamond industry of the region was praised extensively by even the later day foreign travellers who spoke at great length about the revenues received from it (Thevenot, 1971, 93-102). Diamonds and other metals like gold, silver, copper were used extensively for making ornaments and articles. The large-scale construction of temples created work for a great number of sculptors, masons, master builders, carpenters and weavers. The various epigraphical references of the period in Andhra Desa clearly reveal the fact that the temple constituted a large market for the various industrial products. By promoting industry the temple also improved the economic status of various artisan groups. Some important temples of the period maintained artisans like goldsmiths, carpenters, weavers and masons permanently on their roll.

The temple besides encouraging the artisan classes to improve their economic status also encouraged agriculture by irrigation development (Stein, 1984, 68-89). The business community was also benefited because generally pilgrim routes became inland trade routes. It is likely that traders followed these pilgrim routes for carrying out their business (Satyanarayana, 1983, 51). The inland trade was carried out by the vyasas as well as the virbalanjas of the fourth caste (Sundaram, 1968, 46-53). Inland trade was promoted through *Angadis* or the regular market fairs or *Santalu* and *tirunallus* organized fairs on festive occasions near the temple. An inscription dt. 1147, mentions that every Thursday a fair was arranged at Kotyadona (South Indian Inscriptions, Vol. IV, No. 65). Another inscription from Simhachalam refers to a Tirunallu being organized in the temple area (South Indian Inscriptions, 1986, Vol. VI, No. 969). These fairs gave a lot of fillip to trade and commerce.

Besides internal trade, foreign trade also was in a flourishing state during this period and this added to the prosperity of the merchant community. The extension of the Kakatiyas dynasty over the coastal Andhra during 11th and 12th century brought forth a new epoch in foreign trade. Ganapati deva did much to revive foreign trade by offering protection and concession in taxes to the foreign traders as has been mentioned by the Motupalli Inscription.

Expansion of both internal and foreign trade gave employment to large number of traders of both the third and fourth castes and helped them gain a higher economic status. This resulted in their organization into highly developed guilds. There is evidence of much corporate activity during this period. The whole of Deccan was spread with a network of guilds which regulated trade, industry and banking business (Reddy, 1967, 64). Among the prominent merchant guilds of the period were the Pikkandri, Nandesi and the Telikiovuru. Two other merchant guilds of the period were Ayyavole and Manigramam. These guilds were active in handling and distribution of commodities of foreign trade and in some instances; themselves procured goods at the source. Some of these items included luxurious goods like precious stones, pearls, aromatic woods, resins and perfumes and they also traded in commodities like dyes, textiles, processed iron (wootz), live stock, spices and medicinal plants. Of these the manufactured goods the textiles and processed iron became increasingly important from 13th century onwards (Abraham, 1988, 7). So a long with a network of trade and guilds there was considerable economic expansion.

In the Deccan, the later half of the 12th century resulted in marked increase in overseas trade and the development of urban settlement. With the changes in the economy there was bound to be a shift in the social order and changes in the relationship of traders with the state, with the agrahara Brahmana and with the peasant cultivator and landowner (Abraham, 1988, 73).

Besides these there were other communal and professional corporate bodies too comprising of members from different castes and religious corporate bodies as the, "Srivaisnavulu". They functioned more or less as autonomous bodies governing the socio-economic life of their members and in giving grants to some important religious and public purpose (Pande, 1990, 45-46). They even had influence in administration and were provided with arms. They enjoyed certain privileges as having prasastis, banners, seals, corporate property etc. We have an example of the Nagareswara swami temple at Penugonda which was worshipped by the members of the Nakaramu guild (Reddy, 1986, 271-276).

The vasyas also were initially a caste of traders who entered the royal service as bankers and treasures. Slowly they moved into administration. Some of them even served as ministers for minister for military chiefs. A 10th century epigraph of Vemalvada refers to a band of nine sreshtas in the royal court. (South Indian Inscriptions, 1986, Vol. IV, No. 65). They made several endowments and constructed various temples.

It has been argued that India like Europe was affected by profound and rapid changes in the character of its societies and economic and state forms, from at least the 16th century and a fundamental aspect of this development was a local merchant capital which emerged independently of that in Europe, but with a common international theatre of societal and commercial changes (Perlin, 1983, 33). The rapid growth of commerce in the Deccan prior to 16th century proves that the ground was being laid for such a development.

Increasing external and internal trade during this period coincided with urban growth and establishment of an alliance between the peasant farmer and the trader. Bulk assignments of paddy, sugar and a variety of grains and spices came to the towns under the aegis of both the peasant farmer and the trader. Trade brought in wealth which was redeployed into urban centers and into the temples.

Many of the donations made by the rich merchants covered the cost of the temple ritual and food. The oil or ghee used in the rituals as well as flowers and aromatics were supplied by the merchants, as well as textile and clothing. Hence the sacred and the economic geography coincided.

With the improvement in their economic status the lower caste people began to crave for higher social honours inventing mythical origins for each community and keeping Risi gotras similar to Brahmins. The Visvakarma community claimed equal social status with that of the Brahmins. The members of the fourth caste too entered the political world claiming the right to learn, propitiate gods, give grants to Brahmins and temples and assume various titles. Many of the political powers of this time who emerged from the fourth caste claimed descendants from solar and lunar races (Reddy, 1982, 1).

The caste system was in a flexible state and the earlier division of castes based on professions had become impractical. There was a movement for a change amongst the lower caste groups who had money power to back them but no social status. Therefore Sri Vaisnavism had to accommodate these changes and provide equality to all classes in the matter of attaining religious merit.

In spite of these changes the Brahmins never lost their eminent position. They enjoyed the rights of honours and continued their hold on performance of religious rituals. They alone were employed as temple priests and were given land grants for maintaining educational institutions. To continue their strong hold on society they stressed the need for religious observations of vratas, scriptures, making *Danas* and other religious observations. The new movement bhakti helped in foraging a broader cultural unity by integrating tribal and local or regional cults with in the brahmanical framework and the resultant symbiosis even transformed the character of brahmanical religions as they were now based on devotional worship (Jaiswal, 2000, 13).

During this period we find that there was a mutual exchange of honours between the kings and the pontiffs of religious institutions, the former for legitimization of their ritual status and the latter for protection of their tenures. The sectarian religions, Saivism and Vaishnavism, their leaders and institutions like temples, pithas and mathas through the ideology of the bhakti, manipulated the political base of the state. In other words the temple became a nexus of power that gradually transformed into a state in miniature and appeared homologous to political center. It had a huge bureaucracy at its command amongst them were large number of temple girls or the sanis, who were employed in the service of God formed significant officiating dignitaries. These were the most important ritual performers and no festive occasion was complete in the temple with out the performance of the temple girls. The employment of these dancing girls became customary on the part of the *Devasthana,* which gradually institutionalized into a professional organization (Pande, 2004, 26).

The medieval period in Deccan was a period of the rise of various feudatories to power and in order to give legitimacy to their power they used the support of the Brahmin priests, the temples and the tribals. The situation was no different in Andhra. The Andhra region can be defined as an area extending from Mahendragiri in the north to Kalahasti in the south and from Bay of Bengal in the east to Sri Sailam in the west (Sundaram, 1968). Prior to the coming of Kakatiyas the Andhra region especially the deltaic strip formed the peripheral part of the empire either in Karnataka as in the case of the western Chalukyas or Tamilnadu as in the case of the Chalukyas Cholas. The upland region as it was sparsely settled was seldom incorporated. Now when the Kakatiyas came to power with their base in Telengana, we find a shift in the political, economic and cultural activity from the coastal region to the interior Andhra.

The eastern and western ghat regions of the Kakatiya kingdom were covered with deciduous forests and hilly areas. Three major rivers and their tributaries Godavari, Krishna and Pennar flowed through the region and the soil was red loamy with a lot of arable land. The Kakatiyas realized the importance of this and tried to clear the forests by donating land to their officials and Brahmins. As a result many new villages were established and several thousands of acres of land were put under the plough. Irrigation was established in these areas and many new tanks dug. Trichana Pallava granted Lavanpura to one thousand Brahmins who came from Ahichatrapura situated on the banks of Ganges (Satyanarayana, 1983, 25). Virchoda near Pithapuram was granted to about 536 Brahmins (Epigraphia Indica, Vol. V, 1892, 96). This was a continuation of the practices of the earlier period.

It has been pointed out that in the early medieval period when the archaeological data is corroborated with the inscriptional evidences; we find that land grants were given in a large scale to priests and the temples. Most of these land grants, between the 5th to 7th century AD were concentrated in tribal areas of Bengal, Assam, Orissa, Madhya Pradesh, Maharashtra and Andhra Pradesh (Sharma, 1974, 177-179). As a result we have a large number of tribal and sudras also coming into the fold of Brahmanism. The spread of brahmanical ideology in new areas gave a legitimization to the state because the Brahmins by advocating Varnashram Dhrama and respect to the king brought in stability to the empire and removed any dissenting voice. In fact the medieval period saw a gradual establishment of a process started much earlier in early medieval times with the clearance of forests, system of land grants to Brahmins and monastic establishments, recruitment of sudras as artisans and agricultural labourers and contact with different forest dwelling communities (Sharma, 1974, 178). Kingship assumed a dualistic sovereignty incorporating both the political and ritualistic aspect. While the kings stabilized their political power by coercion, they established their ritualistic power by conciliation and giving gifts. The earlier Vedic sacrifices were now replaced by Dana and dakshina as a legitimizing factor for kingship. This reveals a shift from dharmic to ritual kinship. Gifts giving included land grants to the temple, Brahmins, monastic establishments and the construction activities under the ideology of *Saptasantanas.* There are seven pious deeds known as *Sapta Santanas.* These include having one's own son, adopting a son, composing a literary work, and gifting an agrahara, a garden, a tank or construction of a temple (Sastri, 1978, 281). The example of the ruler was followed by the ruled. Thus the state polity backed by the dharmic ideology fostered the temple building activities.

Temple Building Activities

In medieval Deccan the temple served as a multifarious center. It was not only a place of worship but also a center for social, economic, religious and cultural life of the people. It was in fact a nucleus of the village life. There was hardly any village without a temple. Installation of temples was considered as one of the seven acts of righteousness known as Saptasanta. There is a lot of epigraphical evidence of this period to show that these temples were endowed with lands and several gifts of cash and kind.

The kings encouraged temple-building activities giving all possible help to their feudatories. Before the Cholas the power was divided among small segmentary units. The Chola rulers by expressing their symbolic and ritual sovereignty through the brahmadeyas and patronizing temples tried to integrate the segmentary units of power (Stein, 1980, 8). In this process of integration from 10th century onwards the temple and the brahmadayas played a major role and maintained irrigational works also. Many a time the regional kingdoms patronized the religion and deities of the tribals, which surrounded their kingdoms and through the construction of imperial temples to the tribal deities, achieved political integration (Kulke, 1978).

The temples also encouraged education. The big temples used to maintain Vidya mandapams where efficient teachers were employed and free boarding and lodging provided to students (Sarma, 1976, 21). Many of the Siva temples during this period maintained teachers who taught Vedas, Sastras, Agamas, Puranas, Itihasas, Kavyas and Saiva philosophy. In the Andhra region such Kalmukha Saiva mathas existed in Vemulvada where the eminent teachers were employed to impart knowledge to their disciples (Sastri, 1991, 321-322).

The kings and nobles made liberal grants of land and villages for the support of the customary rites and festivals in temples and also for the education in the temples. The

Brahmins who received immense gifts and land grants often invested gold with the village assemblies and received interests thereupon for the maintenance, worship, burning of perpetual lamp and similar other purposes (Sharma, 1974, 120). South Indian temples suggest 12% to 15% as the usual rate of interest for temple investments (Sharma, 1974, 123).

Temples also acted as a tool of urbanization by developing commercial activities in and around the center. Sizeable urban settlements became an adjunct of great temples (Stein, 1980, 246). The inscriptions carved in various temples reveal the benefactors of the Vyasa community. Some of the merchants' guilds like Ayyavolu and Nakaramu in the Andhra region supported temple building activities. Temples were surrounded by numerous shops selling various articles needed by pilgrims for worship. Fairs and Santas were conducted around the temple and these gave a lot of impetus to inland trade. An inscription of 1147 A.D. mentions that every Thursday a fair was arranged at Kotyadona (South Indian Inscriptions, Vol. IV, 1986, No. 65) Another inscription of Simhachalam refers to a *Tirunallu* (fair) being held regularly in the temple area (South Indian Inscriptions, Vol. VI, 1986, No. 969).

For the support of such a social structure a well-knit economic system prevailed during this period. Land was the main source of revenue for the State and by improving the irrigation facilities, it added to its income. Proper care was taken to provide water supply to the cultivable lands. Irrigation was carried through *Cheruvula* (Tanks), *Kalavalu* (canals) and *Bavulu* (wells) (Kumari, 1985, 246). Added to this was the income and wealth received through trade and commerce. As a result of the extensive inland and foreign trade the demand for luxurious goods increased and many industrial arts developed. Many occupations connected with industrial arts developed. These included silversmiths, goldsmiths, sculptors collectively forming the Visvakarma community and artisan communities comprising of the oil mongers, pot makers, barbers, washerwomen etc. We come across not only merchant guilds and craft guilds but also agricultural guilds during this period (Nagabhushanam, 1978, 47). The guilds and their operations, internal commerce and commerce with other regions seem to have catered to the needs of the different stratas of society and generated a large amount of wealth.

During the medieval period the lucrative overseas trade, the trader and agriculturist alliances and the development of towns and temples were interdependent phenomena. The provision of agricultural capital for trade and the influx of gold and copper from overseas trade probably contributed to the establishment and growth of trading interests in already existing towns, particularly the ports and also contributed to the development of many minor redistributing centres through out the peninsula (Abraham, 1988, 118-19). There was a close relationship between the sectarian movements and the development of commerce around the towns.

The various economic functions of the temple made it a citadel of economic power enjoying a status co-equal to that of the state. Temples directed agricultural development, through the endowments it received. Endowments were made in order to provide income for temple maintenance, for festivals honouring the deities and for food offerings to the deities. The endowments involved made provisions for a perpetual service for the merit of the donor or someone designated by the donor. Of the land endowments, which the temple received, it did not have ownership rights but had a major share in the income. The money investments received by the temple were frequently loaned to the village assemblies and commercial firms for a perpetual interest and these added to the income of the temples (Stein, 1984, 282-301). Temple became the citadel of the socio-economic activities of the people. It was the nucleus around which village, towns and commerce flourished. The temple was closely associated with the territorial and communal bodies in the administration of local areas. It was both a landlord and an employer. Its treasury was a bank, which received deposits and lent money.

Hence the medieval period in the Deccan saw a proliferation in the number of temples. Temples were expected to confer on the builder several merits and benefits such as longevity, health, wealth and prosperity in this world and religious merit. We had kings building temples in token of gratitude for victories. Kakatiya king, Rudradeva built shrines for Surya, Rudra and Vasudeva at Hanamkonda after defeating several chieftains (Kakatiya Sanchika Inscriptions, 1991, No. 18, pamphlet, p. 389). Sometimes temples were raised in the name of the dead person. The Kota queen Ganapamba constructed a temple for God Betesvara in the name of her father in 1172 AD (Epigraphia Indica, 1892, Vol. III, pp. 94-103). Many a times vassals erected temples in the names of their overlords. In 1153 AD Jaya the General of the kakatiya king Ganapati Deva, built a temple and installed in it Ganapeswara, named after the king at Dvipa. (Epigraphia Indica, Vol. III, 1892, p. 82). Temples were built for the merit of parents and preceptors. In 1059 A.D. a Reddy of the Kondapamati country built a temple of Somesvara at Goniyapundi for the merit of his parents. (Tirumal Tirupati Devsthanam Inscriptions, Vol. III, 1935, pp 73-74). We also have instances of temples being built for self-merit or to establish the religious merit of their gotras. In 1176 A.D. Hacalamba the daughter of king Allugi, the lord of the town of Morata founded the shrine of Hacalesvara, after her own name. (Pushpagiri, 304 of 1905, p. 25).

Thus there was a total institutionalization of the temple. These temples flourished because the ruling warrior groups provided them with support and protection (Stein, 1984, 348-373). A vast range of officials and warlords came to exercise a lot of control over the temple functioning. Besides these functionaries there was also a substantial participation by pilgrims.

Homologiation of the God and the King

There was now a perfect homologiation of the God and the king. Along with the growth in the number of temples there was a growth in the number of rituals performed in them. It now became necessary to employ a number of specialized priests to perform the daily rituals. They were supported by a large group of people belonging to various professions. These included weavers, potters, carpenters, musicians and a large number of girls. The temple girls were thus a very necessary and integral part of the socio-economic and political set up of medieval times.

The temple firmly established the agrarian feudal order as the honours received by the social groups participating in the temples reveal this on account of the simple fact that in return for their donations; the temple gave redistributed honours thus elevating them ritually and socially. In other words the nearness to the temple meant a higher ritual rank and also honours. The rise of the devotional bhakti literature also suggests this and also the reactions against the same, like in Udipi, where the statue of the presiding deity is positioned towards the wall indicating the struggle of the untouchable worshippers, which according to the prevalent tradition says was not taken kindly by the lord Krishna and hence he turned himself back. There are a number of attempts to authenticate and legitimise the new feudal polity of the period through a parallelism between the deity and the king (Narayanan, 1987, 348-373). In fact the deity in the temple is equated with the king and a parallel world of authority is reconstructed on the spiritual plane. Ritual worship in the temple is conceived on the same lines as ritual services offered to the king.

Since the temple and the God were homologous with the royal court and the king respectively, the *Devasthana* had to maintain the same bureaucracy as that of the *Rajsthana*. Elaborate temple rituals were developed. These were of two kinds, *Angabhoga*-the general worship services and *Rangabhoga*, which were special services performed at the *Rangamantapa*, either daily or on festive occasions and constructed for this purpose.

All these services meant that god was an earthly king and like the king in the court his daily needs had to be taken care of right from the beginning of the day to the mid night service. In both these places the temple and the court women were employed in large numbers. In fact we often find the distinction between the Devas and the kings court diminishing with certain inscriptions alluding to interchangeability of women in the temple services with those of the kings court. An inscription from Sri Kalahasti temple records the orders of the king transferring dancing girls and their descendants from his service to that of the temple (Inscription of Andhra Desa, Vol. II, 1968, Part 1, No. 660). A record from Mukha lingam temple mentions that Vasama the Gudisani of Madhukisvara temple was also the Lanjya of Doddapanayaka, an officer of the Velanaduchoda king Rajendra Choda (Inscription of Andhra Desa, Vol. II, 1968, Part 1, 669). An epigraph dt. 1531 from Tirumala states that Muddukuppayi, who was originally attached to the palace of Achuta Raya, was ordered to proceed to the temple (Soma Reddy, 1984, 260). They were regarded as nitya sumangali, ever auspicious one, who could never be widowed since she was married to an immortal God and they were responsible for preserving the traditional arts in the temple. (Saskia, 1987).

The elaboration of temple ritual and homologiation of God and the Lord necessitated the expansion of the temple hierarchy, especially the *sanis* or dancing girls. All the temples in medieval times had between 300 to 500 of these girls depending on the location and importance of the temple. These girls were employed to perform dance and play music before the deity, sing mangal Gitas and namasankirtanas, wave fly whisks in the presence of the God, carry on administrative responsibilities and clean and decorate the temple premises. These girls played a significant role in popularizing the Bhakti cult and became a link between God and the King. In the feudal political background of medieval times it was these girls who crossed from one boundary to another with ease and were objects of ritualistic exchanges between the King's court and the temple (Pande, 2004, 39). Hence in the Deccan the sectarian religions, Saivism and Vaisnavism, their leaders and institutions like temples, *Pithas* and *Mathas* through the ideology of Bhakti manipulated the political base of the state. The temple became the nexus of power that gradually transformed into a state in miniature and appeared homologus to the political centre

References

Abraham, Meera, 1988, *Two medieval merchant guilds of south India*, Manohar Publications, New Delhi.

Ashraf, K.M. 1959, reprint, 1970, *Life and conditions of the people of Hindustan*, Munshiram Manoharlal, New Delhi.

Appadorai, A. 1936, *Economic conditions in south India* (1000-1500 A.D.) Madras University, Madras.

Bharatiya Vidya Bhawan, 1980, *'The Delhi Sultanate'*, The succession states of the Delhi Sultanate, pp. 155-286. New Delhi.

Bhandarkar, R.J, 1983, reprint, 1913 original, *Vaisnavism, Saivism and Minor religious systems.*

Das Gupta, S.N. 1955, *History of Indian Philosophy*, Vol. V. Cambridge.

Epigraphia Indica, Vol. V, 1892, Calcutta.

Habib, Irfan, 1969, Presidential Address, Section II, "Technological change and society, 13th and 14th centuries, Varanasi Session, *Proceedings of Indian History Congress.*

Habib, Irfan, 1978, "Economic History of India", *Indian Historical Review*, Vol. IV, No. 2, Jan. pp. 289-291.

Habib, Irfan, 1980, "The economic History of Delhi Sultanate" in Devahuti (ed), *Bias in Indian Historiography*, D.K. Publications, New Delhi.

Inscriptions of Andhra Desa, Vol. II, 1968, part, 1, No. 660, (ed.) M. Rama Rao, Tirupati.

Inscriptions of Andhra Desa, Vol. II, 1968, part 1, No. 669, (ed.) M. Rama Rao, Tirupati.

Jaiswal, Suvira, 2000, 'Change and continuity in Brahmanical religion with particular reference to Vaisnava bhakti", *Social Scientist*, Vol. 29, No. 5-6, May June.

Kumari, M. Krishna, 1985, *The rule of Chalukya Cholas in Andhra Pradesh*, New Delhi.

Moreland, W.H. 1929, *Agrarian systems of Moslem India*, Cambridge University Press.

Narayanan M.G.S and Veluthat Keshavan 1987, " The Bhakti movement in medieval South India", in D.N. Jha (Ed) *Feudal Social Formations in early India*, Delhi.

Nirmala, T., 1989, *Nannechoda Kumarsambhava Pariseelamu* (Telugu), Vijaywada.

Nagabhushanam A. 1978, "Agricultural guilds in Medieval Deccan" in proceedings of *A.P. History Congress*, Vijaywada.

Parvathamma, C., 1972, *Sociological essays on Vir Saivism*, Popular Prakashan, Bombay.

Pande Rekha, 1990, *Succession Struggle in the Delhi Sultanate*, Commonwealth Publication, New Delhi.

Pande, Rekha, 1990, 'The socio-economic context of Sri Vaisnavism in 11th and 12th century Andhra", *in Itihas*, Vol. XVI, No. 2, July-December.

Pande, Rekha, 2004, "At the service of the Lord-Temple Girls in Medieval deccan (11th to 17th century), *Deccan Studies*, Vol. II, No. 2, July-December.

Perlin, Frank, 1983, "Proto-Industialization and pre-colonial South Asia", *Past and Present*, 98, pp. 31-95.

Rao, Hanumanth, B.S.L 1973, *Religion in Andhra*, Guntur, Andhra Pradesh.

Ram Chandra Rao, C.V. 1985, *Administration and society of Medieval Andhra* (1038-1536 A.D.) Hyderabad.

Reddy, Soma, 1984, *History of Religious Institutions in Andhra Desa* (1300-1600 A.D.), New Era Publications, Madras.

Reddy, P. Chenna, 1986, "Privileges of guilds in medieval Andhra desa–India", *Past and Present*, Vol. III, No. 2.

Reddy, R. Narasimha, 1967, *Corporate life in medieval Andhradesa*, University Grants Commission, New Delhi.

Reddy, S. Pratap (Telugu), 1982, *Andhrula Sanghika Charitra*, Hyderabad, 1982.

Sachau, reprint, 1983, *Alberunis India*, Vol. 1, Chapter, II, New Delhi.

Sinha, S.K. 1964, *Medieval history of the Deccan Bahmanids*, The Government of A. P. archeological Series, Hyderabad.

Sharma, R.S. 1965, *Indian Feudalism*, c. 300-1200, Calcutta.

Sharma, R.S. 1969, *Social change in early medieval India* (A.D. 500-1200), Delhi.

Sharma, R.S. 1974, *Historical Probings*, New Delhi.

Shobha, Savitri Chandra, 1983, *Social life and concepts in Medieval Hindi Bhakti poetry*-A socio-cultural study, Chandrayan Publications, New Delhi.

Sastri, P.V. Parabrahma, 1978, *The Kakatiyas of Warangal*, Government of Andhra Pradesh, Hyderabad.

Saskia C. Kersen boom-Story, 1987, *Nityasumangali*, Motilal Banarsidas Delhi.

Satyanarayana, K. 1983, *A study of the history and culture of Andhra Desa*, Vol. II, New Delhi.

Sundaram, K. 1968, *Studies in Social and economic conditions in Medieval Andhra Desa* (1000-1600 AD) Machilipatnam.

Stein, Burton, 1984, "The State, The temple and Agricultural Development", in Burton Stein (Ed), *All the Kings Mana:* Papers in medieval South Indian History, New Era Publication, Madras.

Stein, Burton, 1984, "Social Mobility and Medieval South Indian Hindu Sects", in Burton Stein (Ed), *All the Kings Mana:* Papers in medieval South Indian History, New Era Publication, Madras.

Stein, Burton 1984, "The economic functions of medieval South Indian Temple", in All the kings Mana, Papers in medieval South Indian History, New Era Publication, Madras, 1984,

South Indian Inscriptions, Vol. V, 1986, No. 1083, (ed.) Rao Bahadur H. Krishna Sastry, Govt. Press, Madras, 1923, reprint 1986, Mysore.

South Indian Inscriptions, Vol. IV, 1986, No. 65.

South Indian Inscriptions, Vol. VI, 1986, No. 969, (ed.) K.V. Subrahmanya Aiyer, Govt. Press, Madras 1925, reprint, Delhi, 1986.

South Indian Inscriptions, Vol. X, 1986, No. 344, (ed.) J. Ramayya Pantulu, Govt. Press, Madras, 1948, Reprint, Mysore, 1986.

Siddiqui, Y.M., 1980 in "Economic History of Delhi Sultanate-a critique", in Devhuti (ed), *Bias in Indian Historiography,* D.K. Publication, New Delhi.

Surya Narayana, K. 1986, *History of minor Chalukya families in Andhra Desa,* Delhi, 1986

Tarachand, 1936, *Influence of Islam on Indian Culture,* Allahabad.

Temple Inscriptions of Andhra Pradesh, Vol. I, 1980, No. 264, Srikakulam District, Hyderabad.

Tirumala Tirupati Devasthanam Inscriptions, Vol. III, 1935, No. 2, Madras.

Tirumala Tirupati Devasthanam Inscriptions, Vol. IV, 1936, No. 142, Madras.

Thapar, Romila, 1978, *Ancient Indian social History:* Some Interpretations, Delhi.

Thevenot, 1971, *The travels of Monsieur De Thevenot into the Levant,* reprint, F. Gregg, London.

Vaidehi, Krishna Moorthy, 1970, *Socio-Economic conditions in Eastern Deccan,* (1000-1250 A.D.), Hyderabad.

4

Bhakti Movement in the Southern Regions

Historians have studied the Bhakti movement as a pan-Indian movement using concepts and categories that translate to all parts of the country. While this approach no doubt helps us in providing a theoretical framework it does not answer various questions that are specific to the region of south India and one ends up looking at bhakti through a northern centre view. Spatial and temporal differences have seen different historical forces at play in southern India on an already existing base which was markedly different from that of northern or eastern India, two of which may be mentioned at the outset, the relative lesser to almost negligible Muslim influence in many southern regions and the predominance of the temple as an overarching social and religious institution. Hence we have to look at south India in order to understand the different aspects of this movement.

There were three major sects in the South, namely, Vaisnavism the members of which worship Vishnu, Saivism the followers of which worship Siva and Saktas or the worshippers of Shakti. Each of these sects were further divided into different subsects.

It was the Vaisnava saints, Alwars and the Saiva saints Nayanars who made the doctrine of Bhakti popular among their followers in the south between the seventh and tenth centuries against the backdrop of religious tensions between the orthodox sects and the heterodox sects (viz. the Jainas and the Buddhists) which explains the organized and political character of bhakti and the social concern i.e. the need to win over the masses and thus strike at the base of the Jainas. Sri Vaisnavism is one of the subsects of Vaisnavism founded by Nathamuni and developed under Ramanujacharya. Like Saivism, Vaisnavism was also based on perfect faith and devotion or Bhakti.

The followers of this sect have left behind numerous records embodying the teachings, philosophy and other details regarding the sect. Studies made on the subject are concerned with the Vedic origin of the sect, its development in the Gupta period, the concept of Bhakti in Vaisnavism as revealed through the Bhagavat Gita. There are few works that focus on Sri Vaisnavism no doubt, like Sri T. Gopinath Rao's, Lectures on Sri Vaishnavas, delivered by Sri Subramanya Ayyar (Rao Gopinath, 1923), B.V. Ramanuja's, History of Vaisnavism (Ramanuja, 1985) but generally these works concentrate on the history of the Alwars and Acharyas, the tamil origin of the sect. There are a number of other works, which concentrate on the philosophical aspect of the sect. (Bhatt, 1980, Clooney, 1994, Vardachari, 1982, Gonda, 1976).

Though a variety of sources, epigraphical and literary are available for the study of religion and society in medieval period, in south India, no particular work is found regarding Sri Vaisnavism outside the Tamil region. Most of our information comes from the Vaishnava temple inscriptions at Tirupati, Simhachalam, Sri Kurmam and Bapatla. Works like the Ranganadha Ramayanamu by Gona Buddha Reddy, Nrisimhapuranamu by Errapragada and Keyurabahucharitra by Manchana give us a little information about the vaisnava acharyas of this period. Most of the Telugu works of this period emphasize on Saivism. Saivism was the dominant religion of this period and both eastern Chalukyas and Kakatiyas were both Saivites. The abundance of Saivite literature for this period has led scholars to refer to the period from 1100 to 1250 A.D. as, *Siva Kavi Yugam.* (Rao Venkat, 1956, 2). Except for B.S.L. Hanumanth Rao's, general work on, Religion in Andhra Desa, there is hardly any work that concentrates outside the Tamil region and analyses the religion and society in this region, specifically Sri Vaisnavism.

We can clearly see two distinct phases in the development of Vaisnavism in south India. In the pre-Vijaynagara period from 1000 A.D. to 1326 A.D. when it did not receive any royal patronage and finally split into two subsects and in the Vijaynagara period when it received royal patronage. In the first phase though Vaisnavism was popular among the masses it had a more Tamil character to begin with and in the later phase the Dravidian influence on the temple changed and the Temple rituals and observances were changed to Telugu completely. This flowered during the Vijaynagara period.

Vaisnavism-a Background

The antiquity of Vaisnavism is traced back to the Vedic period but it witnessed several changes during the course of its development since the Vedic period. In the Vedic period we have nature worship in the form of Sun, Visnu and Agni who are among the several deities mentioned in the Rig-Veda. From a mere solar deity in the Vedic literature, Visnu emerged in the Epico-puranic period as a supreme power in a composite form of the man-god Vasudev Krishna, the Vedic God Visnu and the cosmic God Narayana.

As the religion became popular among the masses and was spreading far, it was accompanied by growth of devotional literature, iconography, and institutionalization of temple worship and elaboration of sastras relating to the worship of God. This necessitated the composition of *Agamas*. The

Agamas contained principles of worship, installation of deity in a temple, rules regarding the construction of temple structures (Vardachari, 1982). The period between 5th to 7th centuries witnessed the formation of two type's of Vaisnava Agamas–the *Vaikhanasa* and the *Pancharatras* of which the former is termed as Vedic and the latter as non Vedic. The Bhagvata religion was more inclined towards the Pancharatra system.

In the history of Vaisnavism the Pancharatra School, also referred to as the *Bhagavata, Sattavata Ekanatika* occupies an important place. There has been a lot of discussion if the *Pancharatras* is Vedic or non-Vedic in origin. Majority of the scholars believe that major part of the *Pancharatra* literature is non Vedic, but being in a minority the followers of *Pancharatra* dared not revile the Vedas and had to be conciliatory. They took great pains to reconcile the differences and traced the origin of their school to an unknown Vedic school called *Kanava Shakha* of *Shukla Yajurveda* (Bhatt, 1980, 12). The special contribution of the Pancharatra school is the theory of emanation-Vyuhavada, which while bringing in the varying world into existence from the supreme being leaves the latter quite unaffected. The Vyuhavada, doctrine comprises of the worship of five Vrishni heroes, Sankarshana, Vasudeva, Pradyumana, Aniruddha and Samba (Bhandarkar, 1913). All these *Vyuhas* were simply manifested in the central deity, Vishnu whose all pervading powers gave his followers protection from evil and demonic forces. To this was added the concept of *Avatarvada,* where Vishnu is worshipped in various forms and ten forms were recognized as avatars. By the age of Guptas, Buddha also came to be identified with Narayana and was worshipped as one of the ten avatars. This is a perfect example of Hindu syncretism and absorption of rival religions (Rao Hanumanth, 1913). The Imperial Guptas were devout Vaisnavas and they patronized this religion and this is clearly pointed out by their inscriptions and coins.

As a philosophy the system of Vaisnavism grew and developed on the temple foundations of Upanishads,

Brahmasutras and the Bhagvat Gita. The Puranas, notably the Vishnupurana, the Vainava Agamas, Vaikanasa and Pancharatra and the *Nalayiradivya prabandham* in Tamil provided the basis for its religious aspect.

By the 7th century we witness a great religious revival in every part of South India with the two-fold intention of eradicating the influence of popular creeds of Buddhism and Jainism on the one hand and to popularize the new mode of salvation against the monopoly of Brahmins. The emphasis now shifted to the devotion and the use of mantras for purification. It was emphasized that these two aspects were accessible to all and could be used even by the lowly and unlearned to gain salvation. All that one needed was to seek refuge in God, worship him and gain relief (Hopkins, 1971, 117). This new concept of Bhakti brought religion closer to the masses. The separation of the Vaisnava cult from Saivism and its development as a distinct sect was greatly due to Vaishnava saints or Alwars.

The Alwars

Tradition gives us a list of twelve Alwars including a woman. Most of these belonged to the Pallava period and came from different parts of the Tamil country. Some of these were Brahmins and others came from different sections of society. Tiruppanalwar was a saint of depressed castes (pana community of Sudra caste), Nammalwar the greatest of Alwars was a Vellala, Tirumangai Alwar was a kalla and Kulasekhara Alwar was a Kshatriya. Even those of the Alwars who were Brahmins, one of them was a repentant sinner and another Tirumalisai was a person of dubious parentage (Rangacharya, 1975, 163-185). It has been argued by Freidhelm Hardy, that the perception of Alwars as representative of masses", protesting against caste oppression is a popular romantic myth originating in hagiography written in later times when there was a greater penetration of brahmins in the bhakti stream and the varna system had influenced itself in the south. The Alwars belonged to the upper strata and there was no strong reaction against the Varna system as the system was yet to penetrate deeply at the times of early Alwars. Hardy argues that Brahmin contribution to Alwar poetry begins with the 8th century onwards when it is also meant for popularization and facilitating smooth reorientation towards brahmanic normative ideology under the leadership of Vaisnava Acharyas who were the direct inheritors of the Alwar tradition (Hardy, 1983, 412).

The Alwars composed hymns in poetic Tamil and their songs were influenced by the stories of gods of the epics and Puranas. The works of all the Alwars is collected and preserved in the name of *Nalayira Divya Prabandham,* which consists of altogether 4000 verses. The Alwars were ardent lovers of Lord Visnu and worshipped him in all his avatars. They emphasized the universal nature of God. The essence of their teachings was that salvation was attainable to all, even the uninitiated. Nammalwar or Satakopan in his Tirvaymoli is philosophical and lyrical, dispassionately speculative and filled with the outpourings of an anguished heart. (Clooney, 1994).

Soon this movement gathered momentum in the south against Buddhism and Jainism and to a certain extent against agamic Saivism also (Aiyangar, 1981, 266). The Alwars even tried to uplift those classes of society which were considered to be outsiders. They adopted Tamil as the language of expressing themselves with a view to popularize their teachings.

Among the twelve Alwars, Nammalwar is considered by the Sri Vaisnavas as the representative of the teachings of the whole group. His work constitutes the main core of the *Nalayira Divya Prabandham* and is rightly regarded by the Sri Vaisnavas as the, "Dravida Veda", or the Tamil Veda. Nammalwars four poems are the, *Tiruvirattam, Tiruvasiriyam, Perya Tiruvandadi,* and *Tiruvoymoli.* Of these Vedanta Dasika called the Tiruvoymoli the Dravidopanishad. These hymns have shaped the conduct and faith of Sri Vaisnavism. For this reason the Sri Vaisnavas regard him as the founder of their tradition.

The idea of prapatti or saranagati through the guru also seems to have originated with Nammalwar. Its importance lies in the fact that initially for the Alwars Bhakti or devotion was considered as a means of salvation. They aimed at the service in Vaikuntha by performing it in this world in relation to the archavataras (Rangacharya, 1975, 163-185). Subsequently this service that was very simple in the beginning developed certain prescribed methods for its practice and became an organized system of worship with certain rigid methods that are impossible for the common man to follow. This was probably due to the growing Brahmanical control over the movement and the temple organization. Since the lower section could not perform these rituals a guide in the form of Guru was needed to seek salvation. Out of this developed the doctrine of self-surrender or *Prapatti*. This doctrine was developed fully in the age of Acharyas and became an essential aspect of Sri Vaisnava philosophy.

The Acharyas

The coming of the Acharyas started a new epoch in the history of Sri-Vaisnavism. The Acharya parampara seems to have begun in the first half of the 9th century A.D. The Acharyas were learned in Sanskrit as well as Tamil and they tried to interpret the essence of Vedas and Upanishads in terms of Tamil Prabandhams. They combined the gyan and karma with bhakti for realizing god. All the Acharyas were orthodox Brahmins who discharged their duties strictly. They encouraged the study of Vedas, performance of rituals and other temple festivals; strictly according to Vaisnava Agamas but at the same time they also introduced the study of the recitation of Prabandhams (the hymns of the Alwars) in public and private worship. This principle is called *Ubhaya Vedanta Siddhanta* i.e. the duel complex nature of trying to reconcile

Vedas and Upanishads in Sanskrit and interpret the same in Tamil prabandham. Sri Ramanujacharya further developed this philosophy into Visishatadvaita philosophy. They also allowed the members of the other castes besides Brahmins to take part in the ceremonies.

The Acharyas were the makers of modern Sri Vaisnavism, its society, rituals, practices and ideals. The tradition began with Nathmuni (824-924 A.D.) who started the recitation of Prabandhams in Vaisnava temples. He was also responsible for establishing and worshipping the images of Alwars. The next important Acharya was Yamunacharya, the preceptor of Sri Ramanujacharya, the great reformer saint who lived during the first half of the 11th century and under whom Sri-Vaisnavism was established on a firm footing.

Unlike the Alwars the Acharyas emphasized on rationalism. The Acharyas, by and large, followed the inspirational teachings of the Alwars and yet they differed from some of their teachings. The Alwars thought that the grace of God is spontaneous and does not depend on merits of the devotee. The Acharyas however preached that God is free in extending his mercy. He does so as a reward for the meritorious actions of the devotees. It was to the credit of Ramanuja that he evolved the concept bhakti by combining the rich spiritual experiences of the Alwars and the practical methodology of Pancharatras and giving it a firm philosophical background. Bhakti as a full fledged personal emotion had reached its peak in the songs of the Alwars and in the Bhagvata, yet in order to save bhakti from degenerating into a subjective caprice and way wariness of emotionalism he gave it a secure objectivity by placing it on a firm philosophical basis (Pande, 1989, 1).

Sri Ramanuja

Sri Ramanuja was born in 1017 A.D. at Sri Perumbudur to Kesava Somayaji and Kantamati. His mother was the sister of the great bhakta, Tirumalanumbi, who was serving Lord

Venkateswara at Tirumala. (Naidu, 1979, 14). Ramanuja had his early education under Yadvaprakash, a teacher of the advaita school of thought. Soon differences arose between both of them and Ramanuja left him and went to his uncle Tirumalainambi. It was here that he had his strong foundation in Hindu philosophy (Raghavcharya, 1977, 239).

During this period Yamunacharya was occupying the pontifical seat of Vaisnavism at Sri Rangam. He came to respect the great intellect of Ramanuja and desired to entrust the seat to him. However before the two could meet Yamunacharya breathe his last.

At the invitation of the disciples of Yamunacharya, Ramanujacharya occupied the pontifical seat at Sri Rangam, but the political situation was antagonistic to Sri Vaisnavism. The Chola king was a bigoted Saivite and was forcing his subjects to embrace Saivism. On the advice of his minister Nalaran that if Ramanuja were converted to Saivism it would be as good as converting all his followers, the king sent a message to Srirangam inviting Ramanuja. Foreseeing trouble Ramanuja's nephew and chief disciple, Kuruttalvan proceeded, personating as the Vaisnava teacher. Here the eyes of Kuruttalvan were plucked out. This event is placed during the year 1078-79 A.D. i.e. during the reign of Kulottunga Chola (Rao Gopinath, 1923, 34).

However the identity of the persecutor is not clearly established as there is no epigraphical evidence of extreme fanaticism of Koluttunga Chola. On the contrary there is an inscription from Simhachalam temple, which states that two of his generals visited the temple and made donations to god Narasimha (South Indian Inscriptions, Vol. VI, 1986, No. 1144). Most probably the impertinent replies of Kurttalvan under the guise of Ramanuja must have caused the tragedy. This event however clearly brings forth the extreme tensions and conflicts between the followers of different religious sects.

The period of Ramanuja saw several developments in society and in Vaisnavism as well. In north India the rising tantric schools exploited the female principle and emphasized upon the religious values of sexual passion. The Gopi Radha concept became an object for this and this led to a gross perversion of morals and ethics and a general decadence (Yasodadevi, 1980, 215). Ramanuja tried to regain the vigor of Vaisnavism by giving it a solid philosophical grounding on the one hand and also restoring certain moral and spiritual practices of earlier times to avoid the grossly erotic and sensuous practices under the garb of mysticism (Pande, 2004, 268).

Philosophy of Ramanuja

The Vedic faith has been generally described as being action oriented. From Devyajna to Atmayajna, karma to Vidya was a natural and progressive revelation as the unity of Gods was realized in Brahma, as the unity of the inner principle in humans with the cosmic principle. Brahma was stated to be the sole reality. Buddhism challenged this argument stating that if anything is real it must produce an effect and if anything produces an effect it was bound to be momentary and with no permanent soul (Gupta, 1955, 53-60). So the concept of Brahma faced a dilemma. If Brahma was real and produced the world, then it must be held to be momentary. If Brahma was not momentary but eternal, then it cannot produce an effect and must be unreal.

Following Gaudapada, Sankaracharya gave a new principle that, what changes is unreal. The self is real and changeless because it is the undeniable and perceiver of change, whereas illusion is not. Sankara advocated the path of action and this was the advaita philosophy of Sankara (Gupta, 1955, 61-72).

Ramanuja analyzed the various sources of knowledge which according to him were three-perception, inference and testimony. Knowledge directly and immediately perceived is perception-*pratyaksa*. Ramanuja points out that perception will not enable us to obtain knowledge of Brahma and quotes the Kathopanishad that, "His form cannot be seen, no one beholds him with the eyes". Similarly inference-*anuman*, like perception cannot lead us to knowledge of things, which are quality less. After refuting all intellectual proofs for the existence of God, Ramanuja follows the views of Sutrakara and declares that scriptures are the source of knowledge of Brahma. This testimony is called *Sabda Pramana*. This refers to scriptures such as Sruti–the Vedas and Upanishads, Vedanta sutras and Smriti (such as Gita). Ramanuja further states that Brahma is not obtained by mere learning of the scriptures but only by him whom the deities chooses as the recipient of his grace-*prapatti*. Hence meditation and grace of God are revelatory of the knowledge of Brahma. According to him the lower knowledge is a means towards the intuition of Brahma, while the higher knowledge or upasana which has the character of devout mediation (bhakti) consists in the direct intuition of Brahma.

Hence Ramanuja through his philosophy of Visista Advaita defended the reality of the individual, God and the world and the doctrine of Bhakti and *Prapatti*. He emphasized on a personal god, characterized by certain attributes. Two entities that stand in relation to God are nature and the individual souls. While nature or the non-sentient, *achit* is the realm of life both conscious and unconscious, *chit* and *achit* are the two modes–*prakara* in which God manifests himself. *Chit*, *achit* and *Iswara* are the three truths-*tattva-traya* of Visista Advaita.

Therefore with his philosophy Ramanuja brought about a synthesis of Gyan, karma and bhakti to reach *Prapatti* or absolute self-surrender to God. Through such a philosophy Ramanuja could bring about a compromise in society of medieval times because the socio-economic context was such that this was the need of the hour (Pande, 1992). As already mentioned, politically the earlier period was characterized by the intercine warfare and created a political vacuum in the last quarter of the 12th century. The Palnadu war weakened the power of several mandalikas including the

Velanadu Chodas and led to the decline of the Chalukya Chola rule (Krishna Kumari, 1985, 90). The Kakatiyas took advantage of this chaotic political situation in Vengi and extended their empire easily.

Ramanuja's Sri Vaisnavism tried to bring about a compromise between these two groups, the Brahmins on the one hand and the third and fourth castes on the other. He tried to achieve a perfect synthesis by teaching salvation can be obtained by Bhakti yoga leading to prapatti as against Gyan yoga or karma yoga. He insisted on caste rules in food and performing samskars but at the same time converted sudras into Vaisnavism and allowed the untouchables the privilege of visiting certain temples once a year. (Bhandarkar, 1965, 57). He was very eager to carry the message of Sri Vaisnavism to the lower castes by declaring that devotion knew no caste, color or even social status. He even accepted them as Guru or preceptor. He tried to preserve the devotional fervor of the Alwar saints, but their charisma was fit into the framework of brahmanical social system (Hopkins, 1971, 122).

Vir Vaisnavism

We find evidence of a very militant form of Vaisnavism which is referred to as Vir Vaisnavism. However the life span of this movement was very short and was mostly confined to the Andhra region. Many historians refuse to consider it as a sect and attribute it to the ideology of an individual, Brahmanaydu, which was later transformed into Hero worship.

Srinadha, a 15th century poets work, *Palanati Vircharitra,* refers to this in detail. Brahmanaydu was the minister of Haihaya ruler Nalgamaraju, and son of Anuguraju. Nalgamaraju ruled the entire Palnad area comprising of parts of modern Guntur and Prakasam District. Brahmanaydu attempted to bring about radical socio-religious reforms. He married women from all the four castes and adopted Kannamadasa, a person of mala caste an untouchable, as his son. (Rao, 1973, 258) Brahmanaydu was a devotee of Macherla Chenna kesav Swamy. He made the temple at Macherla the center of his activity and threw open the gates of the temple to panchama castes. He initiated people into Vaisnava fold calling them, "Dasa". He encouraged interdinning and intercaste marriages. He seems to have been influenced by the Vaishnava Acharya, Ramanuja and other Vir Saivite practices, pleading for a casteless society (Krishnamoorthy, 1970).

There was much opposition to Brahmanaydu's policies. His own son, Balachandra criticised his father's radical steps and felt that these were responsible for the Palnad war (1176 1182 A.D.) The Palnad war took place between Brahmanaydu and Nagamma a Vir Saivite devotee (Rao, 1983, 223). Many minor dynasties of Andhra also participated in this conflict. This war is also referred to as *Kulamporu* or the battle of castes (Rao, 1973, 258). The literary work, *Kridabhiramam* states that *'Chapacudu'* or the policy adopted by Brahmanaydu that all castes including Velamas the potters, the malas and madigas of sudra castes dinning at one place was the chief reason for the great war of Palnad. (Reddy, 1982, 21). Brahmanaydu was defeated in this war and his son and many other relatives were killed. Along with this defeat Vir Vaisnavism also sustained a defeat in Andhra.

Vir Vaisnavism as a rival creed to Virsaivism attempted to wipe out the caste differences and unite all caste with devotion to Visnu as a factor of unity. A new caste of, "Padmanayakula", a caste of weavers who were originally Velamas belonging to the third caste was created. It had a very short life span but it brought Vaisnavism to the lower caste. The reason for the failure of the movement in Andhra was the lack of a social base, i.e., the absence of strong artisan communities unlike in contemporary Karnataka. It was finally transformed as a hero cult and spread to Telengana and other parts of Andhra Desa.

The Vedgalai and Tengalai

Ramanuja was responsible for making Sri Vaisnavism very popular. Many important temples like Tirupati, Simhachalam, Sri Kurmam, Basalt, and Chodavaram also played an important role. In the Telengana region influence of Sri Vaisnavism could be found in Makhtala, Lingiri, Alampuram and Burugugadda where many temples devoted to Vishnu emerged or the old ones regained their popularity, though when compared to the coastal region, this was less.

Ramanuja's limited attempt at integrating different castes under Sri Visnavism could not continue for long due to the brahmanical control of temples and temple lands. Entry of the lower castes was not conceded though they were provided with certain occupations in the lower level administration.

By the later half of the 13th century Sri Vaisnavism split into two subsects namely the Vadagalai or the northern school and Tengalai the southern school or parabandhic subsect. The Vadagalai sect was more brahmanical and it did not accept Prabandhams as Pancham Vedas. This sect was headed by Vedanta Desika a disciple of Ramanuja. (Rangacharya, 1975, 177). Kanchi, Tiruvanantapuram and Srirangam became the centers of this sect. This sect spread more in the Tamil region. After the death of Vedanta Desika in 1369 A.D. the mantle of leadership fell on his son Kumar Vedantacharya. The Tengalai sect was more revolutionary and willing to accommodate the new changes and also new adherents. Pillai Lokacharya headed it and it expanded to a wider audience on account of the use of Tamil. It made its doctrine easily accessible to all people including the lower castes. This sect developed to a great extent under the active patronage of Vijaynagara rulers.

Sri Vaisnavism during the Vijaynagara Period

The early Vijaynagara kings were Saivite though they were tolerant to other religions. It was in the later half of the

15th century that Vaisnavism superseded other religions and became the dominant religion. It was the rise of Saluva chiefs to power in 1492 A.D. that marked the triumph of Vaisnavism and its emergence as a religion of the royal house (Sarojini Devi, 1990, 89). Saluva Narsimhan was considered as an incarnation of Lord Narasimha of Ahobilam and Lord Venkateswara of Tirupati. He granted a number of villages as gifts to the temple (Tirumalai Tirupati Devsthanam Epigraphical Series, Vol. II, No. 4). He also constructed Vasanta Mandapam in the middle of Swami Puskarini at Tirumala where the image of Sri Venkateswara was kept during the times when it had to be taken out on processions (Tirumalai Tirupati Devsthanam Epigraphical Series, Vol. II, No. 3). He also granted privileges and honours to the Saltada Sri Vaisnavas who were non Brahmins belonging to the Tengalai sect. Krishna Dev Raya was a great devotee of Venkateswara. Achyut Raya also visited the temple at Tirupati many times. He instituted two new festivals Lakshmidev Mahotsvam and the Punarvasu Tirunal in the Venkateswara temple. In order to meet the expense of these temple fairs he granted to the temple a portion of the income from the villages situated in the Kondavidu Sima. (Epigraphica Indica, Vol. IV, p. 5-6). The royal patronage continued to be extended later on and we know from inscriptions of a number of grants. He granted thirty-one villages to the Ramanuja shrine at Sri Perambudur to enable the Vaisnava devotee to carry on their worship with incense, foods, flower, dancing, music and umbrellas. There was also provision made for the distribution of food to the twice born and their families at the hall constructed here (Epigraphica Indica, Vol. IV, No. 54, 58). The critiques of Vaisnava philosophy were answered by Madhavacharya, who further strengthened its philosophy.

Madhavacharya

Madhavacharya was said to be the son of Madhyageha Bhatta and born in Pajakaksetra near Uddipi, near Mangalore. He toured extensively and was aware of the Advaita, Buddhist and Jaina philosophy and had many discussions with them. He founded the Dvaita Vedanta, which was in opposition to the monism of Sankara and the qualified monism of Ramanuja. To Madhava there were five distinctions between God and the individual soul, God and matter. This he refers to as *Bheda*. In refuting his philosophical opponents he adopts a sharp dialectic, while in establishing the structure of Vaisnava faith he relies on the appeal to the traditional scriptures and their interpretation (Pande, 1989, 38).

Madhava recognizes two kinds of reality, Savatrantra and paratantra. God is Savatantra or independentrality, free from all imperfections and possesses infinite excellent spiritual qualities. He is being, *sat*, consciousness, *chit* and bliss, *ananda*. Laxmi as the consort of Visnu is eternally blessed and related to Lord. They are eternally united with each other. The third place is given to *Vayu* incarnated as Hanuman, Bhima and Madhava to, "justify the ways of God to man". The individual soul *"jiva"* is the knower, enjoyer and doer. It dwells in the body and the senses and therefore is the subject to misery and happiness. The soul is eternal but its birth and death are due to its connection with the body. There can never be an absolute identity between God, the worshipped matter and Jiva the worshipping servant. "*Tat-tvam asi*", does not imply identity of soul and God but only suggests a similarity in essence with God. The principle of individuality follows from 'bheda', distinguishing one soul from another.

To Madhava man can find happiness, knowledge and rest in God alone. This incessant pursuit is referred to as sadhana. God is the highest value being sought. He also emphasized the need for a spiritual guru. This probably reflected the social feature of the new monastic life which was being built up (Pande, 1989, 50).

Bhakti becomes the persuasive principle of sadhana. It arises out of a feeling of affection or attachment, which arises from the idea of god as a perfect being. It begins as faith and promotes action in the form of worship and service to God.

Bhakti becomes the golden thread uniting action and contemplation, individual experience and communion with God. Madhava did not dispute the traditional restrictions of Vedic study for sudras but believed they had alternative avenues of spiritual progress especially devotion to god. Madhava enlarged the concept of bhakti. His social outlook was reformist within bounds of liberal traditional, dynamic and activist but not revolutionary (Sharma, 1960, 27).

Many spiritual successors and followers of Madhavaism were much respected during the Vijaynagara period. The most important of these were Vyasaraya (b. 1446) who flourished during the time of Saluva and Tuluva dynasty. An inscription dt. 1513 A.D. found in Vittalswami temple at Hampi records the granting of Sayanapura village to the temple and refers to Vyasaraya as the guru of Krishna Dev Raya. (South Indian Inscriptions, Vol. IV, No. 277).

An important disciple of Vyasaraya was Vadiraja (b. 1480 A.D.) who is the founder of the Haridasa movement which became very popular in Andhra during this period. He occupied the pontifical seat of the matha of Visnu Tirtha. The Haridasa movement made an effort to place a complete code of morality and religion before the people. It condemns both formalism and ritualism in religion and preached devotion to god and recognized spiritual values. It also attempted to remove ills and evil practices from society. (Karmakar et. al, 1989, 71-72).

Thus a number of philosophers and bhakta saints had made the philosophical base of Sri Vaisnavism strong and interpreted it keeping the needs of the time in mind. Once the kings also patronized this religion it became extremely popular with the masses as happened during the Vijaynagara period. During the Vijaynagara period, many of its kings patronized it and gave several land grants to many Vaisnava temples. Krishna Deva Raya visited Tirupati many times and made various gifts during these different occasions. He also visited Kalahasti and is said to have gifted a pearl necklace and another necklace of precious stones, a gold cup inlaid with precious stones and twenty five plates of silver for offering arati. (South Indian Inscriptions, Vol. IX, Plate 11, No. 448). Many of his officers also followed suit and are credited with making several gifts to the various Sri Vaisnava shrines in the kingdom. Due to the royal patronage the temples of Visnu became very popular during this period and Sri Vaisnavism gained a strong hold from the later half of 16th century onwards. The Aravidu dynasty kings besides patronized many important Vaisnava shrines also extended their patronage to many minor shrines. Their patron deity was Kesava another form of Visnu and under them many temples of Chenna Kesava came up such as at Sri Bhasyapuram, Eragudipadu, Kodur, Guntakallu and Moyilla Ceruva. This was helpful in integrating the local elements under the patronage of the temple and the influence of Sri Vaisnavism spread to the interior regions also. Many temples also came up for Laksmi narayana. In many places Visnu was worshipped as Narasimhan and many temples devoted to Narsimha came up.

Besides royal patronage there were a number of Vaisnava families such as Tatacarya, Tallapakams, the Bhattars and the Kandadais who were responsible for admitting into their folds a number of non-Brahmin communities like the Saltada Sri Vaisnavas. There were a number of Tallapakam poets who were a family of musicians, who flourished during the 15th and 16th century and popularized the cult of Bhakti and devotion to Sri Venkateswara of Tirumala. These were Smarta Telugu Brahmins. The musical composition of these poets is preserved in copper plates in the temple at Tirupati. The most important of these was Tallapaka Annamachari who received divine inspiration in 1424 A.D. and composed various sankirtanas. Though there are no epigraphical records to give us more information, these sankirtanas have become very much a part of the modern day spiritual life in Andhra. The various expressions of bhakti like Kirtanas, bhajanas, Harikathas and Kalashepams have left everlasting impressions on the lives of the people and are responsible for the development of various dance drama tradition and forms in modern day life.

Many of these poets composed and wrote during the period of the Vijaynagar Empire and Bhakti gives to these bhaktas a caring correspondent-some one to talk to in a certain way, with love, thanks, longing, reciprocal care and awe and with a dependence need, with hope for helping in coping (Jackson, 1998, 4). In bhakti the Lord and the devotee seem to interact, somehow sharing experiences, even if one is the master and the other dependent.

Annamacharya

Annamacharya was born in a Smarta brahmin family living in Tallapaka village in the Andhra region in 1408 A.D. Even as a child he was a devotee of Venkateshvara, the lord of the Tirumala Hills and neglected the performance of his daily chores but spent his time singing songs to his favourite deity. According to legend, the young boy when he was sixteen went to the Tirumala Hills and on the way rested in a bamboo grove getting very tired. In his dreams he saw goddess Alamelumangamma, who pointed out that had he walked with out his sandals he would not be tired and would not have needed rest. She gave him Prasad and promised that he would be blessed by her consort, Lord Venkateswara. Annamaya is said to have composed a *shatakam*, on the spot consisting of a hundred verses in praise and his devotion. As he sang the verses the temple doors which were closed opened for him.

Annamacharya continued to live in Tirupati and became a disciple of Shathakopayiri who initiated him to Shr-Vaisnava path. On the request of his mother he returned to his native village, Tallapaka and was married to two women, Timmakka and Akkalamma, and continued his composing and singing to the Lord. Once Saluva Narsimha heard Annamacharya sing a shringar Pada addressed to Lord Venkateswara and he was so impressed with him that he asked him to compose a similar song for him. To this

Annamacharya had replied that his tounge could only sing the songs in praise of his Lord and he was not equipped to compose similar songs for a mortal like the King. According to legend the King was very annoyed and ordered Annamaya to be put in prison. Even while being locked up and tied in chains the poet composed songs for his Lord Hari and found himself released from his chains. His songs are called *padas* and it is believed that he has composed thirty two thousand songs which were inscribed on rectangular copper plates only a few of which survive today. His songs speak of devotion being very important and saving one from the calamities of the world.

When ever you'r hungry, whenever you'r tired

Repeat the holy name, there is no other way.

In moments of want, or when you are alone

If someone captures you and you're locked up

The blessed name of Hari is the only support

If you'r forgetful and make mistakes in life. (Jackson, 1998, 44).

He gives importance to God's grace to provide him salvation. He does not understand sin or virtue but wants the Lord's grace.

I am a little nobody, you're the supreme Lord

Your glory alone shall always prevail

I can't understand sin, can't grasp virtue

How can I understand you with my mind?

You are the dweller in my heart

And so I cry-please cleanse me

Of sins-lord you must protect me (Jackson, 1998, 50).

In the path of Bhakti to him like other bhaktas caste does not matter and it is important to have humility and sympathy for others.

Only one knows as being devoted to truth

(not one indulging in doing harm to others

but one who thinks of others as himself)

he is the one with sympathy for all beings

And what if he's born this or that

Doesn't much matter what his caste

Whoever he is-all alone

he comes to know Lord Hari at last (Jackson, 1998, 53).

Bhakti becomes an alternative for him to deal with the miseries of the world and escape suffering.

Having born a mortal

Why achieve nothing but misery

By always serving some other mere mortal?

Arriving at some dismal site

For the sake of your hungry belly

You beg some nobody

For your share of pathetic mush

With grief in your heart you approach

The place you started from

Why go on with this suffering? (Jackson, 1998, 58)

Giving a beautiful similie of a tribal girl, he now does not need any riches of the earth because he has found his true love his God.

What are these jasmine flowers for?

Tell him to wear them himself

For what am I but a tribal girl (chenchu)

My hairstyle has fragrance naturally

What should I do with this silk sari

Shiny leaves are good enough for me

Give it back, tell him that he can wind it

As a sash around his waist-I am tribal

What do I want with a bed with a canopy

Tell him to keep it and sleep on it

What am I but a chenchu girl who'd really

Rather roll around on the earth beneath a tree (Jackson, 1998, 59).

There is a hint of accommodation and a satisfaction that though the Lord may be keeping up with his tricks, he is the ultimate lover.

There may be other women in his life

But I know that I'm his permanent wife

A bee may hover and wander in many fields

But he comes home to his favourite honey petals.

Please won't you go and tell these words for me

When I behave so modestly

Is it right that Lord Venkateswara should get so angry?

The other day I calmly watched him

Talking to another woman-did I make a big to-do?

Did I waste even a precious word

In criticism or suspicion? Still

The Lord has not let up in his trickery. (Jackson, 1998, 67)

After the travails of life there is a passionate union.

When he came to my house

Misunderstandings and stubbornness went away

Why say more?

I bow to Venkateswara

Please.

With love flowering forth in passion

He caressed me O friends

And we joined together in ecstasy

Please. (Jackson, 1998, 68)

There is trace of eroticism in some of his poems describing the union of the God.

With her hair rippling across her shining face

She sleeps until broad daylight

Because she was up until dawn

With unending inventiveness'held the heart of the Lord of the world enthralled

The edge of her sari slipped down charmingly revealing

The goddess breasts, as she sleeps in golden mansion

Her lovely eyes are like the pink lily-red because she is exhausted

From all the intimate exertions she enjoyed with the Lord

Father of the love God-so she is taking rest.

In elegant style she sleeps on a pearl-strung bed, still fatigued!

She embraced Lord Venkatesha so long that her face, exquisite as a

Half blossomed flower, is covered with a fine dew of sweat drops

Our mother whose words are sweet as honey

Is taking her rest

This woman who spent her whole night

In love play with the Lord (Jackson, 1998, 63).

Purandar Das

The time of Purandar Das is said to have been between 1485-1565. His death coincides with the fall of the mighty Vijaynagar Empire and he must have been a witness to the spree of looting, pillage, decoration and vandalism at the hands of Adil Shah and Ibrahim Qutub Shah's forces after the battle of Tallikota. Some of his songs reflect this bewilderment and loss. It is recorded by Annamacharya's grandson Tallpakka Chinna Tiruvenkatnath, that Purandardas arrived in Tirupati as a young man when his grandfather was old and on the latters request Purandar das sang some songs for him. Purandar das also came in contact with Kanka das and they both became good friends.

It is believed that Purandar das composed 475, 000 songs but most of these were lost after the fall of Vijaynagar. This was an oral tradition and it is but natural that most of the form of this would have changed in the intervening centuries. Since Purandar das was a prominent dasa, the Dasakutas, a forum of dasa organized by Vyasaraya probably memorized, taught and compiled these. In the Dasakuta forums these were sung and circulated in towns and villages. In spite of the interpolation, these songs give us an essence of understanding his Bhakti. Purandas used a variety of forms in his compositions such as *pada, suladi, jhampe* and *Chapu* and his verses are highly esteemed for their musical composition and occupy a distinguished place in Karnataka.

There is a reference of Purandar Das's wife playing a part in getting him converted to Bhakti.

Once I was ashamed of holding the staff

May my wife's family increase a thousand fold

Because of her I've come to hold the sadhu staff

What ever has happened all has been for the best.

I used to be so proud feeling like big man

I wouldn't hold a vessel for collecting alms or rice

My wife caused me to take it-may she live long

What ever has happened all has been for the best. (Jackson, 1998, 79).

There is a sense of futility of life and wasting of time in daily pesuits.

Time has passed and I have gotten nothing

Time has passed away and what have I achieved

Under the illusion that this is my wife

These are my children I became foolish.

O imperishable Lord, through constant enjoyment

I am ruined, my mind has lost its purpose

I'm off the path, O highest of all, Lakshmipati (Jackson, 1998, 83).

He is also very critical of rituals and sees no meaning in them.

What's the point of leaving a bitter neem leaf

In sweet brown sugar (spoiling the taste)

What's the use of feeding milk

To a poisonous serpent?

Unless one gives up crooked ways

What is the use of chanting the name? (Jackson, 1998, 83).

There is a feeling of unity of the world and all being equal for a Haridasa.

For us (dasas) the king and the beggar

Are the same, and the one who speaks sweetly

and the one who speaks bitterly are the same

For those always praising Narhari's lotus feet

Its all one, the two are same (Jackson, 1998, 118).

What is important in his Bhakti is to have detatchment.

If you have a virtuous wife

Your home will be like a blissful heaven

But a harsh wife, forever nagging

-you'd better run away from such a woman

The Haridasa should learn

To live in the world but not be of the world (Jackson, 1998, 105).

In bhakti it is important to clean the mind and the heart.

You harbour bad feelings towards others

And wish them ill

You pine for other women, thinking this

Will bring you supreme bliss

Like one observing silence

With firm determination on the outside

But unable to control yourself within

You embody hipocracy on this earth

What if you sit on the banks of a river

Like a crane meditating-so what?

Some people know how to wash away dirt

But not how to cleantheir minds and heart (Jackson, 1998, 124).

Finally what is important is to have humility and this become an essential crieteria for a bhakta.

What good is a tree

Which gives no shelter

What good is shade

If there isn't also water

What good is wealth

If one has no heart to give it

What good is mind

Devoid of spiritual wisdom

What good is life

Lived with out being

A menial worker labouring

For Lord Pundara Vithala (Jackson, 1998, 152).

Kanakadas

Kankadas was born in Bada near Dharwar in present day Karnataka and lived in the sixteenth century. His father Birappa was a feudal chief among the Kurubas, a herding clan. His wife's name was Bachchamma and due to their praying to Lord Venkateswara on Tirumala hills, Kanakadas was born. According to legends, when he grew up Kanaka Nayyaka was severly wounded in a battle and recovered with the blessings of Venkatesa and became his devotee. He went to Vyasaraya to accept him as his disciple and after initial hesitation, he was given initiation. There are many legends related to him. As a low caste person he was not allowed to go inside the Krishna temple and at Udipi he stood by a chink in the wall to look in and due to his intense Bhakti Krishna turned around in his pedestal and turned to face west, to gaze at his devotee. The statue stands as such today.

In one of his songs Kankadas refers to his low status.

I am the son of a servant woman-my mother served

The servants of the servants of the Lord

I'm the son of a dasi at the house of Ranga

The Lord celebrated with the sahasranama

(thousand names of God)

I am just a foolish dasa of Shankuda's home

And I happen to be a doorkeeper dasa

Serving the devotee who worship God

I'm the son of a servant (Jackson, 1998, 179).

In bhakti it is truthfulness, serenity, peace of mind and stopping negative thoughts which are important. This preceds having a son.

Can you really get release by having a son

With out deep search into Vedic meaning?

Can you get release with a son who turns out

To be hideous, a slacker at doing his dharma

A guru abuser, nasty to elders and pious folk

Who fools around with people from othercastes

And with women, and in so doing shoves

His forefathers down in hell?

Can you really get release by having a son

With out deep search into Vedic meaning?

Truthfulness is a good son, serenity is another

Stopping negative tendencies is yet another son

And peace of mind is also a fine son

When you have four noble sons like these

So what if you don't have a biological one. (Jackson, 1998, 194-95).

If one gives into the path of Bhakti then there is nothing to fear because one surrenders to the ultimate God.

If some small town whore commits adultery

When her husband arranges it beforehand

O Hari-what has she got to fear

If the governor of the province finds it out

Arrests her and chastises her?

What damge can Yama's servants do

If a person has knowledge of you.

If a thief shares his loot with the king

Should break into a house to rob it-O Hari

What can the King's night watchman do

If the thief is hauled before him and accused

of stealing the loot which is part the King's too?

What damge can god of death do

If a person has knowledge of you. (Jackson, 1998, 213-14).

Like many other bhaktas befor him Kankadas is also critical of superstious customs.

Ignorant people believe in superstitious customs

Be wise, don't have blind faith in wilderness stones

All the futile little Gods waver and falter

Only one Badadkeshava truly knows

Wherever I look I see Ram

Those who know this secret know

That in their own bodies they can see Ram (Jackson, 1998, 215).

Another major stream in which the Bhakti movement flowed was the Saiva stream and the Vir saiva movement.

Saivism–a background

Saivite tradition has prevailed in India in some form or other and archeological evidence point out to the worship of Siva by the Indus valley people (Tyagi, 1982, 25). In the Vedic period Siva was called Rudra having the power to rule over heaven and earth. He is also Pasupati the protector of cattle. He is also seen as the invisible force behind all sorts of destruction, catastrophes and other sorts of mishappenings (Bhandarkar, 1983, 146). After the epic period, of the Ramayana and Mahabharata he becomes a theistic God and was represented as a God of wide prevalence and becomes very popular (Harendradayal, 1981, 185).

A parallel movement along similar lines like that of the Alwars developed among the worshippers of Shiva. These saints called the Nayanars spread the teachings that salvation could only be won by total self surrender to Siva. By the end of the eleventh century the hymns of these saints were collected together and given the title of *Devaram*. The *Devaram* reached out to a wider audience through ritual singing in the temple and hence its emphasis on social hierarchy, protest against low ritual and caste status and the dominance of *brâhmanas* in the ritual sphere are alluded to. Together with the *Devaram*, the *Tiruvacakam* or sacred utterances, of Manika Vasagar and ancillary writings came to be known as the Tamil Veda. Numbering 63, the Nayanars belonged to all castes though the majority of them were brahmana or velalla, we also have Nandanar who was an untouchable and Kannappar who was a hunter. We notice a strong anti-Jaina sentiment amongst the Nayanars. The broad context of the tamil bhakti movement is located here.

Beginning from the religious conflict of the days of the *Tevâram* hymns, religious dominance was a central aspect of the developments leading to the downfall of Jainism and Buddhism and the triumph of puranic religions, viz., Vaisnavism and Saivism. Towards this end the temple, its ideology and various cultural practices etc. contributed a great deal through a process of appropriation of the ideals of Jainism and Buddhism on the one hand and at the same time the maintenance of a balance between Sanskritic and native sensibilities on the other. These together played a major role in the process of acculturation, interaction and assimilation through which the bhakti of the Saiva and Vaisnava religions developed. As religion was one of the dominant factors defining societal organization, the multi-dimensional aspects of religion are also analysed such as myths, motifs and legends, both sanskritic and Tamil and the syncretic idioms that reached down to the masses.

South India witnessed the spread of Saivite and Vaisnavite faith during the time of the Pallavas. But it was the Cholas who extended the greatest patronage to Saivism in the Tamil country and in the process, made Saivism, the predominant faith. It was the work of the saints under the institutional ageis of the temple and the patronage of an articulate Hindu dynasty, the Cholas. For by this time there is hardly any clear distinction in the institutional role between the *brahmadeya* and the temple although the temple had distinctly superseded the *brahmadeya* as a superordinate instrument of legitimization of the Chola sovereignty and integration of the Chola economy. The early Cholas were confronted with two major problems, one of restructuring the production system and the other of organizing the society under the influences of the brahmanical ideology. They were also faced with the demands of consolidating political alignments with the erstwhile kingdoms of the Pallavas and the Pandyas and many other subordinate chiefs with a long historical past. Hence in their ideological base and integrative instruments one notices a significant transformation from purely brahmanical forms of Vedic religion and *Smriti* tradition to the indigenous bhakti tradition with a strong Tamil idiom and Puranic religion centering around *Siva* and *Visnu*, where temples therefore became the major forces of integration. The role of the temple in the social, political and economic spheres was complex and the interconnections are hard to spell out without the use of contextual analysis of texts of the inscriptions and of the religious literature i.e. the *Tevâram* the texts, particularly the bhakti hymns were more directly concerned with the inequalities in the social and religious spheres and hence constantly brought in the caste status of the bhakti saints in order to establish that irrespective of caste status, salvation was attainable through bhakti and a bhakta's position was superior to that of a *brahmana*. Thus they offered a way out for retaining caste hierarchy through an imagined and elusive equality in society based on the organization of religious community above caste hierarchy.

The Saiva religion in the period had many facets and thus its popularity was due to the fact that it catered to all sections of the people. Bhakti had a bias towards the common person and hence preached them in their own language and gave a direct message which was devoid of intellectual dogma. The popularity was enhanced more by the use of popular drama, *kuttu* or dance and music by the *devaradiyars* who lent colour to the temple functions. This popular appeal can be seen in the singing of the *tiruppadiyam* hymns which was more widely understood than the Vedic rituals as is indicated by the remuneration of the *tiruppadiyam* singers which was higher than that of the priests. The Tevâram also came to be called the *Tamil Veda*.

Other practices of a popular nature like worship of trees, snakes, local festivals, pilgrimages and sacred sites were all included in the religious movement. The bulk of the inscriptions speak of endowments for this rituals and festivals. Thus bhakti could accommodate diverse strands from orthodoxy to radicalism as exemplified by the various forms of Saivism such as the *kalamukhas* and the *pasupatas* down to the folk elements.

The royal association with the divine religious paraphernalia is evident from similar rituals used to wake the king and the deity. The etymology of the word *koil* meaning both the temple and the palace are parallels which cannot be missed. This served to disseminate the royal ideology via the temple. The orthodox element in religion is manifested in the stories of Tirunilakanda Yalpanar and Nandanar which the orthodox attitudes are emphasized and at the same time an imagined equality is established through bhakti. Such attempts at creating an equality in the religious sphere in fact led to the emergence of a Saiva community, redrawing the social boundaries with the exclusion of the Jainas and Buddhists. The temple stood as the centre of this community.

To examine how this reordering of society was achieved, one needs to study the life of the saints and the various devices that they adopted and the context within which they functioned. The evolution of bhakti in Tamilagam was partly due to the challenges posed by the heterodox sects and due to the progress of Saivism and Vaisnavism through a process of acculturation and interaction with the local cults over the centuries beginning with the Sangam Age. Jaina challenge was met with in a dual way, at one level the contestation assumed the character of an open conflict against the Jainas and their gods, asceticism and at another level some aspects of Jaina religion, which struck a receptive chord among the local populace, were appropriated. Conflict and persecution appear as the main process of the change from heterodoxy to orthodoxy. There is a reference by Sambandar that 8000 Jainas were impaled after they were defeated in a debate at the Pandya court (Gopalakrishnan, 1990, 63). Mahendravarman, the Pallava ruler and a Jaina after his conversion to Saivism is said to have destroyed Jain Pallis.

Iyarpakai Nayanar, (one of the 63 Nayanmars) is said to have attacked his relatives violently, since they obstructed a Saiva saint to whom he had given away his wife on the latter's demand (Gopalkrishna, 1990, 20). This indicates that the grace of God could be obtained even through violence and is a noteworthy theme that the use of force could be sanctioned under the approval of religion. Eripatta Nayanar's story of the killing of a royal elephant as it damaged the flowers meant for Siva's worships is another pointer in this direction (Gopal Krishna, 1990, 106) Thus we see the according of religious sanction to this aspect of grace, i.e., through violence is known as, marrakarunai (Gopal Krishna, 1990, 106).

The contestation of the Saivas with the jainas was taking place in all fields and at all levels though there is high visibility in the courts and the urban centers which had by now become Saiva religious centers with the building of new temples and their consecration that later led to the formation of a sacred geography.

In the field of philosophy, the Buddhist view that there was no soul but rebirth and also the Jaina belief of the denial of a universal god was a bit too hard for the tamilian mind to assimilate as it went against the indigenous beliefs (Venkatasubramanian, 1984, 183). The heterodox sects put a great stress on the idea of transmigration but the bhakti sects paid only lip service to the above and stuck to the indigenous concepts of the dead. This was one strand that led to the fall of the heterodox religions (Hart, 1960, 133).

It is also a truism that the Saiva bhakti movement did not concentrate on mere philosophical abstraction, which would anyway not be of much relevance to the common folk. Instead, as said earlier they went a step ahead of the jainas in attracting the common folk by preaching to them in their own language and thus were composed the soul stirring hymns of the 63 Saivaite saints, the *Tevâram* (that has attained a semi-canonical status). Incidentally the number 63 is itself said to be a holy number for the jainas as it denoted the number of the Úalâkapuruúhas (Dehejia, 1998, 1). Indigenous forms of worship were drawn from the Tamil religious practices of the early historical *(Sangam)* period that were current and popular. The religion of the sangham period consisted of the worship of the local gods such as *Murukan, Mâyon, Korravai,* etc. while the Vedic sacrifice was popular among the Brahaman (Da Yalan, 1992, 17). This sacrificial cult could not reach the masses even though the royal houses of the Pallavas and the Pândyas had adopted it (Dirks, 1979, 132). This dichotomy was understood by the bhakti saints and thus their efforts towards integrating the various forms of worship.

Digressing a bit from the main point it would be worthwhile to examine the socio-economic and politico-religious context during the early Chola period and their compulsions that led to the patronage of the orthodox sects, especially the institution of the temple. The early Cholas were faced with two problems, the need to restructure the production process and secondly, to reorganize the society on the lines of the brahmanical social order while at the same time co-opting the rising social groups. Large-scale agrarian expansion took place under the institutional aegis of the temple in the early Chola period and vast tracts of the kaveri delta were colonized. Interrelated to this process was the peaseantisation of a number of castes and thus the need to reorganize the society on the lines of the brahmanical pattern.

The main function of bhakti was to bring in changes in the religious sphere in consonance with the necessities of social adjustments and at the same time asserting the supremacy of the Vedas. Thus the temple cult was the answer to it for it broke Brâhmana exclusivity in religion and gave it a popular appeal (Spencer, 1969, 46). This was a necessity, because in an agrarian society there was a plurality of castes, each with its distinct culture that would stand in the way of integration. Thus the synthesis was achieved through the institution of the temple. Resentment among some sections of the orthodoxy to the temple cult is clear from the ascription of low caste status to the Adisaiva Brahmans (who were priests of the Saiva temples) by the more orthodox Smârta brahamana (Nandi, 1976, 191).

The superiority of the bhakti religion is clearly alluded to many times in literature and the texts and the earliest Nâyanârs, and Appar preaches the superiority of the Saiva faith in no unambiguous terms. Worship in any form was acceptable and earned divine grace. An examination of the mode of worship by the various Nâyanmârs would illustrate this point more clearly. The story of Kannappar who worshipped Siva with flowers and washed the idol with water from his mouth and finally offered his own eye to the bleeding Sivalinga is one of the oft-quoted examples (Gopal Krishna, 1990, 30). A few devotees also adopted socially prohibited ways like gambling, robbery and used that wealth to propitiate Siva (Gopalkrishna, 1990, 70). This shows that all forms of worship get sanction if they pay obesciance to Siva. This then was one of the major hallmarks of the bhakti movement.

The multifaceted character of bhakti can be understood in detail when one sees the two major features of the Saiva religion of this period, the grace of god and the ecstatic mode of worship. The Jaina religion held the view that women were responsible for the degeneration of moral values and thus they advocated celibacy, which was practiced by ascetics. But the bhakti movement stood this theory on its head and did not advocate restraint but was in favour of harnessing several forms of worship, mainly in the form of dance and singing that was a release. This led to the view of salvation as a mystic union with God that could be achieved within the confines of human reality as worship was given a sensual character. There are songs which in characteristic detail describes the attributes of Pârvatî and gives a sensual tinge with talks of her breasts (Dehejia, 1998, 45). Goddess Umadevi is portrayed as wearing the mekalai around her hip (Appar Tevaram, 5.11.6). The Tevâram describes in detail about the worship of Siva by dance and song (Sambandar Tevâram, 3.72.2) The women also joined in the singing along with the men (Sambandar Tevâram, 1.7.3). Tiruvaiyâru was famous as a center of dance and there is a graphic description of this city with its arangams or stages where dance masters taught them Kûttu (Sambandar Tevâram, 1.130.5).

The practice of dancing was prevalent in temples also where epigraphic references speak of grants made for maintaining dancers (South Indian Inscription, Vol. XIX, No. 171). This could reach a wider audience and also pander to the senses. There are references to women who made a lot of noise in a playful and vibrant atmosphere while swimming in the tanks (Sambandar Tevâram, 3.72.4). Mention is made of the sufferings of the love lorn lady and her yearning for her beloved in vain (Appar Tevâram, 4.90.7). Sundarar had two wives Paravaiyâr and Sangiliyar (Rangaswamy, 1958, 97). Tirunîlakanta Nâyanâr's lustful enjoyment with a courtesan was pardoned, as it was perceived as an act of worship to Siva (Gopalkrishna, 1990, 92).

Here one notes that sanctioning of emotional ways of seeking God led to instinctive modes of worship. This served as an outlet for realizing latent energy. It is strongly noticed in singing where bhaktas break into raptures and are taken to a point of ecstasy. As David Kinsley points out in the context of bhakti, the creation of the world, its preservation, destruction etc would be viewed as a play of god (Kinsley, 1979, 51-55). This aspect of bhakti was started by the Alvars who portrayed the Lîlâs of Krishna, his amorous exploits. This emotional bhakti of the Alvars was in fact original to krishnaism and is found in facets in Saivism, particularly among the Nâyanmârs (Hardy, 1983, 45). The Saiva saints led groups of devotees and went on long pilgrimages singing of the Lord and thus were born the concept of pilgrimage (Rangaswamy, 1958, 67). There are many references in the Tevâram to singing and also musical instruments that are described in detail. There is a reference to music and dance with the Yâl (Sambandar Tevâram, 2.187.9) There is also mention of the rhythm of the mulavu that accompanied these songs (Sambandar Tevâram, 1.130.1). There are also very many grants for the singers of the Tiruppadiyam under the early Côlas. The popularity and indispensability of singing the Tiruppadiyam can be gauged from the fact that the singers of Tiruppadiyam were paid more than the temple priests. (Nagaswamy, 1965, 370).

The institution of the Devaradiyars_(South Indian Inscription,Vol.XIII, No., 88) and the dancing girls of whom we get references in the epigraphs added colour and life to religious narrations by propagating religion in the form of an art which was also an entertainment and which like the literature drew on folk themes (Shulman, 1980, 13). Thus the popularity of bhakti among the masses was due to its rejection of ritual formalisation.

Significantly, language that the bhakti poets used created an emotional impact and bound the worshipper to the deity (Sivathambi, 1986, 38). One of the major features of the bhakti movements in India is the concept of a personal god to whom the devotees could address all their yearnings and problems. It is in this context that the relation of the personal god with the devotee is examined to understanding the prevailing power relations in society. God is addressed to as *Peruman, talaivan, Alavan,* all of which are used to indicate positions of power and authority (Dhavamony, 1971, 29-30). The devotee has to just surrender to the lord and his grace will save him. Siva is portrayed as merciful and forgiving (Hardy, 1983, 433). This concept of god enabled the devotee to visualize god as someone who was very near and who would lend an ear to his or her problems. The poetry of the period (7th-9thcenturies) brings this out very clearly. We have seen one segment of the poetic literature i.e. the intense psychological and emotional state of the poet saint (Zvelebil, 1974, 95). The other segment is that of a devotee praying to the all powerful Siva or Vishnu asking for gifts and deliverance (Zvelebil, 1974, 94).

The troubled state of affairs in the society (both in the material and emotional terms) was an important feature for bhakti to triumph, leading it to adopt a bias towards the common person. In short the emotional bhakti alone could not satisfy the common man and hence his material needs were addressed to the personal god. The general character of the hymns shows the longing for a personal relationship with god and a sense of disgust in relation to this world (Pande, 1990, 134). There were not only many things that the common man could not reach out to because of lowly position that is indicted in his sense of despair. In this position there was no way except of surrendering to the God, and God always gave refuge to anyone, as Sambandar says in his padigam that even the Jainas and the Buddhists would get refuge of they submit to Siva (Sambandar Tevaram, 1.66.10). David Shulman has expounded this same view in his analysis of the Asura myths wherein the asura too can get salvation if he submits to Siva (Shulman, 1980, 317). Such is the place of grace in the concept of bhakti. In fact the word 'path' which is a Tamil rendering of the word patti sometimes is used by to signify love (katal), but in the works of the Nâyanmârs we find the use of the word arul (grace) figures prominently (Dhavamony, 1971, 24-28).

This grace leads to salvation and demands single-minded devotion or loyalty from the devotee, which will see the devotee through in all circumstances. There is also a warning that god would not help the insincere (Appar Tevaram, 4.113.4). Siva is also addressed to as Arulâlan or the bestower of grace and this is also seen in temples in the iconographic representation of Siva in the Andhaka Surahamurti form (Rangaswamy, 1958, 535). Cakkiya Nâyanâr was a Buddhist saint but when he accepted Siva's faith he got salvation (Rangaswamy, 1958, 1007). Another aspect of bhakti is the ambiguity of terms that leads to several connotations as we saw in the examples of Katal and Arul. Similar are the groups to whom the messages were intended for.

Such a trend continued during the time of eastern Chalukyas, though the Chalukyas were worshippers of Siva and several Saivite temples came up with immense land grants. The growth of Saivism in the Deccan can be attributed to many factors. The most important among these was the patronage extended by the kings, their subordinates and officials. Vijaya_ditya II, set up a kalasa to the God at the temple of Bhimeswara, built shrines at all cardinal points of the temple and erected Mantapas and Prakaras (Krishna Kumari, 1985, 206). The King Kolottunga Chola Devara also made several endowments to the temple at Draksharama dedicated to Siva. The Kaktiyas were also great patrons of Saivism and Beta and his two sons Durga and Prola II, appear to be disciples of Rameswara Pandit a great Saivite teacher of the Kalmukha sect (Yazdani, 1960, 704).

Vir Saivism

A branch of the Saivism which became very popular in North western parts of Karnataka was Vir Saivism under the leadership of Basavvana around 12th century. Born in the northwestern part of Karnataka region during the 12th century this movement soon influenced the near by regions. This movement assumes a lot of significance because it created an alternate space against the then hierarchical social structures of brahmanical superiority. R.N. Nandi in his work, Social roots of religion in ancient India, Delhi, 1986, opines that the Vir Saiva movement was basically anti brahmanical. This was a movement taken up by the depressed sections against the well off communities. D.A.Pai in, Religious sects of ancient India, Delhi, 1985, feels that the Saiva movement was meant to give the Saivite a more definite theology and a better organization and to win over the Jains to the worship of Siva. A.P.Karmarkar in, Religions of India, Vol.I, Lonavala, Bombay, 1949, believes that the movement originated much before Basava and opines that the concept of Vir Saivism was promulgated by the first five teachers of the sect led by Ekantaka and the philosophical conceptualisation was identified by Basava in the later period. S.N. Das Gupta in, History of Indian Philosophy, Vol. V, Cambridge, 1955, assumes that VirSaivism as a sect is not older than 13th century. He points out that the authors of the Sanskrit text which are quoted as the Virsaiva documents are written under the strong influence of Sanskrit literary tradition and the orthodox philosophical systems of the Brahmins. S.C. Nandimath in, A hand book of Vir Saivism, Delhi, 1979, bases his work on the original kannada and sanskrit sources and tries to find the moorings of the Vir Saiva faith in the earlier texts of Mahabharata and Vijayabhairavi.

Shri Sihtla Ramakrishna Sastri in his work on, Vir Saiva Andhra Vangamayamu, (Telugu), Tirupati, 1948, considers Mallikarjuna Pandita and Pallikurki Somanatha as the first Vir Saiva poets. Sri Pingala Lakshmi Kantam in, Andhra Sahitya Charitra, (Telugu), Hyderabad, 1976, considers the period from 1200 to 1323 as a Saivite poetic era. T. Susila, Andhra Dvipada Sahitya Charitra, (Telugu), also looks at the Vir Saiva literature.

Sources

There is a vast amount of literary sources left behind by the followers of this sect. Though inscriptional sources are not very much helpful in understanding the role of Virsaivism they nevertheless help us in locating the Virsaiva movement in its material context.

Till recently most of the modern day works on this subject have been confined to the Karnataka region. In fact many voluminous works have been coming out with regards to the philosophical, religious, political and economic dimensions of Vir Saivism in Karnataka. As mentioned earlier eminent scholars like S.C. Nandimath, R.N. Nandi, R.G. Bhandarkar, D.A. Pai, A.P. Karmakar, S.N. Das Gupta have contribute a lot to the study of this faith in Karnataka.

In Andhra the works of Sihtla Ramakrishna Sastri, Pingala Lakshmi Kantam and T. Susila only help us to construct the life history of the Virsaiva poets. Their works have basically aimed at looking at the development of Virsaiva literature and the problems related to it. They do not look at this movement from a historical perspective.

Besides these contemporary works there is a rich source of information in the Vachana literature ranging from 11th to 18th century. The vachanas are good specimen of old Kannada and relate to the sayings of early saints. These vachanas and sayings have a peculiar charm and are composed in simple language and are easily understood even by the ignorant and illiterate. They are chiefly meant to convey to the common people soul stirring ideas in a style most simple, terse and convincing. (Nandimath, 1979, 11s) They are in prose but their word magic and cadence lift them to the level of poetry. The primary aim of the vachana writers was apparently not to propound a religious philosophical system but to show to the people the existing social and religious evils in their nakedness. In their strong criticism of these evils neither the Vedas nor the Angamas are spared. It seems that they favored rational ideas and aimed at universal brotherhood. They believed in religious and social elevation through internal purity and strict morality. All vachana sastras seem to be consistent with maintaining the doctrine of unity with the deity in the end. The list of vachana writers comprises of men of all sections from Brahmins by birth to untouchables and women of all ranks from Basava's wives and sisters to humble women earning their own maintenance by labour. We have farmers, basket makers, faggot collectors and washerwomen also among the vachana writers (Nandimath, 1979, 12).

The Vachana sastras literature is more reliable and authentic source of Virsaivism because many of the vachana writers express the real conflict of real persons and represent life more fully than any thing in the older literature (Ramanujam, 1973, 53). These words are not uttered not through a person or mask but directly in the person of the poet himself in his native, local dialect and idiom, using the tones and language of personal conversation or outcry. Compared to the other Indian literature like Vedic hymns, the vachana describe the devotees state directly in relation to the God, thereby showing the concern with the subject rather than the object of worship.

Basavanna

It was Basavanna who popularized Vir saivism around 12th century. He was the Prime Minister of Bijjala of the Kalachuri kingdom of Kalyani. He was born in a Brahmin family but revolted against the inhuman and irrational rituals and orthodox practices. Though born into a privileged class which enjoyed all the advantages and benefits of high society, he nevertheless cared deeply for the upliftment of the under privileged and the unprivileged. He did not internalize the traditional brahmanical values of the family into which he was born and broke away from these and at the age of sixteen he even removed his sacred thread. After this caste did not matter for he says,

"What if one masters the four Vedas,

He is untouchable, who is without a linga" (Ishwaran, 1983, 704).

He is very critical of the variety of Gods.

The pot is god. The winnowing

Fan is god. The stone in the

Street is god. The comb is god. The bowstring is also a

God. The bushel is a god and the

Spouted cup is a god.

God's gods, there are so many

Ther's no place left

For a foot

There is only one God. He is our Lord

Of the Meeting Rivers. (Ramanujan, 1973, 84)

Following Basavanna, all the Vir Saiva saints rebelled against the distinctions of caste and believed a devotee had no caste and all are equal. They asserted that the ideal of equality could only become a fact when the taboos in respect to food and marriage and the unwanted practices of deciding the worth of an individual on the basis of birth or occupation are done away with. Basava says,

"A pariah is the man who slays

A pariah, if he eats the carrion

Where is the caste here-where?

Our Kundala Sanga's, Sarana

Who loves all living things

He is the well born one" (Ishwaran, 1983, 704).

They did not renounce life mistaking it to be maya. Maya was not in the worldly things but in the eyes that sees them and the mind that directs the eye,

"They say gold is maya

Women and land are maya

But gold is not maya

Nor women nor land

The greed before the mind

Is maya, mark it?

O Guhesvara." (Ishwaran, 1983, 704).

They also rejected the Panchasutakas (five taboos or pollution's). They believe that the linga worn on the body is a symbol of fire god which burns all such external impurities from them. Along with removal of caste and death pollution Vir Saivism also removed the three pollution's that affect women namely of menstruation, during child birth and of widowhood (Parvathamma, 1972, 23-29). Even the hindu belief that the birth of a son alone can redeem the father from rebirth and open the doors of moksha is totally absent in Virsaivism (Mulati, 1989, 29).

In no time Vir Saivism became very popular in Karnataka and spread to the nearby regions. Their ideology of protesting against inequalities, differential power and a narrowing of the access to economic power that alienated the Brahmins from the non Brahmins, became very popular. They added immense popularity to their faith by preaching the concept of bhakti to the people. They said that it was not necessary to go to the temple to worship the lord and he is present in every individual. Basava says,

"The rich may build temples for Siva

But what can I a poor man build

My legs are pillars

The body the shrine

The head a cupola of gold

Lord of the meeting rivers

The standing shall fall

But the moving ever shall stay." (Murthy, 1980, 234).

Bhakti is not easy but nevertheless one has to follow it.

Don't you take on

this thing called Bhakti

Like a saw

it cuts when it goes

and it cuts again

when it comes

If you ink your hand

with a cobra in the pit hole

will it let you pass. (Ramanujam, 1973, 79).

Mahadevi Akka

Akka Mahadevi was a contemporary of Basavanna, the founder of Virsaiva movement. She was the daughter of a rich merchant in the village of Udutal. She was a great devotee of Siva and initiated into worship at a very early age by an unknown Guru.She grew up into a beautiful young women and the chieftain of the land named Kausika fell in love with her. Kausiki was an unbeliever. Mahadevi Akka was forced to marry him much against her wishes. Most probably he used coercion and a show of authority to subjugate Akka Mahadevi. Legend goes that she told him that she would leave him if he touched her thrice against her wishes and when he does so she leaves him (Ramanujan, 1985, 112). When she leaves him she breaks all the marital relations leaves behind her clothes and walks about naked and, finally finds solance in the company of saints. She says,

People

Malc and female,

Blush when a cloth covering their shame

Comes loose

When the Lord of lives

lives drowned with out a face

In the world

Of what use is modesty?

When the whole world

Is the lord's eye

What can you hide?

What can you cover. (Ramanujan, 1993, 131)

It was these saints who ultimately helped her consummate her love for Siva by arranging a real marriage to him. This was a marriage of her choice. She died in her early twenties becoming one with Siva at Srisaila. (Ramanuja, 1985, 114). Akka is one of the best poets of Karnataka. The number of her vachanas which can be culled from various sources is approximnatrely 350. Besides these vachanas some songs and two works titled, The vachanas of creation" and Yogangatri are in her name (Dabbe, Manushi, 1989, 42).

By the middle of 12th century Vir Saivism began to gain currency in Karnataka as an alternative to Brahmanism. It had a large Sudra following. Madivala Machchayya, a washer man and Sivanagimayya, an untouchable refused to observe caste pollution. Madhavayya, a Brahmin and Haralayya an untouchable decided to perform an intercaste marriage between their children but the orthodox lobby brought a lot of pressure and succumbing to the pressure Bijjala ordered the blinding and execution of the two men who dared to break caste taboos. This event of 1167 A.D. led to grim reprisals and three Vir Saivite followers, Molla, Bomma and Jagadeva murdered Bijjala. Following this thousands of Lingayats were butchered and the survivors scattered in different directions. (Ramaswamy, 1996, 9). The Lingayat movement was born in the context of a divided and exploited society in order to challenge it in the name of equality, individual freedom and communitarian commitment. This however was very short lived.

In Karnataka the support of the urban moneyed class was particularly relevant to the Vir saivas, who rejected public worship of images, discouraging there by the large-scale employment of professional religious priests. The absence of landgrants to the Vir Saiva monks also suggest their greater dependence on moneyed elite, the artisanal groups. Even in the 1980's most of the Lingayat came from the three commercial districts of Karnataka, Dharwar, Bijapur and Belgaum where they comprised of 40 to 50 % of the population and majority of them belonged to the trading and artisan castes (Nandi, 1986, 142). This movement which in the beginning questioned the Brahminical social order and the division of the society into rigid castes developed social exclusiveness based on privilege of birth and cleanliness of profession much along the lines of Brahmanical caste system which the sect had originally decried. (Nandi, 1986, 142). Thus the Virsaivism of Basavesvara was not the same as Vir Saivism of the post Basava period. It had lost much of its vitality, flexibility, vigor and revolutionary zeal. The classification of Vir Saiva sect into *Samanya, Visesa* and *Nirbhara* also shows the division of the sect on the basis of social precedence (Nandi, 1986, 142).

Vir Saivism in Andhra

Virsaivism entered Andhra when it had declined in Karnataka. Even in Andhra, earlier, we do not come across the term Vir Saivism in the inscriptions or literary sources of the time. Mallikarjuna Pandita uses the term Viravrata, Viramaheswara, showing that the sect did exist in Andhra. Here the sect assumed the form of Aradhya Saivism. This was spread by three Pandita's referred to as Panditatraya, namely, Sripati Pandita, Mallikarjuna Pandita and Sivalenka Manchana Pandita. Since they did not receive any royal patronage they were not able to command substantial following.

There are a number of problems, which a scholar faces while dealing with this subject matter in the Andhra context. The language used in contemporary literature is very complicated. The authors prefer the very complicated Desi, Vernacular style instead of the Marga, Sanskrit style in their writings. But the spoken dialect of Telugu in modern day Andhra is very different from that of 11th and 12th century. Since there is a lack of numismatic evidence one has to increasingly rely on contemporary literature. Certain terms like feudal, caste, superstition, ritual and Hindu are used loosely and one does not always find appropriate terms to replace them in the existing terminology of the period. During 12th and 13th century Saivism gained a lot of popularity in society. It received wide patronage of the rulers and the ruled. There were various divisions among the Saivites also. Of these various sub-sects Kalamukhas and Aradhyas received prominence. However it was only the Kalamukhas who had royal patronage.

There are many contemporary works, which throw a lot of light on the period under study. Mallikarjuna Pandita wrote *Kavyas* such as, *Sivatatvasaram, Lingodbhava deva Gadhyay, Rudramahima, Amareswara Satakamu* and *Parvatavaranamu,* which are important works of Saivite literature (Venkata Subbaih, 1985).

Sivatatvasaram, composed by Mallikarjuna Pandita, begin a new epoch in the history of the Virsaiva movement. This is commonly referred to as *Satakamu.* A *Satakamu* consists of 100 to 108 poems. Here each stanza is rhymes and ends with the poet's message in the context of the social reality. In these he discusses about the decline of Jainism and Buddhism and the subsequent popularity of Saivism has been stressed. In this work it is Siva who dominates and we have explanations of different ways of Siva bhakti along with the life histories of some prominent devotees of Siva. To Mallikarjuna, Siva is always present in Siva bhaktas and they should be therefore looked upon as moving Lingas or the human manifestation of Rudra. He emphasized that no caste should be attributed to Siva Bhaktas. Mallikarjuna also has a serious criticism of advaita philosophy. To him Siva is the lord of all beings from Hari to Brahma down to the smallest ant in the world. He compares Siva to the Universe and Jiva passes through ten different stages of bandhan and moksha. Since Siva is above this the idea of union between Siva and Jiva is subject to the influence of *mithya* or illusion and so it can never be a part of the supreme soul.

Palkurki Somanatha another Saivite poet wrote, *Basavapurana*. (Subramanyam, 1968). This work gives us information on the life and activities of Basavesvara. He describes how Basava condemned Jainism and Buddhism and Vedic religions and how he propagated the faith of Virasaivism. He also welcomed women to participate in religious activities. Besides Anubhavsaram he also wrote Panditaradhya Charitra. This work contains five main sections Diksha, Purantana, Veda, Mahima and Parvata. Here we find information on the life and activities of Mallikarjuna Pandita and the history of Vir Saivism along with the life history of some Saivite devotees which are rich sources of information on Vir Saivism. Besides these we have two other works, *Kayurbahu Charitramu* by Manchana (Vaidehi, 1978). There is also *Palanati Vircharitra* by Srinatha, which give us some glimpse on religious and social life in medieval times (Lakshmikantam, 1991).

Sripati Pandita was a well-versed scholar well versed in the Vedas, Upanishads and other sacred books. He was a great devotee of Lord Siva and lived in Vijaywada. He started Brahmanising Saivism and at the same time he tried to counteract the influence of the Mimamsakas and the Advaitas by upholding Bhakti. His line of thought culminated in Srikanta charya who in his, *Srikanta Bhasya*, openly declared that his system was Siva Visistadvaita (Rao, 1973, 269). In Andhra Desa there is still an Aradhya family which traces its decent from Sripati pandita (Rao, 1973, 289).

Sivalenka Manchana Pandita was another great devotee of Siva. He belonged to a Pandita family in which his father Sambhu Bhatta and his grandfather Sambhu Desika were highly educated and Pandits of highest order. He was a contemporary of Basava.

Mallikarjuna Pandita was the third Pandita who contributed a lot to the Aradhya sect. He was born in a Pandit family at Draksharaman. He accepted Vedic standard and rituals and introduced these into the Aradhya sect. Hence this sect was very different from Lingayat or Basava tradition, where there was no caste distinction and Vedic rituals. Many Brahmins joined this new reformed Virsaivism and the Vedic tradition s gained its stronghold with in the Virsaiva movement. Mallikarjuna Pandita states in his *Sivatatvasa-ram*, "Oh! Lord Siva make it possible, to release people from this earthen bonds for salvation through offerings and prayers in the path of the Vedas."

It is said that Mallikarjuna sowed the seeds of Virsaivism and Palkurki Somanatha developed it to a great extent. He was born in Palkurki in Warangal. Though a strong advocate of Virsaivism he also followed a middle path. His reverence and affection towards Mallikarjuna Pandita made him write, *Panditaradhya Charitra*", and his respect for Basava made him compose "Basavapuranam". Somnatha sarcastically criticized the worship of different Gods by the Brahmins, saying, "Is it proper and accepted to pray or worship various lesser Gods and Goddesses while Sarveswara is there"(Bandaru, 1962, Canto 1) He also attempted to bring into his fold the untouchables, "It cannot be tolerated and justified to keep the Sudras aloof. What dharma and what morality and which Purana supports this (Bandaru, 1962, Canto 7).

Inspite of its zeal and philosophy to bring about a social change, the Virsaiva sect did not make much headway in Andhra. The influence of this sect was limited more to the Telengana region, which was for some time under the rule of the Western Chalukya, and later under Rashtrakutas. It is in this region that we find several Vir Saiva mathas being established (Lalitamba, 1976, 64-67). A large number of Jain monasteries were also destroyed and comparatively this number is more in Telengana than in Coastal Andhra. Inspite of the Vir saiva's objection to the temple a large number of Saivite temples were being built by the kings, feudatories and also individuals (Sastri, 1991, 265). Hence in Andhra this movement had a limited impact. It did not occur, as a radical and violent religious faith as in Karnataka.This was probably because Vir Saivism had declined in Karnataka and it was no longer as radical in its ideology as the earlier phase and had become very divided and exclusive. It is from 14th century onwards that we come across the term Vir Saivism in Inscriptions (Nellore Inscription, Ongole, 112). By the time of Mallikarjuna Pandita and Somanatha many Vir Saiva jangamas of Karnataka had started migrating to Andhra from Karnataka and Tamil nadu and settled here ((Soma Reddy, 1993). The followers of this faith were primarily confined to certain upper sections of the Brahmins and among the Vyasya community, Padmasalees, weavers and Viswakarma and among the few Panchama communities. Though the literature of the Vir Saiva faith appears to be revolutionary, the propagators of this faith were unable to put forth their ideals into practice. Infact Mallikarjuna Pandita continued to wear his sacred thread. Thus their revolutionary ideology was mostly confined to literature. Hence this faith in Andhra took a very mild form of Aradhya sect and in no time merged with the Vedic religion (Pande, 2005, 49).

Disintegration and Development of Social Exclusiveness

The radicalization of the Virsaiva sect did not last for a long time even in Karnataka. The absence of economic equality and the inbuild occupational and income differentiation's between the very poor madigas and Holeyas on the one hand and the very rich Ookkalingas merchants on the other resulted inevitably in the reintroduction of caste hierarchies and social inequalities.

R.N. Nandi has clearly shown that there were three social divisions, which emerged among its followers. The trading communities together with the Jangamas were called Panchamsalis and constituted the top rung even though between the two there was neither inter dinning nor intermarriage. The cultivators and craftsmen constituted the second rung and were known as the non Panchamasalis. These groups had the ashtavarna but could neither interdine nor marry with the Panchamas. The tanners, washerwomen and all untouchables constituted the lowest rung. These were Virsaivites only in name and had no right to the linga dharma or the ashtaavarna. They were excluded ritually and socially and were forbidden to intermix and marry the higher Lingayat groups. So in its original the Virsaiva was professedly a fraternal association overriding all caste discrimination. But it soon developed social exclusiveness based on the privilege of birth and cleanliness of profession, much along the lines of the brahmanical caste system, which the sect originally decried (Nandi, 1975).

References

Aiyangar, S. krishnaswami, 1981, *Contributions of south India to Indian culture*, New Delhi.

Appar Tevaram, 1964, Vol. 4, 5, (Tamil) Tirumurai, Taramapuram Atinam, Tarumapuram.

Bandaru, Tammaiah (ed), 1962, Palakurki Somanatha, *Basavpuranam*, (Telugu), ed. Madras.

Bhattacharya, Chandra (ed), 1995, *Vaisnavism in eastern India*, Firma K.L.M. Pvt. Ltd. Calcutta.

Bhatt, S.R. 1980, *The philosophy of Pancharatra*, Butala and Company, New Delhi.

Bhandarkar, R.G., 1913, reprt. 1983, *Vaisnavism Saivism,and minor religious systems*, Strassburg, Trukner.

Clooney, Francis X, 1994, *The art and theology of Sri vaisnava thinkers*, T.R.Publication for Satya Nilayam Publication, Madras.

Dabbe Vijaya and Robert Zydenbose, 1989, "Akka Mahadevi", in Madhu Kishwar (ed), *Women Bhakta poets*, New Delhi.

Dehejia, Vidya, 1998, *Slaves of The lord-The Path of the Tamil saints*, Delhi.

DaYâlan, D, 1992, *Early Temples of Tamilnadu*, Delhi.

Dirks, Nicholas, 1979, "Political authority and structural change in early south Indian history", *Indian Economic and Social History Review.*

Dhavamony, Maraisusai, 1971, *Love of God according to Saiva Siddhanta*, Oxford University Press, U.K.

Epigraphia Indica, Vol. IV, No.5, 6, Calcutta, 1892.

Epigraphia Indica, Vol. IV, No. 54, 58, Calcutta, 1892.

Gonda, J.1976, *Visnuism and Sivaism-a comparison*, Munshiram,Manoharlal Publishers, New Delhi.

Gopalakrishnan, R.1990, *Religion and Mysticism in the Periyapuranam*, Madras.

Gupta, S.N.Das, 1955, *A history of Indian Philosophy*, Vol. V, Cambridge.

Hardy, Friedhelm, 1983, *Viraha bhakti*-the early history of Krsna devotion in south India, Oxford University Press, New Delhi.

Hart, George L.1960, "The Theory of reincarnation among the Tamils" in Wendy Doinger O'Flaherty,(ed) *Karma and Rebirth in Classical Indian Tradition*, California.

Harendradayal, T.1981, *Ancient cultures of India*, Delhi.

Hopkins, T. J. 1971, *The Hindu religious tradition*, California.

Ishwaran, 1983, *Religion and society among the Lingayats in South India*, Vikas, New Delhi.

Jackson J. William, 1998, *Songs of three great south Indian saints*, Oxford University Press, Delhi.

Krishna Kumari, 1985, *The rule of the Chalukya Cholas in Andhra Desa*, Delhi.

Karmarkar A.P. and N.B. Kalamdani, 1989, *Mystic teachings of the Haridasas of Karnataka*, Dharwar.

Kinsley, David, R. 1979, *The Divine Player A study of Krsna Lila*, Delhi.

Lakshmikantam, P. (Ed), 1991, Srinathas's, *Palanati vira Charitra*, (Telugu), Hyderabad.

Lalitamba, K. 1976, *Vir Saivism in Andhra*, Guntur.

Murthy, M. Chidananda 1980, "Basava and Vir Saivism in Karnataka", in S.P. Sen (ed), *Social Content of Indian Religious reforms*, Calcutta.

Nandimath, S.C. 1979, *A handbook of Virsaivism*, Delhi.

Nandi, R.N. 1975, "Origin of the Vir Saiva movement", in *The Indian Historical Review*, Vol. II, No. 1.

Nandi, R.N. 1976, "Origin and nature of Saivaite Monasticism: The case of Kalamukhas" in R.S. Sharma (ed) *Indian Society: Historical probings*, Delhi.

Nagaswamy, R., 1965, "South Indian Temple as an Employer" *Indian Economic and Social History Review.*

Naidu Gopal Krishna, G.T. 1979, *Lord Venkateswar and Alwars*, Tirupati.

Nellore Inscription Ongole, 850-1350 A.D.in Inscriptional Glossary of Andhra Pradesh, Hyderabad, 1967, entry under, Veeramushtulu, pp. 112.

Pande Rekha, 1992, Ramanuja and Sri Vaishnavism-some observations on its social content, in G.Kamalakar (Ed), *Vishnu in art, thought and literature*, Hyderabad.

Pande, Rekha, 2004, Sri Vaisnavism in Medieval Andhradesa in V. Krishna Rao (ed.) *"Glimpses of our past Historical Research"*, Hyderabad.

Pande, Rekha, 2005, "Some facets of Vir Saivism and aspects of social dynamism in Medieval Andhra Deas", in Satyanarayana and Chenna Reddy (ed), *Recent Trends in Historical Studies*, Pathak Research India Press, New Delhi.

Pande, Susmita, 1989, *Medieval Bhakti movement-its history and philosophy*, Kusumanjali Prakashan, Meerut.

Pande, Susmita, 1990, *Birth of Bhakti in Indian Religions and Art*, Delhi.

Parvathamma, C.1972, *Sociological essayas on Vir Saivism*, Popular Prakashan, Bombay.

Ramanujan, A.K. 1973, *Speaking of Siva*, Penguin, Harmondsworth.

Ramaswamy, Vijaya, 1996, *Divinity and Divine*, Oxford University Press.

Rao Venkat, Nidadavolu, 1956, *Lives of Telugu Poets*, Madras.

Rao, Gopinath T. A. 1923, *Sri Subrahmanya Ayyar: Lectures on the history of Sri. Vaishnavas*, Madras.

Rao Hanumanth, BSL, 1913, *Religion in medieval Andhra*, Guntur. Reprint 1973, Guntur.

Rao, Hanumanth B.S.L. 1983, (Telugu), *Andhrula Charitra*, Guntur.

Reddy S. Pratap, 1982, (Telugu), *Andhrula Sanghika Charitra*, Hyderabad.

Rangacharya, V. 1975, *Historical evolution of Sri Vaisnavism in south India*, Vol. IV (The Religions), Calcutta.

Raghavcharya, T.K.T.Vira, 1977, *History of Tirupati*, Vol. I, Tirumala Tirupati Devastanam, Tirupati.

Rangaswamy, Dorai, 1958, *The Religion and Philosophy of The Tevaram*, Madras.

Sambandar Tevaram, 1964, Vol. 1, 2, 3 (Tamil) Tirumurai, Tarumapuram, Atinam, Tarumapuram.

Sastri, K. A. N. 1991, *History of South India*, Madras.

Spencer, George.W, 1969, "Religious Networks and Royal influences in 11th century south India" *Journal of the Economic and Social History of the Orient*, Vol. XII.

Shulman, David Dean, 1980, *Tamil Temple Myths*, Princeton, USA.

Sivathamby, K, 1986, *Literary History in Tamil*, Thanjavur.

Soma Reddy, 1993, Medieval Presidential Address, *Proceedings of Andhra Pradesh History Congress*, Tirupati.

Sarojini Devi, Konduri, 1990, *Religion in the Vijaynagara Empire*, Sterling publishers, New Delhi.

Sharma, B.N.K 1960, *A history of the dvaita school of Vedanta and its literature*, Vol. 1, Bombay.

South Indian Inscriptions, Vol. VI, 1986, No. 1144, Delhi.

South Indian Inscriptions, Vol. IV, 1986, No. 277, Mysore.

South Indian Inscriptions, Vol. IX, No. 488.

South Indian Inscriptions, Vol. XIII, No. 88.

Subramanyam (ed) 1968, *Basavapuranam*, (Telugu), A.P. Sahitya Academy, Hyderabad,

Subbaiah Venkata (Ed), 1985, *Sahitya Prabandhamu*, (Telugu), Hyderabad.

Tirumalai Tirupati Devasthana Epigraphical Series, Vol.II, No. 4.

Tirumalai Tirupati Devasthana Epigraphical Series, Vol.II, No. 3.

Tyagi, I. C. 1982, *Saivism in ancient India*, Meerut.

Vaidehi, Krishna Moorthy, 1970, "Social and Economic conditions in Eastern Deccan" (1000-1250 A.D.), Hyderabad.

Varadachari, V. 1982, *Agamas and South Indian Vaisnavism*, Prof. M. Rangacharya Memorial Trust, Madras.

Venkatasubramanian, T.K. 1984, "Social Roots of Tamilian Religious Ideology", *Proceedings of Indian History Congress*, Annamalai.

Yasodadevi, V. 1979, "Ramanuja and the Bhakti movement in Andhradesa,", in S.P. Sen (Ed), *The social content of Indian religious reform movement*, Calcutta.

Yazdani, G. (ed.) 1960, *Early history of the Deccan*, Oxford University Press.

Zvelebil, Kamil Veith, 1974, *A History of Indian Literature–Tamil Literature*, (ed) Jan Gonda, Otto Harrasowig Weisbaden, Vol. X, Madras.

5

Bhakti Movement in the Northern Regions

Bhakti had originated in south India and it had then spread to different parts of India in different period. There is a lineal connection in the sense that one of the main founders of the bhakti movement in north India, Ramananda was a disciple of the famous Ramanuja. Thus when Bhakti, entered north India, it was already centuries old and did not have to spend all the energies in evolving but could replicate many of the features that were already a part of the southern bhakti. The similarity cannot be extended further as earlier authors did and we see that north India of the medieval period was fundamentally different from south India in at least two respects viz, the Turkish rule and also the clear demarcation of the varnas. In south India the varna was just a theoretical concept while the jati reflected the local realities. Further, in north India one can see this movement in two streams, the nirgun, monotheistic movement and the sagun, Vaisnava movement. The two main proponets of the monotheistic movement in North were Kabir and Nanak. Kabir was a follower of Ramananda, who was a disciple of Ramanuja and hence one can see an ideological and philosophical connection between south and North India.

The 14th century was a period of regeneration, marked by features like expansion of the agrarian base, increase in trade and commerce, growth of urbanization and an increase in commodity production. Under the Khiljis and Tughluqs, the narrow Turkish domination was replaced by a ruling class which had a broader social base among the muslims. The linking of the Delhi Sultanate to the ports of Gujarat on the one hand and its expansion in to the south on the other and the end of the Mongol menace, freeing the Punjab and Kashmir from their fearsome rule and reintegrating them with the rest of the country opened the way for expansion of trade with central and west Asia (Sobha, 1983, 12). However the 15th century was again a period of political disintegration. The invasion of Timur in 1399, had laid a heavy blow to the stability of the Delhi sultanate. The Sayyids came to power for a short interval and then the Lodi's who were Afghans took over the reigns of the kingdom ending the long rule of the Turks and this too was short lived though the Afghan presence continued for very long. Sufism was very popular during this period and Kabir was very much influenced by this as well as by the Nathpanthis who believed in Yogic practices.

Bhakti Movement in the Indo Gangetic Plain

Before beginning to explore the contours of bhakti in the Indo-gangetic plains, a geographical preface would help us to understand better the bhakti movement and its unique facets in north India. Well watered by the mighty river Ganges and her tributaries, the gangetic plains had large areas under cultivation with relatively dense settlement pattern. The co-relation between well watered and well settled regions is clear in the sense that the settlement pattern here consists of villages with a strong caste hierarchy which was operational in the extraction of surplus. We also find prevalence of pastoralism as evidenced in the braj region, in the northwest of the gangetic plains like the unending river Ganges, the plains were also very vast but by no means uniform as we see diverse culures and dialects ranging from the Braj of the northwest to the avadhi of central plains with an admixture of Persian and the bhojpuri of the middle and eastern gangetic region. All these dialects were earthy and vibrant borrowing from the 'production based' language of the peaseantry and the artisanal class. On this earthy and vibrant template the bhakti saints effectively essayed their concerns that easily struck a receptive chord among the common populace devoid of any formality or sheen that one encounters in the court languages.

In the Indo Gangetic plain one could see the coexistence of both both Nirgun and Sagun forms ostensibly on the basis of a theological difference in the way of conceptualizing the nature of the divine being that is the object of worship. The nirgun Bhakti also develops along two streams of *Gyan marg* and *Prem Marg* and the sagun stream develops into Krishna Bhakti as well as Ram Bhakti. In north India one can find the impact of Yoga and Sufi thinking also on the Bhaktas.

Ramananda

Ramanada belonged to the Visnava school of Benaras. He was the chief inspirer of the worship of Rama in the Bhakti movement in Northern India towards the close of the thirteenth century and the beginning of fourteenth century and he was witness to the spread of Islam in this region and the impact of the Sufis especially under the Khiljis. He seems to have come in contact with learned Muslims in Benaras. (Macauliffe, 1909, 102). He and his guru Raghavananda were very much influenced by the Nirgun ideology of the nath pantha (Badathval, 1950). Though both Raghavananda and Ramananda had moved away from the Sri Sampradaya of Ramanuja in the south they both continued to retain their formal affiliation with the sect. Ramananda is a shadowy figure and not much is know about the historical figure Ramananda. His followers can be grouped into two schools. The first were strictly orthodox and accepted the authority of the Vedas. This school was represented by Nabhadas (the author of Bhaktamal) and Tulsidas. The second school was represented by Kabir and his followers and is more eclectic and sceptic in its approach to Vedas and Hindu rituals and extends the same principle of skepticism and rejection of scriptures and ritual in Islam. He opened the path of Bhakti to all irresespective of caste and stated that Bhakti could be followed by one and all. However he never opposed the caste system and felt that one should work in the society with in the social structure. There are two Sanskrit works, *Vaisnavtabjya Bhaskar* and *Ramarchan Padhati*, which are attributed to Ramanand (Shukla, 1994, 65). The *Bhaktamal* of Nabhadas is the earliest known account of Medieval bhaktas to be found in a single work.According to Ram kumar Verma this was composed in 1585A.D. followed by the commentary of Priya das in 1655 (Verma, 1948). This book states that there are twelve disciples of Ramananada. These include, Anantanand, Sukhanand, Narhayanand, Bhavanand, Pipa, Kabir, Sen, Dhanna, Raidas, Padyawati and Sursuri. It is also believed that Ramananda followed Yoga for twelve years and was very much influenced by it.

The Nirgun School

The Nirgun Bhakti stream which believed in a formless deity but with attributes also developed along two streams. One was the *Gyan marg*, which gave importance to knowledge and yogic practices and the other was the *prem marg*, which gave importance to love and was more influenced by the Sufi thought. Among the former were sants like Kabir, Rai Das, Nanak, Dadu Dayal, Sundar Das, Rajjab and the other lesser known sants like Maluk Das, Jambhanath, Singha Jee and Hari Das Niranjani. Among the Prem margi were sants like Mulla Daud, Qutban, Malik Muhammad Jayasi and Manjhan.

Kabir

It was in 15th century that Kabir established a seperate identity of the Nirgun stream of Bhakti, with the worship of a formless God as against the Sagun stream of Ram Bhakti and Krishna Bhakti. He was a desciple of Ramananda. Kabir can rightly be called the originator of the medieval school of nirgun Bhakti of a formless God. The beginnings made by Kabir were carried further by Nank, Raidas and Dadu.

Kabir's early life is shrouded in mystery, which has contributed more to his popularity as there were always tussles over the ownership of Kabir amongst the hindus and muslims, which was in a sense an anachronism, since it was against these very notions that Kabir campaigned for. It is believed that he was born to a hindu widow, who in order to hide her shame abandoned this child and it was adopted by a weaver couple Neeru and Neema, who were muslims. According to legend, Kabir was found in a lotus leaf, although only some aspects can be substantiated as historical truths (Scott, 1985, 101-103). The date of birth ascribed to Kabir has been 1398 A.D. corresponding to the month of jeth 1455 of the Vikramaditya era (Maculiffe, 1989, 122-123). It has been held that Kabir died in 1449 (Vaudeville, 1974, p.36).

Kabir himself was unlettered and he has left nothing in a written form. This was mainly an oral tradition that was handed down. It was his admirers and disciples who treasured his poems and repeated them to one another and perhaps in some cases wrote them down. When the Kabir panth was definitely organized and there was a need for a definite authentic scripture steps were taken to collect Kabirs works and it was his pupils who put down his sayings and thoughts in a collection known as *Bijak*. Tradition has it that it was dictated by Kabir to his disciple Bhagwan Das though other feel that this was done in 1600 A.D. The *Bijak* is the most authoritative record of Kabir's teachings. The language used here is the dialect which was spoken in the neighbourhood of Benares, Mirzapur and Gorakhpur. It also has a large number of Persian, Arabic and Turkish words. All these words found their way into the writings of Kabir because there must have been daily interactions between all these groups.

From the modern point of view Kabirs language is full of grammatical mistakes but even today his words along with those of Tulsidas can be heard in the villages of Northen India. Kabir Panthis recognize three other works of his, *Kutavani, Taksara* and *Mulijana.*

Kabir spent his early life in the midst of both hindus and muslims and offended both the communities by his so called, "blasphemous" utterances. Muslims called him. Kafir, when he uttered "Ram, Ram, Hari, Hari". He also attracted the wrath of the orthodox Hindu sections by his unorthodox practices. The Brahmins disliked him for wearing the symbolic thread normally worn by them (Westcott, 1953, 5). Kabir was so involved in his religious pursuits that he was often rebuked by his family members for neglecting his work.

Thou art always rising early and bringing fresh utensils

Thy life hath gone in plastering cooking squares

Thou payest no attention to thy weaving

Thou art engrossed in the pleasures of saying God, God

Who in our family had even uttered the name of Ram?

Since this worthless son of ours began to wear a

Roasary, we have no peace

Hear wife of my eldest brother in law

Hear wife of my younger brother in law

A wonderful thing hath occurred

This boy hath ruined our weaving business

Why is he not dead? (Keay, quoted in Hedayetullah, 1977, 176).

Though illiterate Kabir was well versed in the religion of the Hindus. He lived and was brought up in Benaras. He was witness to the pigrims from all over the country gathering here on different festive occasions and was familiar with the numerous temples, shrines and bathing *ghats* of this city. Kabir was brought up by a muslim family and hence he would have been aware of Islam also. Kabir had settled in Manikpur Kara and came under the influence of Shaikh Taqqi. There is evidence that he met many other Sufis also.

Through Manikpur Kabir passed

There he heard of the fame of Shaikh Taqqi

At the place which is called Jaunpur

And Jhusi I heard the name of many Pirs

There are written twenty one pirs

They were giving discourses in the name of the prophet. (Ramaini, 48 as quoted in Hedayetullah, 1977, 183).

It was because of his interaction with the two communities that Kabir has the basic concept of unity of God.

He is one, there is no second

Rama, Khuda, Sakti, Siva are one, tell me

Pray how will you distinguish them? (Bijak, Sabd 43, as quoted in Hedayetullah, 1977, 203).

Again he says,

Rama, Khuda, Sakti, Siva are one. Then to whom

Do the prayers go? The Vedas, the Puranas and

The Quran are only different manners of description

Neither the Hindu, nor the Turk, neither the Jain

Nor the Yogi is cognizant of the secret (Bijak, Sabd, 28 as quoted in Hedayetullah, 1977, 205).

By means of his instructions to Hindus and Turks alike Kabir was trying to spread the message of brotherhood of mankind. He showed no partiality to either and never tried to please any one. Kabir was very appreciative of Persian mystics and on account of this he had a desire to synthesize Muhammadan mysticism with Hindu thought. Great Persian mystics like Attar Sadi, Jalauddin, Rumi and Hafiz played a significant role in forming opinions and views held by Kabir and exercised a powerful influence on the religious thought of India (Tagore, 1945, vii). Kabir was well versed in mysticism and was a follower of Sufism and took a liberal approach towards Islamic traditions.

The Sufis regarded all ordinary religious duties as mere forms and attached no importance to them. Divine rewards and punishments such as paradise and hell and human standards of right and wrong are regarded as non existent for one who has found union with God. Many of these ideas of the Sufis are found in the teachings of Kabir. In order to obtain union with God as the supreme reality, he condemns pride and declares the uselessness of the ordinary religious rites. He also advocates the value of a guru or spiritual guide and the repetition of the name of God (Keay, 1931, 91)

To Kabir religion (dharma) with out devotion (Bhakti) was no religion at all (a dharma). Bhakti is a matter of feeling and experience.As his Bhakti is rooted in mysticism, he condemned every external and ritualistic form of religious devotion. He says there is no dearth of saints,(Bhaktas) who have little knowledge about the true nature of Bhakti but pride themselves in it (Sunder Das, Shyam, 1959, 115). To Kabir Bhakti is difficult and it is not one's aunt's house and in this house of God's love is not with in easy reach (Sunder Das, Shyam, 1959, 62). To attain Bhakti one has to take ones head in ones hand and feel pain like being cut by a sharp blade of steel or burnt by a tong of fire (Sunder Das, Shyam, 1959, 62). With out Bhakti in ones heart a person becomes heartless.

O Kabir all spoiled Bhakti

By laying stones and pebbles

With in they stored up poison

And poured away the amrit (Shah, 1977, 208).

Bhakti for Kabir meant human love, love of God and complete faith in almighty and this meant paying obeisance to him. There should be no restrictions placed on such a love. Every individual should seek shelter in the abode of God who is an embodiment of love. With out this the world has no meaning.

This world is bound in error

No one considers

Knowing not the Bhakti or hari

All the world is drowned

And dead (Shah, 1977, 88)

Bhakti means surrendering to truth and it also means an affirmation of truth. Search for this truth or God is not an easy path. It is full of suffering and only he who knows the anguish of suffering can obtain God (Sunder Das, Shyam, 1959, 8). He refers to his God as Ram, but he clearly points out that this Ram is not the avatar of Vishnu nor is he the son of Dasaratha who married Sita and destroys Lanka (Shastri and Prasad, 1950, 66). This Ram is omni present and can be found with in one self. Even the Vedas, the Smritis and the Puranas cannot solve the mystery of this Rama (Sunder Das, Shyam, 1959, 92).

There is great trouble

A mine of trouble

Thou wilt escape only when

Thou knowest Rama

Know Rama and find the

Path of union then the noose

Will not fall round thee (Shah, 1977, 63).

One cannot realize this God through scriptures but one has to know the truth of inner experience. He scorns at the learned man who repeatedly recites the Vedas but is ignorant of the fact that reality resides but with in himself (Sunder Das, Shyam, 1959, 90).He is like the all pervading spirit and lives in man like the pupil in the eye. The deer wanders in the forest searching for musk which rests with in itself, similarly an ignorant man wanders around searching for God with out realizing that he resides with in himself (Sunder Das, Shyam, 1959, 72).

Since God resided in all, Kabir believed that all men were born equal. All human beings were sustained by the same air, water and light. All were formed by the same dust and all had the same creator. He asks the Brahmin, who claims to be a superior by birth if he was born in some other fashion. He wants to know if the Brahmin has milk in his veins while he has blood. How is it that one is a Brahmin and another a Shudra (Sunder Das, Shyam, 1959, 42).

Kabir is also very critical of the Muslim and their rituals, particularly clerical Islam. He believed in oneness of God and peaceful coexistence between various religious orders which is well reflected in his verse of God being one and the same, whether a Hindu or Muslim Each may be called differently but they are pots of one clay.

Brother, whence came two

Diverse masters of the world?

Who led you astray?

Allah, Rama, Karim, Keshava,

Hari, Hazrat are but names

That are given.

Jewels are made of

One gold bar, but in

It is one nature only

Only in speech and hearing two

Are made one Namaz, another Puja

He is Mahadev, He is Mohammad

And Brahma is called Adam.

One is called Hindu, one Turk,

Both live on the same earth.

One reads the Vedas, another Khutba.

One is Maulvi, one is Panda

Each is called a separate name

Both are pots of clay

Kabir says both alike have

Gone astray

None has found Rama. One sacrificed a goat and one food

In arguing both have lost their lives (Shah, 1977, 110).

Guru is considered to be very important in Kabirs scheme of things because it is the guru who is the guide and provides his desciple with knowledge and reason. In fact Kabir says that infront of him stand both God and Guru and he does not know whose feet to touch first but then he decides he will touch the feet of his Guru because it is through his Guru that he has found God.

Kabir is very critical of the power and privileges enjoyed by the Brahmins. He says the rich use costly clothes, wear pearl and dimonds and sleep on soft beddings, while the poor wore rags and slept on the ground and were ridden with disease (Sunder Das, Shyam, 1959, 92). He makes a contrast between the lofty mansions of the rich with Naubat or ceremonial music being played outside their house and the poor living in mud huts and only tatters shielding their doors from the strong winds. Hence Kabir was questioning the very feudal structure of his times which gave the rich and the powerful many privileges and the right to rule and exercise authority, and Bhakti becomes a tool for this questioning.

Ravi Das

Ravi Das also known as Rai Das probably lived in 15th century but not much is known about him. Tradition holds it that he was a tanner by profession and hence occupied a very low position in the caste hierarchy as the members of this caste handled dead animals. His songs are filled with reference to his despised occupation but along with this is an expression of gratitude that one so lowly has been given the power to teach others including the proud Brahmins, the true path.Ravi Das followers have formed a sect to perpetuate his teachings and many ot the modern day reform movements of the 20th century like the Harijan Sevak Sangh, Schedule Caste Federations regard him as a hero of such a social reform movement which talks of a vision of equality. To the many followers of Ravi Das their worship of Ravi das is not just a religious phenomena but a vehicle of social, religious and political protest against the inequitable distribution of power and wealth in a social order. Some of Ravi Das's writings are found in the Guru Granth Sahib.

He talks of an utopian city that is free from pain and oppression and is the ideal city.

The regal realm with the sorrowless name

They call it Queen city, aplace with no pain

No taxes or cares, none own property there,

No wrongdoing, worry, terror or torture.

O my brother, I have come to take it as my own,

My distant home, where every thing is right.

That imperial kingdom is rich and secure,

Where none are third or second-all are one,

Its food and drink are famous, and those who live there

Dwell in satisfaction and in wealth.

They do this or that, they walk where they wish,

They stroll through fabled palaces unchallenged.

O says Ravi Das, a good for nothing tanner

Those who walk beside me are my friends (Embree, 1991, 376).

He also opposes rituals and believes in the worship of a formless God with the help of a Guru and a God that can be worshipped with body and mind.

Mother she asks, with what can I worship?

All the pure is impure. Can I offer milk?

The calf has dirtied it in sucking its mothers teat

Water, the fish have muddied, flowers, the bees-

No other flowers could be offered than these.

Even the sandalwood tree where the snake has coiled is spoiled

The same act formed both nectar and poison

Every thing's tainted; candles, rice and incense-But still I can worship with my body and my mind

And I have the guru's grace to find the formless Lord.

Worship and offerings-I cannot do any of these.

What says Ravi das, will you do with me? (Embree, 1991, 377)

He makes fun of the Brahmin and says that they come to him to find the way to God.

Oh well born of Banaras, I too am well known,

My labor is with leather.But my heart can boast the Lord.

See how your honor, the purest of pure

Water from the Ganges, which no saint will touch.

If it had been made into intoxicating drink-

Liquor is liquor, what ever its source.

And this toddy tree you consider impure,

Since the sacred writings have branded it that way

But see that writings are written on its leaves

The Bhagavata Purana you so greatly revere.

And I, born to be a carrier of carrion, am now

The lowly, the one to whom the brahmans come

And lowly bow.

They seek

The shelter of my name, servant of the sun,

Whose service is the service of the Lord. (Embree, 1991, 377-78).

Dadu Dayal

There is a lot of controversy about Dadu Dayal. Some regard him as a Brahmin and others as a shoe maker. He was probably born around 1544 A.D. and it is generally believed that he was a follower of Kabir as he mentions Kabir many times in his poems. He traveled to different places like Amer, Bikaner, Marwar and probably died in Bharane around 1603 A.D. He uses a lot of Arabic and Persian words in his writings while he talks of a nirgun god who gives his grace to the devotee. He is also opposed to rituals and the division of society on the basis of religion. Dadu says," I am neither a Hindu nor a Muslim. I am not attached to any philosophical school for all represent only the mask of deceit." (Narayandas, 1959, No. 10/85). To Dadu it is only a saint who can be praised for his lack of attachment ot worldly goods. Compassion, charity and kindness towards the poor, the helpless are advocated as acts of virtue (Narayan das, 1959, 15/84). Dadu criticizes the Hindus for going to Dwarka, Kashi and Mathura and the Muslims for going to Mecca and Medina. All the holy places he says are with in one self (Narayan das, 1959, 9/309).He also denounces all external forms of rituals and ceremonies like fasting, feasting, pilgrimage, taking dip in the holy rivers, going to the temple or mosque, performing Namaz (Narayandas, 1959, 13/42). Even book learning becomes a hindrance in the path of attaining God. He is equally critical of the pandits and Brahmins on one hand and the sheikhs and mullas on the other for they take their stand based on the letter of the scriptures and loose sight of the truth (Narayan das, 1959, 16/27). To him the Hindus and Muslims are like two maddened elephants fighting each other and since he adopted the path of *nipakh,* nirgun every one has become hostile to him. According to him one who abandons the narrowness of faith *(pakh)* and concentrates on the name, would always stand face to face in near proximity to God and a person who having adopted the path of *nipakh*, again identifies with a particular faith, would go to hell. (Narayandas, 1959, 16/48). Dadu uses a lot of Persian, Punjabi, Sindhi and Gujarati words in his writings and his language is of the common people.

Sundar Das

He is said to be a follower of Dadu Dayal. He was born in 1516 in Dhausa near Jaipur. From the age of ten till thirty he studied the holy scriptures by staying in Kasi. He returned to Rajasthan and died in 1689 in Sanganer. He was well versed with Persian and his most famous work is *Sundar Vilas*. He has composed many small poems on nirgun Bhakti, social relationships and need for a moral character of individuals.

Rajjab

Rajjab was a disciple of Dadu Dayal and belongs to the seventeenth century. He was also well versed with Persian and uses it extensively in his writings. We have very little historical information about him.

In the *Prem Margi* stream of Nirgun Bhakti there is more emphasis on love. The important thinkers and poets of this stream were as follows:

Mulla Daud

He lived in Dalmau, on the banks of ganges in Rai Bareilly. He completed his work *Chandayan* 1379 A.D. Firoz Tughluq is the ruler at Delhi during this period. Badauni the court Chronicler of Firoz Tughluq also speaks very highly about Mulla Dauds literary achievements. The story of Chandayan revolves around the romance of Chanda, the daughter of the *mahar* of Govar and Lorik who was an *ahir* or cow herd. It was George Grierson, who was the first scholar to discover the Lorik legend and publish it as The birth of Lorik in 1929.

Chanda was married to another Chieftain when she was four years old but after moving to her husbands place when she was twelve years old she returned back to her parents with in a year. She fell in love with Lorik, who had successfully defended the city against the attack by the neighbouring Raja. Chanda then eloped with Lorik and lived in kalinga for a year. She returned to Govar after a year with Lorik as her husband. The story tells us about the newly emerging groups and their alliances with the traditional ruling groups.

The ahirs were nomads. They moved about from pasture to pasture in their heavy chariots. They had no roof over their heads but temporary shelters, made of straw and thorny bushes and surrounded by trenches to keep away wild beast. Though cattle rearing was their main occupation, stories about them deal mainly about their immorality and their wild ways. There is a continuity in the ahir tradition and all of them refer to their northern origins, the ancient land they call Vraj, meaning a flock. They were the ones who gave northern India its first popular culture and its first literary language, Braj a language in which many of the sants of medieval India composed their songs. Daud's work tells us about the expansion and proliferation of the castes. It talks of artisan groups like Sakligar, Sisgar, Hawaigar, Kagadi, Dhunis, Thathera etc. that were new professional groups but now forming castes and sub castes. More than thirty six caste groups or Jatis are mentioned as invitees to the mass feast on the occasion of the birth of Chanda. These include Thakurs, Rawats, Tiwaris, Joshis, Chauhans, Khandelwal, Agarwal, Banjara and Sonar.

Malik Muhammad Jayasi

He is one of the greatest poets of this stream. He was born in Awadh in a village named Jayas around 1493 A.D. Jayasi was very ugly to look at and he could not see with one eye. Half of his body had suffered a paralytic stroke. According to legend once Jaysai visited the court of Sher Shah and the King began to laugh looking at his face. Then Jayasi is said to have answered, "Is the King laughing at me or at the

Almighty who has made me like this". The King felt ashamed at his behaviour and asked for forgiveness. Jayasi led a married life but after the death of his son became much inclined towards spirituality. Muhammad Jayasi was a disciple of the famous Sufi saint Seikh Moinuddin who traced the lineage of his other disciple to Seikh Nizamuddin Auliya. Jayasi was very familiar with the nath Panthis. In some of his writings there is a mention of Hath Yog, *Ila, Pingla* and *Sushumna Nadi.* (Shukla, 1999, 5). He seems to be well versed with Yoga and was in touch with many yogic seers. This point illustrates the fact that Jayasi, though being a Muslim was well aware of the subtlties and philosophical intracacies of the Yogic practices and their symbolic meanings. This fact mitigates against the common sensical understanding of closed Hindu and Muslim identities in medieval India. The reality was otherwise showing considerable give and take which led to syncretism. He died around 1542 A.D in Amethi in Uttar Pradesh. Though Jayasi wrote about twenty two books his most famous works are *Padmavat, Akhara wat* and *Akhiri Kalam.* He follows the style of the Persian Masnavi in the writing of this work. The story revolves around the love of Allauddin khilji and Rani Padmavati the a queen of Chittor. Padmavati is a unique case of the secession of a muslim mind from its own culture and choosing self expression through non synthesis in rival Hindu cultural heritage (Ahmad, 2002, 241). Jaisi's language is the purest Awadhi dialect of the time, though generally considered to have been written directly in the Persian script. Here we find a very good amalgamation of Sufi heritage and hindu mystical leanings and Jaisi is said to have been influenced by Kabir also.

Qutban

Qutban was a follower of the Chisti silsila of Sufism and the disciple of Seikh Burhan. He was patronized by the King of Jaunpur Hussain Shah. His famous work is *Mrigavati* and it is believed to have been composed before *Padmavati.* Its plot repeats the pattern of the Sita legend, a fair princess in the clutches of the demon and ends with the self immolation of the two queens on the pyre of the dying raja and the ending seems to have influence Jaisi also to end his Padmavati in the same fashion.

Manjhan

Another poet whose work is available is Manjhan. His work *Madhumalti* is said to have been composed between 1550-1590 A.D. The plot here follows the similar pattern of Padmavati and Mrigavati. His work is also written in Awadhi language. Anthers like Jaysai's, Qutban's and Manjhan's works point to interesting facts of a shared composite culture that freely borrows effective literary genres like the enduring legend of Sita. This may be because of the fact that since every literary work pre-supposes an audience—in this case the Awadhi audience was already familiar with the Ramayana as a performative tradition. Hence the easy identification by the audience must have motivated the authors to use these imagery.

The Sagun School

In the Indo Gangetic plains we find in sharp contrast to the almost radical postures of the Nirgun school, a complete reversal in the case of the Sagun school. Chief determining characteristics of the Sagun school were the conception of god in an anthropomorphic form, establishment of temples for the worship of this God and elaborate rituals to be carried out in the daily worship of this personal God. The Sagun School was divided into two branches, the Krishna Bhakti with Krishna as its chief deity and Ram Bhakti with Ram as the chief deity.

Krishna Bhakti

Vallabhacharya

Vallabhacharya whose period was around 1479-1531 A.D. also played an important role in strengthening the philosophical base of Sri Vaisnavism. He was a Telengana

Brahmin whose family had settled in Benaras. He traveled incessantly preaching, debating, the latter was an established form of settling disputes among members of rival religious sects. It was primarily due to the efforts of Vallabaha Charya and Jiv Goswami and their disciples that an active center of Krisnaism arose in Mathura and Vrindavan. It seems to be in these circles that a new theology of Vrindavana evolved, the mysteries of which according to the sacred scriptures took place in the mythical past and came to be regarded as earthly manifestation of the eternal Vrindavna where beyond space and time Krishna enjoys himself in Radha's company (Hardy, 1983, 567). It would be pertinent to come back to Vrindavana once again and connect with the theme of preaching and debating, as the above said activities contributed to the enhancement of personal charisma among the saints. In an earlier chapter, we had seen the saivaite bhakti saints in the Tamil country performing miracles to outwit the Jainas. Similarly in the gangetic valley of the mid 15th century it was not the books that contributed to the creation of a charismatic personality rather personal fctors like austerity, effective preaching and debating would connect to the rural masses directly. Thus, an exercise in reconstructiong bhakti purely from the textual traditions would be incomplete since the 'texts' co-existed with the oral traditions and secondly the prevalence of the texts was largely among the literate class which was a small base. Therefore the orality we are reffering to must have been set in a pre-textual consciousness and this can be located in the effective transmission of the bhakti saints in their earthy rustic dialects, freely borrowing metaphors from the surrounding countryside and the production language.

Vallabhacharya is attributed with writing eighty-four works and as we had argued earlier, both the oral and textual,(which later became a semi-canonical class of literature) continued to co-exist While upholding the Vedic faith, including the ritualistic practices, Vallabhacharya recognized that the times had changed and he advocated a practicable personal religion of the heart compatible with domestic life as well as spiritual detachment. He was a strong proponent of monism rather than dualism and he labelled his version of monism as Suddhadvaita. Vallabha's suddhadvaita was a progressive harmony and interaction between religious thought and practice (Hardy, 1983, 557). To him the whole world in its infinite diversity is nothing except the self expression of Brahma. The soul also has the same nature as Brahma. Vallabhacharya recognized Brahma but his Brahma was much different from the Brahma of Shankracharya. He recognized Brahma as the creator of all the deeds *(Leela)* on this universe. Shankracharya had evolved the concept of Maya to explain the phenomenal world as illusion. Expaining the world on similar monistic lines, Vallabhacharya rejected the category of maya. If all was Brahman he argued, there was no need to explain any part with the aid of extraneous concept. According to Vallabha the Universe is neither an illusion nor a manifestation of Brahma, but it is a natural emanation. God is the whole and an individual a part of this and the relation between the two is that of a spark and fire.Brahma is the Supreme inner ruler of the universe (antaryamin) and the material world is only a manifestation of his existence and knowledge. Brahma as bliss remains obscure in the material world but from his nature as bliss springs forth the anataryamins who are the residing deities of the individual souls and are as numerous as the souls (Gupta, 55, Vol. IV, 331).

He propounds the view that unaided reason cannot guide us into the mysteries of creation. Scriptural revelation is the only source of knowledge about God. To him knowledge and action are distinct powers of the same being. Bhakti as pure love is distinct from bhakti as a mode of worship. His concept of Bhakti is of pure love assimilated to Rasa. This was a great development because earlier bhakti was considered to be a bhav, which could not rise to the status of Rasa. Rasa belongs to a state of imaginary experience and is not at par with the experience of reality. Did this mean that bhakti was an imaginary experience? Vallabhacharya gave a lot of importance to the concept of spiritual love. The love of God was not an imaginative imitation of human erotic love. The real love of God arises from pure grace of god, the love of worldly things disappears and increasingly a kind of intoxication takes hold of the soul. The Gopis are said to illustrate this highest kind of love possible for the human soul. This love or prema arises as sneha or affection and culminates as Rasa in the vision of nitya lila.

Vallabha finds a connection between prema and rasa leading to nitya lila. He states that when the mind and all the senses have taken on the form of Bhagwan, who creates pure bliss then alone one processes Bhakti rasa (Gupta, 1940, Vol. III, 352). According to Vallabah the idea of God as the highest rasa is best explained on the lines of Bhakti, representing the best of the sentiments and the only sentiment. It effects the mind and the body with intense delight whereby feeling of one ness with the lord arises. This one ness is not the real end in view but a means only since it is but a transitory feeling meant to deepen and enhance the permanent one ie. Devotion itself which is the highest attainment and the root of the rest (Mafatia, 1967, 85).

Surdas

We get information about Surdas from the work, *Chaurasi Vaisnavo Ke Varta,* that he inhabited Gau Ghat, the region between Agra and Mathura in the Indo Gangetic plain. According to legend he met Vallabhacharya when the latter visited Gau Ghat and recited one of his compositions. Vallabhacharya was very impressed with him and accepted him as his disciple. Most probably his period is between 1540 to 1620 A.D. His important works are *Sursagar, Saravalli* and *Sahitya Lahiri.* In *Sahitya Lahiri* there is a poem in the end which gives us some information regarding the family of Surdas.

According to this Surdas belonged to the family of the poet Chandbardai who was the court poet of Prathavi Raj Raso. They were six brothers and the youngest of these was Surdas who was blind by birth. His elder five brothers were killed fighting the muslims and he became an orphan after the death of his brothers and wandered here and there. Now he became a devotee of Lord Krishna and composed poems in his praise.

After the death of Vallabhacharya his son Gosain Vitthal das became his successor. He established a group of eight famous poets called the *Ashta Chaap* and these included Surdas, Kumbhan das, Parmanand, Krishnadas, Chitswami, Govind swami, Chaturbhuj Das and Nand Das. It is believed that it was on the orders of Vallabhacharya that Surdas composed and sang poems based on the *Shrimad Bhagvat.* The emotion of love dominates the writing of Surdas. His Krishna is a small child and he has written a large number of poemes describing the mischief of Krishna, the love of the mother Yasoda for him (Pandey, 1993, 171-211)

He talks about life being meaningless unless it has a purpose.

Life has stumbled, unraveled,

Roped to politics and salary and sons.

With out my even noticing, my life has ambled off

And tangled in a snare of illusion so foolproof

That now I cannot break it or loose its grip.

Songs of the Lord, gathering of the good

I left myself hanging in air with out either,

Like an overeager acrobat who does just one more trick

Because he cannot bear to close the show

What splendour, says Sur, can you find in flaunting wealth

When your husband, your lover has gone? (Embree, 1991, 361).

The path of Bhakti is not easy. A devotee has to give up all conventional ways of life for the love of Krishna but Krishna remains elusive.

Gopal has slipped in and stolen my heart, friend.

He stole through my eyes and invaded my breasts

Simply by looking-who knows how he did it?

Even though parents and husbands and all

Crowded the courtyard and filled my world.

The door was protected by all that was proper,

Nor a corner, nothing was left with out a guard.

Decency, prudence, respect for family-

These three were locks and I hid the keys,

The sturdiest doors were my eyelids gates-

To enter through them was a passage impossible-

And secure in my heart, a mountainous treasure,

Insight, intelligence, fortitude, wit.

And then, says Sur, he'd stolen it-

With a thought and a laugh and a look-

And my body was scorched with remorse (Embree, 1991, 364)

Surdas lived and wrote during a period of violence and strife when the Lodi Sultanate was crumbling. In this climate of uncertainity the nobles had become very selfish and had placed their interests above that of the State (Pande, 1990, 177). Hence it was primarily due to their intervention that Ibrahim Lodi lost the throne and the Mughals under Babar were able to enter into India. In such an environment Surdas brought the message of love and devotion.He was responsible for the revival and growth of Krishna in his Sagun form. To him the love of Radha for Krishna is the essence of Veda, the Gita and the Puranas. For a devotee caste does not matter for a bhakta should not bother about caste or family while he is heeding the teachings of the Vedas and the Puranas.It does not matter if he is a king or beggar, if he is high or low for infront of Hari both the high and the low are alike (Surdas, 1969, 290). How ever Surdas could not completely rise above his caste leanings and he is not vehement like the nirgun's in denouncing cast. In fact he almost advocates the caste system for according to him, people from the higher castes are not supposed to partake meals or intermarry with the lower castes. The shudra dining with the brahmana is like a crow living with a hansa (swan) or garlic mixing with camphor or glass mingling with gold. (Surdas, 1969, 3770). According to him the brahmans were to be honoured, fed, and given gifts of cows and villages on various occasions (Surdas, 1969, 440, 649). Surdas talks about the different castes in Mathura and Braj. He refers to Gokul and Nand's place of residence as *pura* (town) and *Shahar* (capital) (Surdas, 1969, 648). This is bigger than the qasba or the village with its grain collecting center (*mandi).* A number of poems of Surdas talk about the ahirs or Pastrolites who are referred to as *gwal* (cowherds) or *gwalin* (milkmaid). Though Krishna is the son of the village chieftain he spend all his time in playing with the other children of the cowherds and there seems to be no major difference in his life and that of the other children. They all graze cattel on the banks of the river Yamuna the whole day and come home in the evening. They are able to distinguish between the various colours and breed of the cows and the patterns of behaviour of the old cows and those that have come to graze for the first time (Surdas, 1963, 1063-66) The process of cows being milked, butter being churned and the preparation of ghee are described in detail. The persons involved in agriculture are referred to as *khetihar* or *haldhar.*He discusses at length the land being leveled, not leaving any depressions (*Khal*) and how the cultivators weed the crops after the first rains. There is also a mention of natural calamities like floods and famines and the oppression by the local officials like *patwaris, amins, mustaufi* and the *mahajan* and *thakur* all who made life very difficult for the farmer. Though Krishna spends all his time with the other cowherds and the society is egalitarian in a broad sense yet the poems of Surdas also tell us that his father Nand had a very luxurious life style and a very high standard of living. Nand is referred to as *Shiqdar, thakur,Sardar, Mahar* and *Chowdhry* indicating his status as the head of the village (Surdas, 1963, 1433-35)

Thousands of milkmaids work in their house churning curds and doing other household chores. The clothes they wear are made with silk and gold thread *(zari)*.They wear costly ornaments of gold, pearls and rubies on their body. Their food is laced with a lot of dry fruits almonds, raisins, sweetmeats and pan. Three meals are mentioned morning breakfast, *Kaleva,* Mid day meals, *jeonar* and an evening meal, *bayari,* where different varieties of food made with wheat, milk products, curds, lentils, *dal,* and sweets are served. During important festivals all the residents of Braj, who are the clansmen of Nand are invited to the feast (Surdas, 1963, 1511). The different and costly clothes worn by all the people especially Gopis show that there was a brisk trade in textiles. The *hat* or *bazaars* were a major source of the markets and it was here that most of the purchases were made. Obviously such a life style was only available to the rich and the nobility and the poor peasant had a difficult life and was oppressed with taxes and had to struggle to make both ends meet.

Nand Das

Nand das is also regarded as a contemporary of Surdas and probably died around, 1625 A.D. We get some information about him from the book, *Do sau Vaisnavo Ke*

Varta. According to this book, Nandas was the brother of Tulsi Das and since Tulsi was a disciple of Ram and Nand Das worshipped Krishna they did not get along However this cannot be proved with certainity (Shukla, 1994, 95). His most famous work is *Ras panch Dhyani*, in which he describes the childhood of Krishna in beautiful verses. A lot of works are attributed to him and these include, *Rukmini Mangal, Siddhanta Panch dhayayi, Rup Manjari, Ras Manjari, Virah manjari, Anekath Manjari, Gyan Manjari, Dan Leela, Man leela.* However only four works of his are available namely, *Ras panchdhyayi, Anekarth Manjari, Brahmar Geet and Anekartha nam mala.*

Ras Khan

Ras Khan was a disciple of Gosai Vithal Das and it was under his influence that he became a devotee of Krishna and composed beautiful songs for his friend Krishna. Two of his books which are available include, *Prem Vatika* and *Sujan RasKhan*. We get some information about him from *Do saw Bawan Vaishnavo ki varta*. Ras Khan is said to have composed *Prem Vatika* around 1614 A.D. We find a mixture of Sufi and Hindi mystical thinking in his writings. His love for Braj is all pervading in his writings.

Rahim

Abdur Rahim Khan-i-Khana was a Mansabdar in the court of Akbar. He was the son of the famous Bairam Khan and a brave warrior in his own right. He became very much involved in Krishna Bhakti. His work includes, *Barawe Nayika Bhed*. He was a friend of Tulsidas and it is believed that *Ramcharitramanas* is also influenced by him. The other works of Rahim include *Rahim Dohavalli, Sringar Soratha, Madnashtak* and *Raspanchadyayi*. Rahim was comfortable in both Awadhi and Vraj and his poems in both the languages are beautiful and a tribute to the composite culture heritage of India.

RAM BHAKTI

Tulsi Das

Tulsidas was born in 1554 A.D in the village of Rajapur in Banda District near Prayag, Allahabad. His father, Atma Ram Dubey was a well known Saryupari Brahmin and his mother's name was Hulsi. When Tulsidas was born he did not cry and there were teeth in his mouth. Considering this a bad omen his mother sent him to her in laws place to be brought up and she died the next day. This child was lovingly brought up by a servant named Chunia but after she died when the child was five and a half years old he became an orphan and would just roam here and there. Shri Narhaya Nandji a saint found him and gave him protection and took him to Ayodhya with him. The young boy soon impressed every one with his sharp intellect. Then for fifteen years Tulsidas remained in Kashi and studied the Vedas. After this he returned to his native place and married a beautiful girl named Ratnavali. Legend has it that he was so engrossed in his wife that he would not leave her alone and once when she went to visit her parents he crossed the river Ganges which was flooded with the help of a dead body and reached her. His wife was very angry with him and she remarked that he was so much in love with her body which is made of mere skin and bones and which will soon be destroyed and had he had this kind of love for Shri Ram his life would be free of worldly things. This struck a cord and Tulsidas immediately returned back and became a sanyasi leaving behind his married life. He came back to Allahabad and then traveled to Chitrakoot and sitting on the banks of Ganges he became enlightened. He started composing the *Ramcharitra Manas* in 1631 A.D. and all the seven sections were over in 1633, A.D. after two years, seven months and twenty six days.Tulsidas died in 1680 after he had composed Vinay Patrika.

The *Ramcharitramanas* is the most influential and famous writing of medieval Bhakti tradition. It expresses par excellence the religious sentiment of bhakti to the Vaisnava avatar, Rama, who is regarded as the chief means of salvation. Although Tulsidas was above all a devotee of Rama, he remained a Smarta Vaisnava (a follower of the more generally accepted traditions and customs of Hinduism rather than a strict sectarian), and his poem gives some expression both to orthodox monistic Advaita doctrine and to the polytheistic mythology of Hinduism though these are everywhere subordinated to his expression of bhakti for Rama. His eclectic approach to doctrinal questions meant that he was able to rally wide support for the worship of Rama in northern India, and the success of the *Ramcaritmanas* has been a prime factor in the replacement of the Krishna cult by the cult of Rama as the dominant religious influence in that area.

Ramcharitramanas, tells the story of Ram, who is an incarnation of Visnu. The exploits of Ram, his wife Sita and their faithful Hanuman form the story of the *Ramcharitramanas*. This work summarizes many of the themes of Indian social and religious thought that good and evil are both powerful but unreal. Maya obscures reality and in the end it is fate which controls the destiny of human beings and that of the God's. Even Ravana the villan of the piece has been shown grace because though he is defeated he has found place in Ram's own realm and thus Ravana wins the "final liberation that contemplatives hardly win" (Embree, 1991, 358).

Though not a religious reformer or founder of any sect or creed, Tulsidas championed the worship of Rama, by citing the works of sages. In one of his *dohas* he says how a person attains happiness through God's grace and loses it without that grace. He was great advocate of devotion (bhakti) and preached monism or *Advita* School proclaiming that Rama's worship alone could lead to eternal bliss. (Salatore, 1989, 1476-77).

In his Vinay Patrika, he talks about life being a river, a trappers snare and escape from all this through Bhakti.

Madhav, you will find none duller than I

The moth and the fish, though lacking in wit

Can scarcely approach my slow standard

Transfixed by the shimmering shapes they meet

They fail to discern the dangers of fire and hook

But, I who see the peril of fiery flesh

And still refuse to leave it, have wisdom even less.

I've drifted along in the grand and entrancing river of ignorance,

A stream that knows no shores

And abandoned the rescue raft of Hari's lotus feet

To grapple and grasp after bubbles and foam

Like a dog so hungry that he lungs for a bone

Grown old and marrowless

The bone scrapes his mouth and draws blood

His own blood, yet he tastes it with delight

I too am trapped in jaws.........

The goddess of learning could count my sins for countless ages

And still not be done

Yet Tulsidas places his trust in one who rescues the destitute

And in trusting hopes to live. (Embree, 1991, 358-359).

Though Tulsidas at times states that an untouchable who recounts the name of Shri Ram is superior to any one else he is not very critical of the existing class and caste divisions. In fact he says that in Kali yuga the Shudra consider themselves as learned as the Brahmin, they enter into discussions with them and adopt an overbearing attitude and participate in *Jap, tap* and *Vrat.* (Manas 2004, 7/99/5). Though Tulsidas is very critical of the Brahmins who had forsaken the study of the Vedas and were very much engrossed in worldly pleasures, and yet he says that it is preferable to worship a brahmin, though he may be lacking in qualities to a Shudra. He is critical of a Shudra wearing the sacred thread and advising the Brahmin (Manas, 2004, 7/99/1). Tulsi attempts to synthesise the prevailing ideas in a framework which would reject the inequalities of the caste system, yet be acceptable to a powerfully entrenched orthodox element in Hindiu society The task was not easy and in attempting it, Tulsi takes up contradictory positions (Shobha, 1977, 169-184).

Bhakti Movement in Punjab

Like the northeast, the north western part of the country also witnessed the influence of Bhakti tradition resulting in the emergence of Sikhism in Punjab due to the spread of the teachings of Guru Nanak. Of all the Bhakti movements which arose in different parts of India this was the only movement which survived as Sikhism. The main principles of Sikhism evolved out of the contemporary heterodox tradition in the background of Hindu cultural context.

Guru Nanak

Guru Nanak was born in a Khatri family in AD 1469 at Talwandi in Lahore district, Nanak laid stress on moral virtues in order to put an end to the religious conflicts. "Religion consisteth not in mere words', said Nanak, "he who broketh on all men as equals is religious. Religion consisteth not in wandering to tombs or places of cremation or setting in attitudes of contemplation. Religion consisteth not in wandering in foreign countries or in bathing at places of pilgrimage. Abide pure amidst the impurities of the world, thus shall thou find the way to religion. Three things you must inculcate in your panth repeating the divine name, giving charity and regular bathing. Keep yourself unspotted while yet remaining a householder (Mcbod, 1976, 30).

Nanak's ideas were reminiscent of the Upanishad principles when he propounded that God is simply one without a second (*Ek Onkara sat nam karta purukh nirbhau nirvair akal Murat ajuni saibhang Guruprasad)* (Pande, 1989, 134). These lines are known as *Mula Mantra* or the basic formula of the Sikhs. In keeping with the true Nirguna bhakti tradition, Guru Nanak describes God as pure light through which every other thing is illuminated and as *sat*. He says that "Eternal truth is His name, Ram, Mohan, Hari, Gobind or Allah are names of the ultimate reality which is *sat* (Pande, 1989, 135). Another important area where Nanak laid special emphasis was on service or *seva*. He says that this leads to purification of body and mind (*Kirat karani wand chakna te nam japna*). A devotee should follow the ethical teachings, Nanak said. "Truth is higher than everything but higher still is the living of truth". Nanak also laid stress on equality and brotherhood. He died in AD 1538.

Guru Nanak, the founder of the religion of Sikhs lent a new dimension to the Bhakti movement. The first and foremost was the territory where the bhakti of Nanak originated. The area of present day Punjab (Northwest region) was characterized with innumerable movements and migrations of the people and this made the matters of religion, beliefs and social behavior less rigid. Brahmanical influence could not make much headway into this land compared to the Gangetic valley or other areas of the country. This can be considered as the reason that the saints (bhakthas) in those areas could not make bhakti a distinct movement, which shortly after succumbed to the brahmanical influence. For example Chaitanya's Vaishnava movement became brahmanical in its nature and tone under the direction of his disciples who shifted the scene of activity to *vrindavan*.

Even the Kabir's movement fell from its ideal. Nanak's bhakti on the other hand was different in which he worked independently for the people. (Gandhi, 1978, 60,). Further the impact of Muslim conquest and the effect of Islam added impetus to the already growing bhakti movement. Its influence was more profoundly felt in Punjab because of its geographical location and comparatively less religious atmosphere. Though the challenge was more serious, the response was soft and solid. Guru Nanak's bhakti was more positive in its outlook, clear in its spiritualism and emphatic in the ethics. (Gandhi, 1978, 62,).

In this environment Nanak also speaks of spiritual deliverance,

This age is a knife, Kings are butchers

Justice hath

In this completely dark night of falsehood

Justice hath taken wings and fled

In this completely dark night of falsehood

The moon of truth is never seen to rise

I have become perplexed in my search

In the darkness I find no way

Devoted to pride I weep in sorrow

How shall deliverance be obtained (Maculiffe, 1909).

Guru Nanak's thought revolves around the understanding of the nature of God at the very beginning of the *Adi Granth*. This is considered as *Mul Mantra*, the basic creedal statement. Of all the Sikh scriptures none is more important than Guru Nanak's. *Jappi*, and this work of surpassing beauty the theme is God, the one whom human beings must praise and who far exceeds the most exalted conception, which the mind of man can form. (McLeod, 1968, 148). For Guru Nanak, the meaning and purpose of human existence centers in the Divine existence of the eternal one, He who creates, sustains and destroys, He who having created reveals himself in His creation, he who by His grace communicates to man the way of salvation and calls forth the response which enables him to appropriate that salvation. He also gives a lot of importance to Guru and to Nanak serving Guru meant serving God. The Adi Granth states that the world is my Guru and the mediating mind the disciple. By dwelling in him I remain detached. The cherisher of the world is my Guru. It also gives importance to Nam Simiran which is not interpreted as just repetition of God but a sadhana, or concentration leading to God realization.

The message of Guru Nanak was a clear response to the large scale socio-economic changes in the form of intensive agrarian expansion which led to the emergence of the Jats. It was the Jat community that formed the base of the Sikh movement and this phenomenon is related to the changing material base of the Jats from that of of a semi-nomadic hunter gatherer economy to that of a peaseantry who colonized the areas of the present day Punjab in large numbers. This colonization and the subsequent material prosperity led to the emergence of a wealthy jat peaseantry who were a force to reckon with but their ritual ranking was not co-equal to their new found status that led to a tension and search for a dignified identity. Therefore it is often suggested that the protest of the jats under the guise of religion was in fact a social protest. We can add that since the Jats constituted the bulk of the Sikh community, their social protest was an effective articulation and creation of an alternative space through the devices of bhakti as these were the only contemporary forms available.

Sikhism

Sikhism, which is the youngest religion, underwent evolutionary process for more than two centuries after Guru

Nanak, its founder. Sikhism acquired a definitive martial identity under Guru Govind Singh the 10th Guru. While tracing the evolution of Sikh religion, some scholars have gone beyond the time and teachings of Guru Nanak Dev. In this sense, the origin of Sikhism goes back to the *sant* tradition of North India and further traces back to antiquity. W.H McLeod has expressed one such view in his book *"The Evolution of Sikh Community"*. He says "To Sikhs of all subsequent generations Guru Nanak is the founder of Sikh religion." In another term the term founder could be mislead, for it suggested that Guru Nanak originated not merely a group of followers but also a school of thought or set of teachings. If we make a comparison of His teachings with those of other contemporary or earlier religious personalities, it could be visualized that he stands with in a well-defined tradition of bhakti.

The Sacred Formula or the *mul mantra*, which occurs hundred times in the Guru Grant Sahib, occupies a very significant and high place for the Sikhs. The very first word of this formula i.e. *Ik Omkara* is significant. It conveys the Unity of Brahman and also its two aspects i.e. the unmanifested (*Nirguna)* and the manifested (*Saguna).*

Ik Omkara (The One *Omkara*, the manifested as well as unmanifested Brahman) *Satnam* (His name is Truth) *Karta Purakh* (A *purusha*, who is the Creator) *Nirbhau* (without fear) *Nirvair* (without enmity) *Akal Murat* (A being whom death cannot assail) *Ajuni* (unborn) *Saibham* (self–existence) *Gurprasad* (with the grace of Guru, the preceptor). (Kohli, 1990, 31). The above formula presents the nature of Ultimate reality.

The *Adi Granth*, the scripture of the Sikhs is considered as sacred book of Asia. It holds a unique position among the scriptures of the world. It was given the status of the Guru by the tenth and the last Sikh guru, Guru Gobind Singh in AD 1708 thereby ending the line of personal guru ship. The *Adi Granth* thus became *Guru Grant Sahib* and it contains the *bani* of the Sikh Gurus and the radical saints of the

Bhakti Movement. Besides the hymns of the first, second, third, fourth, fifth and ninth Sikh Gurus, it consists of the verses of some prominent Indian saints including those of Jaidev of Bengal (12th century AD), Shaikh Baba Farid of West Punjab (12th-13th centuries), Namdev and Trilochan of Maharashtra (14th century) and Kabir and Raidas of Uttar Padesh (15th century). These compositions manifest synthesis of Indian thought, an exposition of the ideal life of an individual and society and unity of Indian culture. Also the path of life enunciated by the Sikh Gurus and the saints of *Adi Granth* is the product of a definite period of Indian history, its tenets and beliefs is universal.

Sikhism rejects asceticism and lays stress on the life of a householder. It is the religion of activity, not only in the world, in which we are born, but also in the inner spiritual world. God does not live away from humanity and from the world of *jives.* The Lord resides in the heart of every being and he who runs away from humanity causes the displeasure of the Lord, who lives in humanity. The Sikh dictum "*Kirt karo Wand chhakoate ate Nam Jappo*" (Work for a living, share your earnings with the needy and remember the name of the Lord.) gives us the insight into the life of a Sikh. Of the four stages of life viz. *Brahmacharya, Grahastaya, Vanaprastha and Sanyasa*, the Guru rejected the first and the last two giving preference only to the householder life. For him, only those people tread on the path of God, who work hard for sustaining themselves and their families and even perform certain duties for the welfare of the needy.

Sikhism rejects all formalism and ritualism and lays emphasis on the adoption of ethical qualities. Of the three parts of Vedas i.e. *karma kanda, Upasana kanda* and *Gyan kanda*, Sikhism accepts only the last one. There is no priestly class in Sikhism. The devote and learned Sikhs perform services at temples (*Gurudwaras).* Sikhism insists on poise and balance of life, equal stress on the physical and spiritual well being of individual and society and a balanced combination of devotion, action and knowledge.

Sikhism preaches Fatherhood of God and brotherhood of man. It rejects all prejudices of caste, colour and birth and lays emphasis on equal status of man and woman in the society. It speaks against all types of exploitation. Gurus and saints condemned the hierarchy in society based on *chaturvarna*. The intensity of revolt can be seen in the words of Guru Nanak. He said, "How are you a Brahmin? And how am I a Sudra? How I am the blood and how are you the milk?" "No one asks for the caste and birth in the home of the True Lord".... The caste and honour are determined by the deeds. The tenth Master Guru Gobind Sigh said, "they have the same eyes, the same ears, the same bodies and the same habits and are composed of the same elements." then how they are different from each other? They are the sons of the same father and the caste, birth or colour cannot make one inferior or superior.

Sikhism advocated significant importance to women and imparted all the rights in the society to them. Stress was given on education and the evil of sati was very much-condemned. Amardas spoke severely on sati. The woman has same soul as the man and she has an equal right to attend religious congregations and recite divine hymns at the temples. Monogamy was preferred and the golden principle of 'One man and one wife was propagated.

Sikhism advocates the excellence of utility of human life, the necessity of education, true preceptor and truthful living, the building of character, the inculcation of love, truth, contentment humility and the achievement of the spiritual greatness by following the path preached by the preceptor. The seeker had to concentrate on the Name of the Lord or the word given by the Guru. The union with the Lord through his name is the *Srut Shabad Yoga*.

A significant feature of Sikhism is its view regarding the extent of cosmos. Guru Nanak did not accept the idea of the delimitation of the universe expressed by the contemporary religions. He argued with the theologians of his day that the "Creation of the infinite Lord cannot be finite." He said, "There are lakhs of nether-worlds and lakhs of skies. Even the Vedas declare unanimously that the ends of creation cannot be determined. The eighteen thousand *slokas* of *Bhagvat Purana* and the Muslim scriptures say that there is only 'One reality'. He is unaccountable. Those who make an account of His creation destroy themselves. The Lord is great and He alone knows His Greatness." Modern scientists like Hoyle and Gold believe that universe is expanding and Nanak held the same view five centuries earlier. In its finalform, Sikhism contains elements taken from Islam (equality in the faith, opposition to iconolatry, extreme reverence for the sacred book) and probably also from Christianity (the Sikh baptism and communion meal), but its theology is still essentially Hindu.

In the subsequent period after Nanak, the main consequence of Sikh belief has been a gradual breaking away from the Hindu social system and the development of Sikh separatism. The singular worship of the Adi Granth excludes worship of all other objects common among Hindus (i.e., the Sun, rivers, trees, etc.) and also puts a stop to the practice of ritual purifications and pilgrimages to the Ganges. Since every Sikh is entitled to read the scripture, Sikhs do not have a priestly caste similar to the Brahmans in Hinduism. Sikh insistence on commensality (eating together) at the *Guru ka langar* (kitchen of the Guru) destroyed the traditional Hindu pattern of caste among them and substituted a far less rigid social structure. Sikhs are grouped into three broad categories based largely on ethnic differences: Jats (agricultural tribes), non-Jats (erstwhile Brahmans, Kshatriyas, and Vaisyas (the three highest groups of the traditional Hindu social system), and

Mazahabis (untouchables). The Jats, though low in the caste hierarchy, are preeminent; the Mazahabis, though converts from Hindu outcastes (untouchables outside the caste system) and still discriminated against, have a much higher status than untouchables in Hindu society.

Bhakti Movement in Kashmir

It was in 1342 that Kashmir came under the Muslim rule and remained thus till 1827. The first two ruling houses, the Shahmiris and the Baihaquis both were originally non Kashmiris. The Chaks who followed the Baihiquis were originally highlanders from Drav or North Kashmir.The last Muslim rulers were Afghans (Pandita, 2004, 137-138). It was in this process of Islamization that the Bhakti movement entered Kashmir.In Kashmir it was Saiva Bhakti which flourished from the ancient period and some of the saints associated with Shaiva philosophy were Vasugupta, Somanand, Bhatta Kallata, Utpal Dev and Abhinavgupta. Saivism in Kashmir also flowed into two streams, the Spanda and the Pratyabhijna. Spanda stream advocated both Gyan and Bhakti as a means of salvation. The Spanda school advocated Non-Dualism but this philosophy differed from Shankara that it did not subscribe to the Universe as being maya, stating that the universe is but the manifestation of Brahma and as Brahma is real his manifestation also has to be real. Vedic dharma was also followed and medieval Kashmir saw an increase in rituals in the temples which became more ostentatious and profound.

It was in this environment that Lal Ded the Saivite saint preached in Kashmir. Lal Ded lived during the fourteenth centuries during the reign of Alluddin. Like many other saints elsewhere her life is also shrouded in myth, miracle and legend. She was born in a Brahmin family at Pandrenthan near Srinagar and was educated at home in her fathers house. She was married at the age of twelve into another Brahmin family surnamed Nica Bhatt at Pimpore. According to the Kashmiri custom she was renamed Padmavati. We have a number of legends which talk about the cruelty meted out to Lal Ded. She endured this torture for twelve years and finally left home. Her Bhakti provided her a space to renounce her domestic hell. Padmavati is supposed to have danced naked singing in frenzy. She now came to be known as Lal Ded, Lal in Kashmiri referring to the lower part of her belly, which increased in size and hung loose over her pubic region. She expressed her thoughts through four liners known as *Vakh*, from the Sanskrit *Vakya* meaning a sentence.Her *Vakh* are remarkable for clarity and co herence and depth of thought. She was highly respected by both hindus and muslims. She died at an advance age at Bijbehara, another village south of Srinangar. The social environment in Kashmir was very much influenced by the Islamic influences much before the establishment of the Sultanate in 1320 A.D. (Khan, 1986, 189).

There are a number of stories and legends related to Lal ded. It is stated that she visited the household of Nunda Rishi, her junior contemporary when he was born. Nun Rishi's mother complained that the child was not taking milk from her breast. Lal Ded then held the baby in her arms and told him that he was not shy of coming to this world and then why is he shy of sucking his mothers breast. The baby started sucking the milk. Lal ded had to suffer a lot in the hands of her mother in law and she was always served food filled with stones, and her writings speak of this cruelty.

Like the Bhakti saints in other region, Lalded also is critical of rituals,idol worship, false show of religiosity and animal sacrifice. Animal sacrifice had become very rampant under the influence of some Tantrik practice. She opposeses this stating, "who has given this preposterous advice to you Pandit,. To sacrifice a living sheep for a lifeless stone idol? (Kundan, 2004, 197)

It covers your shame

Saves you from cold.

Its food and drink-

Mere water and grass

Who counseled you, O Brahmin,

To slaughter a living sheep

As sacrifice

Unto a lifeless stone? (Kaul, 1973, 110)

She has a large number of *Vakhs* which speak of tolerance. She swept aside all the illtreatment meted out to her and people speaking ill of her behind her back by stating that it is human nature to speak ill of others behind ones back just as it is the nature of water to flow and the nature of sun to give heat and the nature of moon to wax and wane (Kundan, 2004, 194). She also says in another Vakh that people have been speaking ill of her in her presence and behind her back but she has tolerated all abuse sportingly.

They may abuse me or jeer at me

They may say what pleases them

They may with flowers worship me

What profits them what ever they do?

I am indifferent to praise or blame. (Kaul, 1973, 102)

She further states, I have no rancour for a person who speaks ill of me or makes fun of me. If lord Shiva bestows grace on me how can these adverse remarks of people affect me.

Let them mock at me and call me names

If a true devotee of Siva I be

I shall not feel distressed nor hurt

Can a few ashes a mirror be foul (Kaul, 1973, 102)

In another *Vakh* she states, If you wash off all your dirt with the purifying water of tolerance, you will shine like a mirror and become spotless like snow. You will control all your birth and death as also all your sense organs once you revel in conversation with Siva (Kundan, 2004, 195). She goes searching for her god and finds him with in.

For love that would not let me be

I Lalla, set forth in search of him

And toiled and toiled for days and night

Then lo! the most auspicious moment of life

I saw the Pandit in my own home (Kaul, 1973, 120)

Once she finds her God there is light all around.

Gently, gently, I trained my mind

To suspendits processes and thoughts

Then (in the windless calm), the flame of the lamp

Shining steady and bright

Revealed my true nature un to me

In the dark recess of my soul

I seized upon him and held him fast

Then I diffused the inner light

(and with in and with out, all was light) (Kaul, 1973, 120)

Lal Ded also is very critical of idol worship and rituals as were evolved by the Brahmins and most probably she was influenced by Islam.She says, that idol is a stone and the temple is a stone structure. It is the same above and below, which one shall you worship?

The idol is but stone

The temple is but stone

From top to bottom all is stone

Whom will you worship, O stubborn Pandit?

Let prana and the mind unite. (Kaul, 1973, 110)

To her there was no difference between the stone found on the road and the one used in the shrine as well as the one used in the grinding mill.She is also critical of the Brahmin and says that, "you have put on a mask of goodness but in reality you are like a stone with no impression. You have studied a lot but your inner malice is still there". She is also critical of fasting for she says, "Useless is your fasting and all your studies that you are torturing your self. Do not keep your self thirsty or hungry. Maintain yourself by eating and drinking properly. She says,

Let not your body suffer

From hunger and thirst

Feed it when ever it feels famished

Fie on your fasts and religious rites

Do good, there in your duty lies (Kaul, 1973, 100-101)

Lal Ded advocates moderation in food and drink.

By pandering your appetites

You get nowhere

By penance amend fasting

You get conceit

Be moderate in food and drink

And live a moderate life

The gates of heaven will surely be

Thrown open wide for you. (Kaul, 1973, 99).

God is omnipresent, 'You are the sky, the earth, the air, the day and the night. You are the offering, the sandlewood, the flowers and the water. You are everything, what is there to offer you?" God is to be found with in and not outside, "Do trust my straight forward word and go inwards. Why are you groping in the dark like a blind man? Siva is inside you and you need not look for him elsewhere (Kundan, 2004, 200).

Who is the florist, who is the flower girl?

With what flowers should he be worshiped?

In what water should he be bathed?

With what mantra should we awaken Shankara,

Who abides in the self (Kaul, 1973, 111)

She is critical of fasting as a means to obtain God.

O fool, right action does not lie

In observing fasts and ceremonial rites.

O fool right action does not lie

In providing for bodily comforts and ease

In contemplation of self alone

Is right action and right counsel for you (Kaul, 1973, 107-8)

She gives her own example by stating,

In life I sought neither wealth nor power

Nor ran after the pleasures of sense

Moderate in food and drink, I lived a controlled life

Patiently bore my lot, my pain and poverty

And loved my God (Kaul, 1973, 98)

She does not just preach but practices what she preaches.

I practiced what I read,

And learnt what was not taught.

From its jungle abode

I brought the lion down

As I a jackal would

(From pleasures of the world

I pulled my mind away)

I practiced what I preached,

And scored the goal (Kaul, 1973, 104).

It is very interesting to note that Lal Ded's name is not mentioned either by the Sanskrit chronicles or the commentaries on Shaivism of the fifteenth to eighteenth centuries. Birbal Kachru was the first Brahman scholar to mention her in the nineteenth century (Khan, 2004, 132). Most of Lal ded's *vakhs* have come down as an oral tradition and were written much later. With regard to the reception of Lal Ded and Nunda Rishi by both the Hindus and the Muslims, the earlier writers have assumed that it was their message of bhakti that were drawn from both Hinduism and Islam and therefore the mass popularity of the two saints. While the above reading may not be wrong in substance, it only obscures some facts that emerge when we view the same from a different angle. Islam has often been understood from the perspective of oil rich Arab countries and viewed through Arab lenses which is a textual reading wheras we find that wherever Islam went it had to negotiate with the local cultures and this produced a rich tapestry of cultural plurality that borrowed from the pre-existing local cultures which was the canvas through which the people operated. In other words, traditions cannot be wiped out overnight and they only become reformulated and hence survive. Thus, the popularity of Lal Ded and Nunda Rishi can be explained as an active relationship between their audience and the message which was not wholly religious but also cultural and in this culture, the Muslims too shared the same concerns and hence were attracted.

Nunda Rishi

Another important saint of Kashmir and a very young contemporary of Lalded was Nunda Rishi. He is remembered by the Hindus as Sahazananda and by the muslims as Sheikh-ul-aalam. He was married and had two children. He practiced penance in a cave very vigorously seeking for truth. He travelled from place to place preaching about love and devotion to God. He is said to have composed *Shrukhs* (from the Sanskrit Sholaka), which are again verses of four lines.

Roop Bhawani

Her period in around seventeenth century having been born in the house of the Brahmin Madhav Joo Dhar in 1621 A.D. She also traveled from place to place and made Manigam and Vaskur her place of worship. There are lots of legends attributed to her. Once her mother in law distributed the pudding sent by her father freely out of vengeance but still this never got exhausted. She has left behind a fund of profound knowledge known as *Rasasyopadesha.*

Bhakti Movement in Rajasthan

Mira Bai

Of all the bhakti poets of the Middle Ages, Mira shines out in pure splendour.The period of Mira was a period of upsurge of Krishna cult in Rajasthan (Ganguly, 1983, 226-27). The dates of Mira's life are uncertain and much disputed According to one account she was born in AD 1498 and died in AD 1546, and hence lived during the end of fifteenth and beginning of sixteenth century. She belonged to the Rajput aristocracy of Rajasthan. She was the daughter of Ratan Singh and his wife, Vir Kunwari of Medtiya of Rathor clan. Mira's paternal grandfather Jodhaji was the founder of Jodhapur. Her paternal grandfather, Dudaji had conquered Medata city and 360 villages around it. He gave Mira's father Ratansing twelve villages of which the central village was Kudki. Mira was born in this fort. Her paternal family were Vaishnavas and hence Mira inherited Vaisnava Bhakti as part of her family legacy.

Mira was an ardent devotee of Lord Krishna (Giridhar Gopal) and sang in praise of her lord in Vraj bhasa. She is said to have written about four hundred *padas* or song verses. Her poems are found in three languages—Hindi, Gujarati and Rajasthani (Jain, 2003, 237-38). The subject of bhakti is intensely personal 'I' in the form of Mira and her personality is vividly felt in all her verses. The ideal of the true devotee mentioned in Gita who, by dedicating all the actions to God transcends the realm of Karma can be seen in Mira (Pande, 1989, 141). Mira does not appear to have been a patronized by a court related biographer and neither Rajput chronicles, nor religious hagiography is available for her. Mira's history has been reconstructed much later.

Tradition has it that as a young girl Mira pestered her mother to tell her who was her bridegroom when she saw a marriage procession. To avoid her persistent questioning Miras mother pointed at a statue of Krishna and told her this was her bridegroom. Mira hence considered herself wedded to Krishna. When she grew up she was married into the royal family of Sisodia Rajputs of Mewar. The identity of her husband is not well established. Some identify him to be Maharaj Kumbh and others with Bhojraj the son of the famous Rana Sanga. Most probably the marriage was a part of the political alliance between Rators of Jodhpur with the Ranas of Mewar. Legend has it that when Mira arrived in her inlaws house she was asked to worship godess Shakti for the well being of her husband and his family an she refused. Naturally her husband and inlaws were very angry.

Mira even refused to consummate her marriage regarding her self already wedded to Krishna. This was an open defiance and her inlaws could not tolerate this. There were various attempts at her life. Some of her songs talk about this.

I am colored in the color of dusk, O Rana

Colored with the color of my lord

Drumming out the rhythym on the drums, I danced,

Dancing in the presence of the saints

Colored with the color of my Lord

They thought me mad for the wily one,

Raw for my dear dark one

Colored with the color of my Lord.

The Rana sent me a poison cup of poison

I did not look I drank it up

Colored with the color of my Lord

The clever mountain lifter is the Lord of Mira

Life after life he is true-

Colored with the color of my Lord (Embree, 1991, 365-366).

Mira finally left the palace and went and stayed in the temple of Krishna but here too she did not find solace because her inlaws family disapproved of her Bhakti. She then started wandering around in the company of other saints and visited many temples and places associated with Krishna. She went to Dakur, then Vrindawan and finally Dwakra. According to legend Akbar and Tansesn travelled to Dwarka to visit her and Tansen sang one of her Bhajans.

Some of her songs talk about her intense love for Krishna.

Murali sound on the banks of Jamuna

Murali snatches away my mind

My senses cut away from the moorings

Dark waters, dark garments, Dark Lord.

I listen close to the sounds of Murali

And my body withers away-

Lost thought, lost even the power to think.

Mira's Lord, clever mountain lifter

Come quick snatch away my pain (Embree, 1991, 367)

To Mira there is no heaven that one has to go after death but her portrayal of another life pictures a realm which is filled with the love of Krishna and all his devotees sing and dance here.

Let us go to a realm beyond going

Where death is afraid to go,

Where the high flying birds alight and play,

Afloat in the full lake of love

There they gather-the good, the true

To strengthen an inner regimen,

To focus on the dark form of the Lord

And refine their mind like fire.

Garbed in goodness-their ankle bells

They dance the dance of content

And deck themselves with the sixteen signs

Of beauty, and a golden crown-

There where the love of the dark one comes first

And every thing else is last (Embree, 1991, 369).

Due to her involment in Bhakti now riches and expensive clothes have no meaning for Mira.

Rich clothes, silk and Gold

Have no use for me now

For Mira now, the saffron coloured clothes

And in these I shall move about openly (Pal, 1974, 65)

According to legends, when Mira was staying at the Ranchhorji temple on the sea coast of Dwarka, her natal and marital families sent a group of priests as emmisarries to persuade her to return. When she refused the Brahmin priests started a fast unto death outside the temple. Mira was now in a delimma and did not want to have Brahmin blood on her hand. She then composed *Hari tum haro jan ke pir* and entered the temple and is said to have absorbed in the statue of Krishna.This is interpreted by many scholars as emerging from the western door of the temple which faces the sea and having lept into it (Kishwar, Manushi, 1989, 85).

Bhakti gave Mira entry into religious field as a passive follower but this movement gave the more capable woman leadership of other women and sometimes of the entire sect (Mulati, 1989, 8-10). Bhakti had five important features and these were in tune with Mira's Bhakti. This was the only sufficient and powerful marga or method of religious life. It was the development of purity in menatal and physical action in every field. Use of religious philosophy in Sanskrit was not a pre requisite for Bhakti. The deputations of Brahmins as mediators between the devotee and God was totally unnecessary and caste and brahmanically prescribed "sin-cleanship", was found unnecessary for Bhakti (Mulati, 1989, 9). Hence this ideology suited Mira.

By fifteenth century the Rajputs had occupied the whole of Rajasthan. The change from varna to jati went hand in hand with colonization of new areas with in which the process of the expansion of agrarian economy occured. It was then that the term Rajput began to be employed (Chattopadhyay, 1976, 62). Even muslims were included in the term Rajputs, as they were deemed to be part of this jati. The jati was Rajput and under this were included muslims and Hindus (Ziegler, 1976, 59). Merta where Mira spent her childhood was a flourishing trade center from 16th to 19th centuries. As it was on the main route connecting Gujarat to Agra it was also a flourishing financial center. It had weekly markets for indigo, cotton wool, yarn and cotton cloth and it was an important center for textile and leather goods (Bhidwani, 1975, 224). Merta ceased to exist as an independent state when it was incorporated in to the state of Mewar in 1556 A.D. The Rajput system of political power and sovereignity was linked to the structure of *kul* and *bhaiyad* which was interwoven with land ownership.Where as the *kul* consisted of all those related to a common ancestor by ties of male blood, *bhaiyad* was the brotherhood composed of sons and the brothers of the ruler who held power over land conquered by them. Highly complex notions of fidelity to this brotherhood were evolved. (Mukta, 1997, 59). Marriage became a very important instrument in forging new alliances. A woman was always married into a family of superior status than the one they were born into. Hence when Mira is married into the Sisodiyya family it is a marriage in to a superior family. In such a society there were two alternatives to the man woman relationship. One was the emergence of a romantic love, which formed the theme of legends and epics such as *Dhola Maru ra Duha,* which expressed the yearning of the two people but who were thwarted in realizing it. The other alternative was the world of Bhakti. This had an intense emotional thrust. This would have been attractive to a woman of sensitivity who sought to escape the hatred and domination which underlay the Rajput system of marriage. Mira's Bhakti must be seen essentially as an enunciating principal of love in an age and society marked by war, vendetta and the rising power of the state (Mukta, 1997, 64-65).

Mira is very much aware of the fact that her Bhakti would bring in a reaction from the society at large and the aristocracy.

If Sisodiya is angry, what will he do to me?

I will sing the virtues of Govind, friend.

If Rana is angry, he will stay in his own country

If Hari is angry, I will wither, friend

I don't care for worldly position,

Fearless, I will beat the drum, friend

I will sound Shyam's name on the castanets

I will cross the ocean of life, friend

Strong Giridhar is Mira's refuge,

I will cling to his lotus feet, friend (Manushi, 1989, 79).

Her path to Bhakti is strewn with a lot of pain.

I am mad in love

And no one understands my plight

Only the wounded

Understand the agonies of the wounded

When a fire rages in the heart

Only the jeweler knows the value of the jewel

Nor the one who lets it go

In pain I wander from door to door

But could not find a doctor

Says Mira, Harken my master

Mira's pain will subside

When Shyam comes as a doctor. (Alston, 1980, 63)

She publicly dances in the temple and faces many difficulties

Sister I will sing the glories of Govind

I will rise regularly at dawn

And go to the temple to have a sight

And drink the water that washes his feet

I will dance in the temple of Hari

Making my anklets jingle

I will sail the boat of the name of Shyam

And cross the ocean of becoming

This world is a thorny briar bush

And the road to the beloved is blocked

Mira's lord is the courtly Giridhar.

She will reach him through singing his glories (Alston, 1980, 46-47).

Mira is conscious of the fact that she is married to Krishna in all previous lives and she begs him to come and unite with her in this life.

I have talked to you, talked

Dark lifter of mountains

About this old love

From birth, after birth

Don't go, don't

Lifter of mountains

Let me offer a sacrifice-myself

Beloved

To your beautiful face

Come here in the courtyard

Dark Lord

The women are singing auspicious wedding songs

My eyes have fashioned

An alter of pearl tears

And here is my sacrifice

The body and mind

Of Mira

The servant who clings to your feet

Through life after life

A virginal harvest for you to reap (Embree, 1991, 366).

Mira continues to reign popular imagination even today through legends and supportive reinterpretation of her songs.She is seen as a saint, a mystic, a devotee of Krishna and one who had the courage to live life according to her own terms. Her Bhakti provides her this alternative space. Mira also became a favourite of Mahatma Gandhi and he refers to her in many of his writings and speeches. To Gandhi Mira was a symbol of non-violence resistance to injustice and a formost follower of non-co-operation. Her leaving a royal life and becoming a bhakta to Gandhi meant her liberation, and he wanted the fearless Mira to be the role model for the young girls.

Sahajo Bai

Sahajo Bai was a disciple of Sant Charan Das. She was born in a Vaishya family in Dehra village in Rajasthan and moved to Delhi later on. It is generally agreed that she was born in 1683 and died in 1765. Her father Hari Prasad was a trader. Sahajo Bai did not marry. In many of her verses she describes the hard work that she does grinding corn,carrying water, sweeping, digging. She says that one can walk on the guru's path only if she is a brave warrior and frees one self of the fear of death. Sahjo's verse are collected in *Sahaj Prakash*, the major text of the Chandradasi sect. She extols meekness and humility as true strength and greatness. Both nirgun Bhakti and prem Bhakti occupy an important place in her teachings. She is for meditation.

Bliss comes not from book knowledge

Bliss comes not from debate

Blissful the wise, Sahajo says

Who in solitude meditate. (Manushi, 1989, 102).

The Guru has a very important place in her Bhakti. In fact she places the Guru above God and one can find a similarity here with Kabir.

I can give up God

But not my guru.

I cannot see god

As equal to my guru

God gave me five thieves

For company

I was helpless, the guru rescued me,

God ensnared me in the soul's form

God hid from my sight

The guru showed me the soul's form

God hid from my sight

The guru lit a lamp to give me vision

All I am I would give for Charan Das

I can give up God

But not my Guru. (Manushi, 1989, 102)

Her joy knows no bound when she discovers Bhakti

Joy prevails in my mind

Each part of my body is drunk

Neither is Sahajo with any one

Nor is any one with her. (Manushi, 1989, 102)

Hence to conclude, when bhakti entered north India, it was already centuries old and did not have to spend all the energies in evolving but could replicate many of the features that were already a part of the southern bhakti.The similarity cannot be extended further as earlier authors did and we see that north India of the medieval period was fundamentally different from south India in at least two respects viz, the Turkish rule and also the clear demarcation of the *varnas*, wheras in south India the varna was just a theoretical concept while the jati reflected the local realities. Further, in north India one can see this movement in two streams, the nirgun, monotheistic movement and the sagun, Vaisnava movement.

In the Indo Gangetic plain one could see the coexistence of both both Nirgun and Sagun forms ostensibly on the basis of a theological difference in the way of conceptualizing the nature of the divine being that is the object of worship. The nirgun Bhakti also develops along two streams of *Gyan* marg and *Prem* Marg and the sagun stream develops into Krishna Bhakti as well as Ram Bhakti. In north India one can find the impact of Yoga and Sufi thinking also on the Bhaktas. Sagun Bhakti worshiped the different manifestations of Vishnu, Siva. The nirgun worshipped the unmanifested God with out any attributes.Though the social base of the two bhaktis can be clearly distinguished there were many overlaps also. Sagun Bhakti represents a liberal reform of the early Vedic and Sastric Hinduism, which had become the exclusive privilege of the Brahmin to practice and had left out a large mass of people from practising it. With out challenging the Brahmins control over the Vedas the sagun Bhakti did make an attempt to open the doors of salvation to the non privileged classes but this was very limited. This was carried forward by the nirgun sants. The nirgun sants accepted the idea of the cycle of birth but they treated all human births as rare and equally valuable. To the Sagun bhaktas if one behave properly in this life they could expect a better birth in next life or birth into a higher caste. Sagun Bhakti was more agrarian based and nirgun Bhakti was confined and practiced by the urban classess who practiced a profession for their living.

References

Alston, A.J., 1980, The devotional poems of Mirabai, Motilal Banarsidas, Delhi.

Ahmad, Aziz, 1964, reprint, 2002, *Studies in Islamic culture in Indian Environment*, Oxford University Press, U.K.

Badathval, Pitambar Dutt, 1950, (Hindi), *Ramananda ki Hindi Racnayen*, Nagari prachar Sabha, Kasi.

Bhidwani, Bhanwar, 1975, "Economic conditions in Pargana Merta (Rajasthan) (A.D. 1658-63) in *Proceedings of Indian History Congress*, Aligarh.

Chattopadhyay, B.D. 1976, "Origin of the Rajput: The political, economic and social processes in early Medieval Rajasthan", in *Indian Historical Review*, Vol. III, No. 1, July.

Das, Shyam Sundar (ed), 1959, *Kabir Granthavali*, (Hindi) Nagari Pracharini Sabha, Kasi.

Embree, Ainslie, T. 1958, reprint, 1991, *Sources of Indian Tradition*, Vol. 1, From the Beginning to 1800, 2nd Edition, Viking, Penguin Books, USA.

Ganguly, K.K. 1983, *Cultural History of Rajasthan*, Sundeep Prakashan, New Delhi.

Gandhi, Surjit Singh, 1978, *History of the Sikh Gurus-A Comparative Study*, Gurdas Kapur & Sons, Delhi.

Gupta, S. N. Das, 1940, *A history of Indian Philosophy*, Vol. III, Cambridge Univeristy Press.

Gupta, S.N. Das, 1955, *A history of Indian Philosophy*, Vol. IV. Vols, Cambridge University Press.

Hardy, Friedhelm, 1983, *Viraha Bhakti*-an early history of Krsna devotion in South India, Oxford University Press, New York.

Hedayetullah, Muhammad, 1977, *Kabir: apostle of Hindu Muslim Unity*, Motilal Banarasi Das, Delhi.

Jain, Simmy, 2003, *Encyclopaedia of Women through the Ages*, (Vol. 2), Kalpaz Publications, Delhi.

Kundan, Dhar, T.N. 2004, "Saints and sages of Kashmir', in M.N. Kaw (ed), *Kashmir and its people*, A.P.H. Publishing Corporation, New Delhi.

Kaul, Jayalal, 1973, *Lal Ded*, Sahitya Academy, New Delhi.

Kohli, S.S. 1990, *Sikhism and Guru Granth Sahib*, National Book Shop, Delhi.

Keay, F.E, 1931, *Kabir and his followers*, Associated Press, Calcutta.

Mafatia, Mrudula, I, 1967, *The philosophy of Vallabhacarya*, Munshiram Manohar Lal, New Delhi.

Manas, Ramcharita, 2004, Geeta Press, Gorakhpur.

Mukta, Parita, 1997, *Upholding the Common Life*, Oxford University Press.

Mc Leod, W.H, 1968, *Nanak and the Sikh Religion*, Oxford University Press. Delhi.

Mc Leod, W.H, 1976, *The Evolution of the Sikh Community*, Clarendon Press, Oxford.

Macauliffe, Max. Arthur, 1909, *The Sikh Religion*, Oxford University Press.

Maculiffe, Max. Arthur, 1989, *The Sikhs-Their Religion, Gurus, Sacred Writings and Authors*, Cosmo Publication, New Delhi.

Mulati, Leela, 1989, *The Bhakti movement and the status of woman-The case of Virsaivism*, Abhinav Publications, New Delhi.

Narayan Das, Swami (ed) 1959, *Shri Dadu Vani*, Varanasi.

Pandey, Susmita, 1989, *Medieval Bhakti Movement*, Kusumanjali Prakashan, Meerut.

Pandey, Manage, 1993, (Hindi), *Bhakti Andolan aur Surdas Ka kavya*, Vani Psrakashan, New Delhi.

Pandey, Rekha, 1990, *Succession in the Delhi Sultanate*, Common Wealth Publication, New Delhi.

Pal, H.B. Capt. 1974, *Historic Rajasthan*, Sagar Publications, New Delhi.

Pandita, K.N. 2004, "Some fallacies of Medieval Kashmir History", in, M.N. Kaw (ed), *Kashmir and its people*, A.P.H. Publishing Corporation, New Delhi.

Rangarajan, Haripriya, 1996, *Ramanuja Sampradaya in Gujarat-a historical perspective*, Somiya Publications, Bombay.

Shastri, Hans Das and Prasad, Mahabir, 1950, *Kabir Saheb Ke Bijak*, Kabir Granth Prakashan Samiti, Harak, Barabanki District, Uttar Pradesh.

Shobha, Savitri Chandra, 1976, "Two aspects of Hindu social life and thought as reflected in the works of Tulsidas", *Journal of the Economic and Social History of the Orient*, xix, pt. 1, pp.48-60.

Salatore, R.N, 1989, *Encyclopedia of Indian Culture*, Vol. IV, Sterling Publishers Pvt Ltd, Delhi.

Scott, G.H, 1985, *Kabir and the Kabir Panth*, New Delhi.

Shah, Ahmad, 1977, *The Bijak*-(or the completer works of Kabir) New Delhi.

Surdas, 1969, *Sursagar*, Kashi Nagari Pracharini Sabha, 4th edition, Kashi.

Sundardas, Shyam (ed.) 1959, *Kabir Granthavali*, Nagiri Prachar Sabha, 7th ed., Kasi.

Shukla, 1994, *Hindi Sahitya ka Alochnatmak Itihaas*, Nagiri Pracharini Sabha, Varanasi.

Shukla, Ramchandra, 1999, *Jayasi Granthawali*-Atharth Padmavat, Akharavat aur Akhiri Kalam, (Hindi) Nagiri Pracharini Sabha, Varanasi.

Tagore, Ravindranath, 1945, *One hundred poems of Kabir*, assisted by Evelyn Underwill, India edition, Macmillan and Co. Ltd. St. Martins Street, London.

Vaudeville, Charlotte, 1974, *Kabir*, Vol. I, Oxford Press.

Verma, Ram Kumar, 1948, (Hindi) *Hindi Sahitya Ka Alochanatmak Ithihas*, 4th edition, Ram Narayan Lal, Prayag.

Westcott, G.H.1953, *Kabir and Kabir Panth*, Sushil Gupta (India) Limited, Calcutta.

Ziegler, N.P. 1976, "Marwari Historical chronicles: Sources for the social and cultural history of Rajasthan", in *Indian Economic and Social History Review*, Vol. XIII, No. 2, April-June.

6

Bhakti Movement in Western, Eastern and North Eastern Regions

Medieval Indian society witnessed a great ferment in the socio-political sphere with the rise of new social groups who were becoming increasingly vocal about their status in society and also their place before God. Far removed from the cultivated Sanskritic, ordered and formalized ritual services to God to end their dilemmas, there were other voices. Initially they would seem as the echo of the south Indian saints in different languages since they displayed the same concerns viz use of the vernacular, emotional reunion with the god and an informal and direct relationship that bypassed the feudal structures. Based on these practices of the saints and their devotees all over India, historians are emboldened to label this phenomenon as bhakti. Thus the pan Indian character of bhakti also reveals to us the different concerns and issues which can be explained as being fundamentally a product of the regional diversities and also the product of the times, as the bhakti movement travelled through the centuries. Thus we can locate the diverse regional specifities better and analyse them meaningfully if we view them in their temporal and spatial contexts. It is with this purpose that we look into this movement which having originated in South India and then spreading to Northern India, also spread to Gujarat, Maharashtra, Bengal and North east.

The origin of the new forms of Hinduism has been attributed to the influence of Islam, but the proposition that the rise of popular emotional bhakti was a response to Islam is impossible, for the practice of singing ecstatic hymns in the current local language was well-known in South India even before Prophet Muhammad. All the features of this form of bhakti are found in the Bhagavata-Puran and in the commentaries of Ramanuja. The earliest bhakti literature in a living Indo-Aryan language is from Maharashtra and was composed before Muslims occupied the area. Thus, passionate bhakti existed long before the Muslim conquest. However, the presence of rulers of alien faith and the withdrawal of royal patronage from the temples and Brahmanic colleges may have encouraged the spread of new, more popular forms of Hinduism. The psychological effect of the Muslim conquest may also have predisposed the people to accept the powerful teachings of the poets, but Islam was only a contributory factor in the spread of the new movements.

The poets and saints of medieval bhakti appeared throughout India. Although all have their individual genius, the bhakti lyricists share a number of common features whatever their language. The Sanskrit education needed for authors of Sanskrit texts limited them largely to the Brahman class and thus put a definite stamp on them. Because bhakti poets could use any language, they might come from any class. They brought to their poetry a familiarity with folk religion unknown or ignored in the Sanskrit texts. The use of the spoken language, even though it was formalized, made possible the immediate expression of an unmediated vision that needed no further context; thus the lyrics are short, intensely personal, and precise. These works illustrate the localistic and reformist tendencies evidenced throughout India in the vernacular literatures, especially in Tamil, Bengali, and Hindi.

Bhakti Movement in Gujarat

Bhakti movement in Gujarat begins from the fifteenth century and there are two major streams here. One is of sagun Bhakti around Krishna beginning with Narsinh Mehata and Mira and developed further under the Vallabha sect and the Swami narayana sect of Sahajanand Swami. Here the Vallabha sect which owed its philosophical origins to Vallabhacharya found a lot of mass following. It was Narsimha Mehta (1414-1481) who popularized this and he found a large number of following among the merchant class. The wave of Bhakti gave way for the growth of outstanding literature related to Vaishnavism. This wave swept Gujarat somewhere around the end of fourteenth and beginning of fifteenth century as a highly developed bhakti in which the concept attained a new dimension. The two important personalities who led the growth of Krishna bhakti cult in Gujarat were Mirabai and Narasinh Mehta. The other strain of Bhakti cult was of Yoga which was strongly influenced by the nath cult of Guru Matsyendra Nath and Gorakh Nath, who preached pursuit of ultimate truth and joy by treating the world as an illusion.

Narasinh Mehta was a Nagar Brahmin born in AD 1412 and was a native of Talaja near Palitana in Bhavnagar district. He gave a new impetus to Bhakti in Gujarat. The main contributions of this saint poet constitute the valuable resources of Gujarati literature. They are *Haramala, sudamacarita, caturi, Sodasi, samaldas, danalila, Govindagaman*, about 2000 padas on devotion and erotics (*srngar*) and *Surata sangrama* (Rangarajan, 1990, 19). However his works are divided into love poems and bhakti. But both are said to have merged together ultimately in his descriptions.

According to Narasinh Mehta, Vaishnava is not one who worships Visnu but who feels others sufferings as his own is the real Vaishnava. (*Vaishnava jana to tene kahiye je pida paraye jane re....)*. Gandhiji realized the importance of this pada and made it the hymn of his life. Narasinh was a great bhakta and philosophic saint who changed Gujarat poetry from an impersonal to personal art. Narasinh Mehta died in AD 1480.

Though there is no historical evidence to support the fact that Sri Ramanuja or his disciples visited Gujarat it is generally believed that Ramanuja visited Dwarka on his way to Kashmir. However after 17th century there is a continuous movement of acharyas from Tamilnadu and Karnataka into Gujarat. Towards the end of seventeenth century some of the individual Acharyas from Tamilnadu and Karnataka went to Gujarat. They influenced many Gujaratis to follow the Sri Sampradaya and thus encouraged many merchants, business men and other saints to become the followers of Ranmanuja. Two of these Acharyas were the acharyas from Sri Rangam in Tamilnadu and they belonged to a family popularly known as Tatacharya. The other belonged to the Ananthalvan family which hailed from Doddabalam now in Karnataka. Of the Tatacharya family Srinivasacharya (1816-1887 A.D.) played a very important role in Gujarat. Some of the very important disciples who helped him in the missionary work in Gujarat included, Divan Gopal Rai, a resident of Jodhpur, Vijaysimha Mehta, the Divan of Jodhpur, Trikamdas the eleventh descendent of the Bhakti poet Narsimha Mehta (Rangarajan, 1996, 38-39). As a result the followers of this sect increased in numbers and they came from far off places like Jamnagar in Saurashtra, Baroda, Nandod (North Gujarat) and Ahmedabad.The followers included different castes of people such as Brahmins, Patels, Panchals, Vaisyas, Mali, Sonar and Thakurs. The followers of the Sri sampradaya set aside the the taboos of interdinning and touch by taking prasadam in the presence of each other irrespective of caste and creed in the temple (Rangarajan, 1996, 161). The followers of Sri Vasinavism in Gujarat continue to follow the five ceremonies introduced at this time till today. These include *tapa* (branding), *Pundra* (sect mark), *nama* (giving a name) *mantra* (repeating sacred chants) and *yajna* (worship of special deity). However today most of the Gujarati hindus are followers of the Swami Narayana Sampradaya, which they consider as an off shoot of Ramanuja Sampradaya. The founder of this sect was Sri

Sahajananda Swami who was born in A.D. 1780 at Chhapaiya in Uttar Pradesh. He was a virtuous, self controlled, austere, ascetic and philanthropic man with a great aptitude for learning. He soon had a large following and made Jetalpur about 20 Km. south of Ahmedabad as his headquarters. He took the name Swami Narayan and established the worship of Nara-narayan and Narayan Lakshmi. He laid stress on the purity of personal life and the essence of devotion in daily life. Many were attracted to this sect because they consider it as an off shoot of Ramanuja sampradaya. His work, *Siksapatri* or manual of instructions written in Sanskrit in Sanskrit has a long commentary which constitutes the religious directory of the sect (Williams, 1974).

Of all the women bhakta poets in Gujarat, Mira stands out and there is mention of her name only, but Gujarat did have some women saints, who practiced and preached Bhakti. The earlier anthologies and books on the history of literature mention only Gujarat based women poets like Gaurabai and Diwalibai, whose poetry is not popular among the masses, but do not mention a powerful poet like Ganngasati from Saurashtra at all. This is due to the fact that serious research on medieval literature and collection of manuscripts started over 100 years ago in the more advanced areas and the literary people who undertook this task were more concerned with poets of their own areas and neglected the folk literature (Shukla, 1989, 64). Most of the women based in the Gujarat region were Brahmins. They sang the sagun Bhakti of Krishna and Ram. There was one muslim Ratanbai among them and another Maharashtrian Radhabai, but all the other women poets from Kathiawad and Kutch were non Brahmins and some like Loyal and Amarbai were from the lower castes. All of them sing of Nirgun Bhakti and emphasise the relationship of *atma* with *parmatama*. There is a touch of Sufism also in their writings.

Ganga Sati

Gangasati was a devoted Rajput woman married to Kahlubha, who shared her love for *bhajan* and *satsang*.

Kahlubha according to legend was asked by his fellow Rajputs to prove his faith by bringing a dead cow back to life. He started chanting and singinging invoking God to perform a miracle. The cow did come back to life but after this he decided to take *mahasamadhi* and renounce his life for he felt that he would not be allowed to practice Bhakti for its own sake but would become a miracle man. Ganga sati also wanted to join him but he prevented her saying that she had not passed on her knowledge and wisdom to their daughter in law Panbai. Gangasati composed a set of *bhajans* for this purpose and this is the only recorded case of a woman who is respected for her knowledge passing it on in a formal way to another.

Cleanse yourself, come out in the field, Panabai

Learn of what stuff your soul is made

To know your kind from others I teach you

I print you on another design

String the pearl...

Beyond self and world is a teacher, Panabai,

I show you his land

Ganga sati says

There no trace of illusion remains

String the pearls (Shukla, 1989, 66).

Gangasati further states that devotion and compassion become a major requirement in the path of Bhakti.

Before teaching others, show devotion,

Thus dissolving their illusions

Extend to them always compassion,

Address them with respect, attention

Cast no seed...

When their doubts disappear, mind is at peace,

When they do not hate or envyany,

Gangasati says, only then,

To such a one, show the land of God (Shukla, 1989, 67)

Sant Toral

The legend of Sant Toral has all the trappings of medieval classic chivilry, laced with myths, sacrifice which finally unfolds in the dramatic scene of giving away ones wife.

Sant Toral is the better half of the famous Jesal Toral pair that were know as the legendary lover as well as the saint pair. Toral was a Kanthi woman married to Sansatia, who were considered a lower caste than Rajputs but were also martial. Jesal was a Rajput dacoit from Kutch who was dared to acquire Toral. According to legend he was dared to acquire three things, *Tati, Toli* and *Toral. Tati* was the famous sword, *Toli* the famous mare and *Toral* the woman known for her beauty and piety. Jesal reached Sansatias house and hid in the stable. When Toral distributed Prasad one extra helping was left and the search revealed Jesal who told Sansatia why he was there. Sansatia willingly gave his wife and mare. According to legend Toral agreed to go because she was born with the mission of changing the lives of three fallen men. But a wife was considered a chattle by the patriarchal system and she could easily be given away. She had no identity of her own and had to confirm to patriarchal values.

On their way to Kutch by boat a heavy storm arose and began to rock the boat. While Jesal was terrified of death Toral remained calm and she addresses him in bhajans which teach that the attachment to the material world is pointless and one must find Bhakti.Jesal confesses to his sins which include robbing the wedding processions, killing bridegrooms, stealing and dragging away grazing cows, hunting deers, killing peacocks and letting down his sisters and their children. As he confesses the storm subsides and the boat stops rocking. Anecdotes relate how Jesal is transformed and he gives up arms and violence.

Sea shells form in the sea

Of no worth are they

Rain under Svatis ray

Falls in them turns to pearls

Do come, Jesalrai.

Rising at dawn, bathing in rivers

Coals do not turn white.

Whom can a whores son call father?

Stray rains grow no grain.

Do come, Jesalrai.

Look not to another light

He who does is incomplete

Lamp in hand he falls in a well

Four eras tale Toral Rani tells

Do come, Jesalrai (Shukla, 1989, 68).

Sant Loyal

Loyal was born in a community of blacksmiths in the latter half of eighteenth century and is said to have been very beautiful.Her lover Lakha was an ahir a cowherd of Saurashtra and they could not marry due to the difference in their castes. It is believed that Lakha planned to overcome this hurdle by pleasing his family and community by giving many gifts through his robberies. Loyal became a devotee under the influence of guru Selansi who belonged to the revered sect of Pir Ramdeo.Lakha could not stand the change in Loyal and he tried to attack her and grab her but he was struck with leprosy. Loyal is supposed to have sung 144 *bhajans* to Lakha, talking about the emptiness of life, greatness of guru and the fruits of Bhakti. Her bhajans usually begin with "Ji re Lakha...."

Shed your pride, O Lakha, enter the field

Bow your head at the Guru's feet

O Lakha, shed your lordly ways,

Make into your choices and your resolves

Make the guru's word your touchstone, Lakha

Else you sink in the sea of being.

Many the views and opinions here-

Submerge these continuous ways of seeing (Shukla, 1989, 71)

Bhakti Movement in Maharashtra

The main trends in bhakti in Maharashtra took the form of a number of *sant* traditions that developed between 13th to 17th centuries. More emphasis was given to Guru and *satsang*, the company of the good, as a path to self-realization. Verses were composed in *abhang* form based on an old folk song form called *Ovi*. There were five main sampradaya or sant tradition in Maharashtra. The *Mahanubhav Sampradaya* was established by Chakradhar Swami in 13th century, in Vidarbha and acknowledged no other deity other than Krishna. Mahadamba, (1233-1308 A.D.), the first Marathi woman poetess belonged to this Sampradaya. She composed two narrative poems on the wedding of Krishna and Rukmani. The *Nath* tradition was an ancient Shiva cult and became very popular among the lower castes. The *Datta* tradition combined the worship of Shiva and Vishnu in the form of Dattatreya, an incarnation of the three Gods, Brahma, Vishnu and Mahesh. The *Samarth* tradition was founded in 17th century by Ramdas, a Brahmin devotee of Ram and he became Shivaji's Guru. His famous disciples include Akkabai and Venabai (1627-1678 A.D.) However of the five main sant traditions, the most popular tradition was the *Varkari* tradition, which, was founded by Namdev (a sant of tailor community) and Jnanesvar (son of a socially outcaste Brahman) (Manushi, 1989, 47). The Varkari tradition preaches non violence and vegetarianism and an annual pilgrimage to Pandharpur. They use a lot of musical devotional singing *(bhajan)* and congregational gathering *(kirtan)* as a means to God realization.

The main characteristics of Maharashtrian bhakti may be summarized under three headings.

1. The all embracing importance of the Pandharpur image (*Vithoba)*, the Pandharpur *kshetra* (sacred land)and the Pandharpur piligrimage in this form of Vaishnava bhakti.

2. The peculiar features of the central deity, the God, Vittala or *Vithoba* of Pandharpur as *Svarupa* (i.e. original form) of Visnu rather than the *avatara* of the same God.

3. The absence of codified scriptures and all importance of the popular religious lyrics known as *abhangs* composed in middle Marathi by the poet saints of Maharashtra between fourteenth and seventeenth centuries AD.

In Maharashtra it was *Bhagavat Puran* which was the basic inspiration behind the movement. The Bhakti movement in Maharashtra has to be viewed against the background of the lack of an indigenous mercantile community and the traditional base of its chiefly agrarian economy in a variant of the Jajmani system, known as balutedari, which was made for a largely self sufficient village economy. The jati pyramid of Maharashtra is composed of Brahmins, elite Marathas claiming Kshatriya ancestry, peasant Marathas (Kunbis), artisans and service jatis (of Shudra Varna) and a number of formal untouchable Jatis technically outside the Varna system such as Mahars, who are known by their generic term Dalit or the Oppressed (Kosambi, 2000, 7). The saints of the Varkari movement were drawn from different sections of the society. Jnaneswar and Eknath were Brahmins, Tukaram and Namdev came from peasant and artisan classes, Savatra was a gardener, Tukaram a sudra and Cokhamela was a Mahar. Hence the Bhakti philosophy which provided them an alternative space for egalitarian devotional space away from the harsh realities of caste had a powerful appeal in Maharashtra. However many of these saint poets were not very vocal about the Varna-dharma. In fact many of them compromised and accepted their existing status instead seeking an egalitarian world in the realm of the sacred.

Namdev

Namdev is regarded as a link between the northen Bhakti movement and the Maharashtra Bhakti movement. He was born nearly two hundred years before Nank and one hundred and thirty years before Kabir and his period is said to have been between 1270-1350 A.D. His father's name was Damaseth and his mothers name was Gaurai. Namdev also followed the profession of his father and became a tailor in Narsi Bamani. From his childhood Namdev had a spiritual bent of mind. According to a legend, his father would always worship the image of Vitthal by pouring milk over it. Once he had to go out and asked Namdev to perform the worship. When Namdev pored milk and it remained as such he was very upset that God had not accepted his offerings and he cried a lot and voved that he would not move from that place till Vitthal accepted his offerings. It is stated that due to the firm devotion of the child the milk vanished. Namdev was married to Rajai and he was not able to earn enough to support his family and his wife often complained about this. He accepted Visobha Kechhar as his guru. In one of his abhangs he says that Kechhar is like a mother giving love and it is only after meeting him that he is rid of the fears of life and death. Not he is free from the worldly attachments and through Samadhi he has got a very fruitful experience. Namdev says that I have found every thing through Kechhar and now I will not leave his feet (Puri and Sethi, 2002, 39). He was against idol worship and elaborate rituals as a means to attain God. He says in another abhang, only those ignorant people talk of God being near or far, who do not have real knowledge. This is as false as saying that a fish has climbed up the date palm tree and is eating dates. Those who have realized God know the truth. Pandits talk about the Vedas but Nama says I am a fool, I know only Ram and nothing else (Puri and Sethi, 2002, 71). He says that God is present with in us but men forget this and worship stones, which do not have life (Puri and Sethi, 2002, 98). Namdev refers to his God in different ways, Vitthal, Ram, Hari but his God is a Nirgun God that does not have a form. Another prominent saint was Janeswar (1275-1296): He taught that the only way to attain God is through Bhakti and there was no place for cast distinctions here.

Mukata Bai

Mukata Bai lived during the thirteenth century and was the sister of Nivritti, Jnandev and Sopan who are considered the founders of the Varkari tradition. Their father was a Brahmin and a disciple of Ramanand but he was ostricised by the Brahmin community because after having taken sanyas he reverted back to a householders life. He then committed suicide. Though Mukata Bai according to tradition was a beautiful and intelligent girl she did not marry but lived with her brothers. She is said to have composed over 100 abangs.

In her abhangs she talks about God realization coming not through false rituals but having a pure heart.

What are mountains and cave to one

Who has not given up anger and desire?

Such a one is not a sanyasi

Who envies another's state.

He may live in the mountains

But wanders door to door for pleasure.

What use is yogadharm

When the heart is not desireless?

Make your heart pure as ganga water,

Open the door, O Jnaneswar. (Manushi, 1989, 53).

Unlike many other women bhaktas Muktabai does not emphasise her womanhood or talk about the conditions of her life as a woman. Her many songs are cast in the form of dialogues with other sants and she discourses with them as an equal. In *Nivritti Mukti Samvad,* she and Nivritti instruct one another. In *Tatiche Abhang* (Song of the Door) she tries to persuade Jnaneshwar, who has got annoyed by peoples comments and locked himself in his hut, to open the door. She does not adapts the tone of a younger sister pleading with the younger brother but a sant addressing another.

Brahma is the one reality,

All else but the five elements.

If your hand happens to hit you

You do not get annoyed do you?

If the teeth happen to bite the tongue,

Does any one break the thirty two (teeth)?

Even the biggest sorrow or insult

Is a lesson for the future.

Only one who can chew iron gram.

Can establish the mind in Brahm

Kill the mind, be unattached

Open the door o Janeshwar. (Songs of the Door, Manushi, 1989, 53).

She died at the young age of eighteen. In a verse Cokhamela says that if he has a son the son should be a sant and if a daughter she should be like Mirabai or Muktabai, other wise he would rather not have children at all. She is one of the most revered saints of Maharashtra.

Janabai

Janabai was a contemporary of Muktabai and was a maid servant in the house of Janadev. Janabai was the daughter of a sudra and was taken into the house of Namdev's father Damshetti when she was very young and she grew up there as a maid servant. Not much is known about her except her life as depicted in the abhangs. Namdev had taken a vow to compose one crore verses in praise of Vithoba and he divided the task amongst his household members. Janabai also composed a number of abhangs and these appear in *Namdev Gatha*. She is very much aware of her position as a maid servant but she is happy that she is in the house of a sant.

Tukaram

The other prominent saint of Maharashtra was Tukaram (1598-1649). Tukaram's parents died early and he had to shoulder the burden of maintaining a huge family. He tried to carry out his hereditary profession of petty trader cum mony lender but he suffered heavy lossess due to his over generous nature. His first wife Rakuma and son Santu died due to starvation. Tukaram went to Bhambanatha and other places and gave himself to spiritual readings. His second wife was more practical and kept nagging him for his ways. All this made him turn to God in order to seek internal peace. In one of the abhangs few admirers approach Tukaram to enlighten them about his own spiritual life and how he developed into a saint, he first scorns at the idea but then tells us something about his life. He was born into a family of sudras and worshipped his family deity. He lost all prestige and money in a famine and his wife and son died of starvation. He spent his time in singing devotional songs to his God Vitthal. He states that he is content with the present and his future is in the hands of God who is merciful and will never neglect his devotees (Tulpule, 1992, 150-151). Tukaram's abhangs tell us about his spiritual journey, the difficulties in the path of Bhakti, his heart rending experiences in his path to Bhakti and as he realized God the gleam of light that began to shine on him. In fact there is a kind of Hegelian dialecticism in Tukarams soul. He first withdraws himself from the world with a determination to win spiritual knowledge. Then comes the stage of negetation, the dark side of Tukaram's soul where he is warring with his own self. Finally there is a stage of affirmation, namely the transforming the original determination and following negation to the final vision of the God head a stage which supersedes them both (Ranade, 1933, reprint, 1982, 281-82).

Tukaram and many of the other Varkari saints were not indifferent to the existing caste system and accepted it, with out challenging it. According to legend Tukaram had dared to comment on the Brahmanical scriptures and a Brahmin had ordered him to throw them in the river Indrayani and he had obliged. In fact when Tukaram is describing a person who does not follow the path of Bhakti, he uses the castes of those who are not included in the traditional four Varna system.Hence he who is not aware of Panduranga is a Mang, he whose mouth does not pronounce the Name is a vessel of a Chamar, Tuka says on the day such a man was conceived, his mother who is a harlot paid a visit to a Mahar (Glushkova, 2000, 48). In a period of spiritual disharmony, he even accuses Vitthal of not possessing a caste for he does not follow his Karma (Glushkova, 2000, 49). He also meekly accepts the fact that he belongs to the lower caste. He says," O God it is good that you have made me a Kunbi, otherwise I would have died of vanity. A low state is a state which no one would envy for a flood washes away trees but bushes, remain (Glushkova, 2000, 49).

The Varkari tradition is again very critical of women though there were many who were also seeking Bhakti and writing abhangs. Rarely do the women mention their names, especially if they are from the lower classes. Soryabai hence calls heself as, "Cokha's Maharin" janabai as "Nama's Jani". However some of the Brahmin saints like Muktabai and Bahina bai inscribe their poems with their own names. (Glushkova, 1996).

The direct impulse of spiritual life must have come to Tukaram from his spiritual teacher Babaji. Tukaram himself tells us that his spiritual line may be traced from Raghava Chaitanya to Kesava Chaitanya and to Babaji Chaitanya. (Ranade, 1933, 1982, 264). Bahina bai, one of the greatest diciples who had seen him and lived under his instruction says that Raghava Chaitanya was a spiritual descendent of Sacchidananda Baba who himself was a disciple of Jnanadeva. From this it can be seen that Tukaram was directly related to the spiritual line of Jnanadeva. If we ponder into Tukaram's mystical carrier and teaching as a whole we could find a typical illustration of what is called 'Personalistic Mysticism'. Tukaram exhibits all the doubts and the disbeliefs, the weaknesses and sufferings, the anxieties and the uncertainties through which every aspiring soul has to pass before it can come into the life of light, spirit and harmony. There is no other instance in the whole galaxy of Maratha saints barring Namdev, which contain this human element that we find in Tukaram. (Ranade, 1982, 269) Of the important aspects to be pondered is whether Christianity influenced Tukaram. Mr. Murrey Mitchell has no hesitation in saying that Tukaram having definitely influenced by

Christian doctrine. The reason was the violence of Portuguese in India in propagating their religion and this must have attracted the attention of Marathas to Christian religion.

Bahina Bai

The next important saint from Maharashtra was Bahina Bai (1628-1700 A.D) and she was a disciple of Tukaram. She lived during the seventeenth century and is the only woman saint who has written an autobiography. She was born in a poor Brahmin family of Deigoan. When she was three years old she was married to Ratnakar Pathak who was thirty years old and was a priest and an astrologer. For him this was a second marriage. At the age of seven Bahina Bai came to Kolhapur to live with her husband and his parents. Here too she had to suffer a lot due to her Bhakti and she is the only woman saint who remains married through out her life. Her life eases only when her husband gets converted to her way of thinking. She also wrote her abhangas in the popular Marathi *ovi* meter, which is used in songs when women go about their daily work like doing the household chores, grinding the corn or husking the grain.

Cokhamela

As the concept of bhakti attached great importance on the concept of Personal God, the early *sants* or the Vaishnava bhaktas were mostly lowborn sudras. Some of them were ranked even lower in the social hierarchy and were known as *atisudras* since they belonged to Polluting castes and were addressed as *Harijans* by Mahatma Gandhi. (Vaudeville, 1999, 221). Between the two untouchable saint poets, two have risen to great fame. One was Raidas, who lived in Kasi in the fifteenth century and the other was Cokhamela, a *Mahar* of Pandharpur. While Raidasa composed a number of *padas* in archaic Hindi (of which some were recorded by Sikhs). Cokamela, or Cokha composed a large number of short archaic poems in Marathi known as *abhangs*. These were the inspiration by his devotion to the supreme Lord, God Vittala of Pandharpur to which, he belonged. A few elements of Cokhamela's biography are found in his own verses and in the verses composed by his family members (his wife, Soyara and son Vanka) (In the compilation of Marathi *abhangs* known as *Sakalasanta gatha*, ed. By Sakhare, 1961, Vol 1, 192 *abhangs* are found attributed to Cokhamela). Cokhamela's biography that is in vogue in Maharashtra even today is largely based on accounts found in the *Bhakta Vijaya* of Mahapati, the eighteenth century poet of Maharashtra. It was translated into English by J.A Abott and N.R Godbole, Poona, 1933.

Cokhamela was born in Pandharpur itself and was one of the outstanding Vaishnava bhaktas. According to legends, as he had no access to temple, he brought the Lord in his thoughts and worshipped him from afar standing at the *Mahadvara* of the main temple. To the Brahmins who reviled him, Cokha is said to have replied that 'Krsna himself loved him and Vithoba constantly cared for him. One night *Vithoba* is said to have taken Cokha by hand and led him into His own shrine in the temple. A priest overheard the conversation between the mahar and the God. Thereupon the enraged Brahmins due to this sinful act, exiled Cokha to the other side of the Bhima river opposite Pandharpur. Cokha remained worshipping the Lord in his heart. The God unable to bear the separation came to him and both of them dined together in Cokhamela's hut. Some curd is said to have fallen in the middle of the meal on the Lord's garment. A Brahman saw this and he slapped Cokha for this act. Later when the Priest came to the temple, the Lord's garment was still having the stains of curd and the marks of the slapped fingers that were given to Cokha. The priest realizing the fondness of Lord for the mahar brought Cokha inside the temple. It is said that Cokha had an accidental death due to wall collapse in which many other workers of his community also died. When Namdev with others was not able to recognize the bones of Cokha, the Lord Himself is said to have come and told Namdev to hit the bones with stick and whichever sound resembled *Vithoba* were the bones of Cokha. Finally he was buried at the entrance of the great temple at Pandharpur from where he used to worship the Lord.

In his songs Cokha talks about his low birth.

O God, Vile is my birth

How then could I serve you?

People shout at me Go away, get away.

How then could I meet you?

If they happen to touch my hand

They pour water on themselves

O my Govind! O my Govind!

Cokhamela cries for your mercy (Vaudeville, 1999, 230)

He talks in very distressed voice about his being impure and wants to find out what is pure.

All the five elements are equally impure

The same impurity pervades the whole world!

If that be so, what can be called pure or impure?

The body itself is the very source of filth-

At the beginning and at the end, nothing but filth

Who is then, who could get pure? I do not know!

Says Cokha, I myself wonder,

How can any one ever get rid of impurity? (Vaudeville, 1999, 231)

Cokha is very critical of the Brahmins and the Yogis.

Cursed be their actions, cursed be their thinking

Cursed be their birth and their life!

Curse be their knowledge of Absolute

Tis all but vain talk

There is neither pity nor forgiveness nor peace in their hearts

Cursed be those postures and those hair knots of theirs

In vain did they put on ascetic garb!

Says Cokha, cursed be the birth of such people

In the end they'll endure the torments of hell! (Vaudeville, 1999, 232)

Bhakti Movement in Bengal

In Bengal it was the Vaishnava Bhakti tradition which had a lot of impact. It emphasized on Bhagvata Purana with its emphasis on Krishna lila and Sahajiya Buddhist tradition and the Nathpanthi tradition on the other. As in other parts of India the Bhakti tradition had a much longer history, beginning with Jayadeva's *Gita Govinda* written around 12th century. He highlighted the erotic mystical dimension of love with reference to Radha Krishna. Chandidas and Vidyapati came under the influence of the Non-Vaisnava cults. However it was Chaitanya who popularized this cult in Bengal through the Gaudiya Viashnava school and broadening its base to include social reforms.

Bengal has a rich cultural tradition in itself that got into shape due to the efforts of different dynasties that ruled the region. The Palas were one among these, who developed the area and made it very wealthy. They also patronized Buddhism which led to the growth of universities like Vikramasila which gave this region an intellectual boost.

Sri Chaitanya

Vaishnavism began to get popularity due to the effort of Sri Chaitanya earlier known as Visvambar Misra, he was born in Nudia district of Bengal in AD 1485. Chaitanya adopted an ascetic life in AD 1507 and began to practice the passionate bhakti of the *Bhagavata Purana* by Isvara Puri, an ascetic of Madhva sect (Hedoyetullah, 1977, 120). He was given the name *Gauranya* on the occasion of his sacred thread ceremony and later came to be known as Sri Krishna Chaitanya at the time of his sanyas. He came under the influence of the Nimbarkas and Visnuswamis and sang delightly the songs of Jayadeva (the author of *Gita Govinda*), Chandidas and Vidyapati. Chaitanya gave Radha, the imaginary consort of *Krsna* a prominent place in his worship and made the Radha-Krishna myth the basis of his teachings and worship. So intense was his desire to be to *Krsna* as Radha was to her divine lover that he was sometimes heard to murmur "I am He" (Hedoyetullah, 1977, 121). Sometimes he used to dance with his disciples chanting the name of Krishna. His power over men came from the reality of his mystical religious experience which he exhibited through overpowering his emotions and an impassioned love for God.

Chaitanya was the originator of the *Gaudiya* school of Vaishnavism. The formation of this school was a direct outcome of the religious ideas of Chaitanya which took shape during his lifetime. He felt the need to re interpret the Vedanta on dualistic Vaishnava lines and accepted Srimad Bhagavata as an independent source of knowledge by providing it with scriptural status (Chatterjee, 100, yr). Chaitanya also seems to have believed in the brotherhood and equality and it is probably due to this reason that he had many Muslim disciples. Chaitanya died in AD 1533.

Chaitanya disregarded all cast distinctions and expanded his following to include people of all cast and communities. He popularized the practice of sankirtan or group devotional singing accompanied by esoteric dancing. His favourite disciple was Haridasa who was a muslim. Inspite his reform zeal Chaitanya did not give up the traditional brahmanical values and upheld the class prejudice of his Brahmin disciples against the lower caste disciples. Six of his Sanskrit knowing Brahmin Goswamins reorganized caste restrictions in their devotional practices and rituals when they established a religious order near Vrindavan in Mathura. Yet in spite of this Chaitanyas movement remained popular in Orissa and Bengal.

Bhakti Movement in Assam

In Assam it was Sankar deva, who introduced the concept of Bhakti in the Brahmaputa valley as in Cooch-Bihar. Shankardeva's Neo-Vaishnavite movement was the first organized attempt in Assam at breaking down the age old bondage to the restrictions of caste, superstitions, ignorance, poverty and uncleanliness through the medium of Bhakti. Known as the land of Kirta-Mlecchas, the society of North East consisted of various tribes who were all regarded as outcastes. Due to a confused admixture of different Hindu and Buddhist tantrik cults a mysterious atmosphere was created and this region came to be known to the outside world as a land of mysticism and sorcery (Neog, 1965, 91).Tribals including the ruling chieftains like the Chutiyas, Ahoms, the Kochs and the Kacharis were patrons of Saktism and accustomed to sacrifices. It was in this environment that Neo-Vaisnavism with ideals of humanism and non violence and simplification of heterogenous religious beliefs called for injunction against blood sacrifices.

In Assam the decline of the Pala dynasty was followed by the rise of various dynasties. The political geography of Assam in 13th century was marked by Chutiya Kings who ruled the country east of Subansiri and Disang, a Kachari Kingdom on the south banks of the Brahmaputra, a number of independent Bhuyans who occupied the land west of the Kacharis on the south bank. Although there was no unity amongst them they joined together in the hour of peril and in the interest of honour and self respect and fought as one against a common enemy. Invasions by Muhammad Bhaktiyar towards the close of 12th century and Ghiyasud-din in 1227 A.D. resulted in terrible bolood shed and large scale plunder in this region. After this were followed the invasions of Ikhtiyauddin Tughril Khan in 1257 A.D, Muhammad Shah in the second quarter of 14th century and

Hussain Shah in the first half of the 16th century. The Ahoms, a group of Shan invaders under the hegemony of Sukhapa (1228-1268 A.D) penetrated in the north of Brahmaputra and soon established a considerable influence over portions of eastern Assam by subjugating Nagas, Morans and Borahis. The Koch took the help of the Ahoms in driving out the muslims and in a peace treaty that was drawn in 1638 A.D. the Koch kingdom was divided between the Ahoms and the Muslims.

15th century Assam presented a motely collection of diverse shades of culture, religion, race and political status. There was neither political unity nor social solidarity.To the tyranny from with out was added the social tyranny from with in (Murthy, 1973, 29). The domination of the Brahmins over much of the society was a crowning feature of the social order of medieval Assam. A sudra was debarred from even chanting the vedic mantras. Giving instruction to the tribe by a Brahmin was regarded as mean. None of the highest nobles had a right to wear shoes or to carry an umbrella or to travel in a palanquin but the last mentioned privileges might be purchased for a sum of one thousand rupees. Persons of humble origin who wished to wear *chaddar* or shawl were obliged to fold it over the left shoulder and not over the right as the upper class did. The common people were not permitted to build houses of masonary or with round ends, Musalmans, Morias, Doms and Haris were forbidden to wear their hair long and members of the two latter communities were further distinguished by having a fish or broom, respectively tattooed on their forheads (Gait, 1926, 242). With these wide difference in society the Bhakti philosophy which spoke of equality between all the castes and classes in matters of devotion and faith was largely welcomed in Assam and helped in the creation of an alternative space.

Sankardeva

It was Srimantha Sankaradeva who spread the Vaishnava bhakti and its ideology in the northeastern part of India (Kamarupa). He was born in AD 1449 at Alipukri which is around 15km from Nawgong.His fathers name was Kusumavara, the chief of the Sirmomani Bara Bhuyana. His mother was Satyasandha and she died three days after the birth of Sankar deva. He was brought up by his grandmother Buri Gosain Khersuti. From his childhood Sankara was very different from other children. He never cared about food or sleep and spent all his time in sports and swimming. In school Sankara impressed every one with his extraordinary intellect and imaginative power to quickly grasp things. He soon mastered Sanskrit grammer, lexicography, Vedas, Smritis, the two epics, Puranas and the Kavyas. When Sankar was twenty two years of age he took to Yogic practices and soon mastered this art. He learnt other yogic practices like *pranayam, dhyan, asana, dharana and Samadhi.* On account of these practices the strength and beauty of his body and mind increased considerably. After this Sankara went on various pilgrimages to different parts of the country. Here he came in contact with Vaisnavism as practiced in different regions. At these holy places he had discussions regarding Vaisnavism with different learned men. All this must have prompted Sankardeva to introduce Neo Vaisnavism in Assam.

Deeply religious by nature Sankaradeva desired to lead a life of devoted service towards bettering the society but he had to lead a married life due to the pressure of his grandmother. At the age of twenty three he married Suryavati but she died with in four years after giving birth to a daughter. Meanwhile Shankardeva also lost his father and his mind was filled with grief and he became disgusted with worldly pleasures. The death of his wife deepened Sankaradeva's sense of detachment with the worldly ways. However he desisted from going on a pilgrimage until he got his daughter married.He soon composed himself and regained his calm and spent his energies in bringing up the motherless child. In AD 1481 at the age of thirty two Sankaradeva set out on a pilgrimage. This provided ample scope for him to exchange thoughts with various Vaishnavite schools. It was at Badrikasrama that he composed a baragit *mana meri Rama charanahi lagu* (My thinking is solely centered on the feet of Rama) (Rastogi, 1994, 32). Sankaradeva benefited a good deal from the discourses of Jagdish Misra who had enviable knowledge of scriptures and who came from Puri. These discussions helped him to reach the conclusion that the religion consists in 'supreme surrender to *Krsna*'. Now Sankara began drawing attention to what he called *Ek Sarana Dharma*. It rests on four pillars i.e. *Deva* (deity), *Nama* (recitation), *Guru* (preceptor) and *Bhakti* (devotion) (Rastogi, 1994, 33).

Sankar deva belonged to the family of non Brahmin Bhuyan chiefs. He became an ascetic in late life and traveled all over south and Northern India. He preached absolute devotion to Vishnu and his incarnation Krishna. He had to face persecution at the hands of the orthodox priesthood of the Ahom kingdom and took shelter in the territories of the neighbouring Cooch Bihar where the king gave him the freedom to preach Bhakti. The brahmanas were upset with Sankardeva because he questioned the authority of the priests who were regarded as indispensable mediators of salvation. Sankardeva, expounded the supremacy of Bhakti. He was very much influenced by the monistic ideas and his concept of Bhakti is known as, *eka-sarana-dharma*,, religion seeking refuge in one. He denounced the caste system and preached his ideas in Assamese. He founded the institution of *Satra*, which means sitting during which people of all classes assembled for religious and social purpose. Later the *satras* grew into full fledged monastries. His sect is called Mahapurashiya dharma.

It can be said that Sankaradeva's Neo-Vaishnavite movement was the first organised attempt in Assam in breaking down age old restrictions of caste, superstitions, ignorance and poverty that pervaded the society. Since the social background of the northeast was characterized by the existence of numerous tribes and outcastes, this gave an opportunity of them being uplifted. Sankaradeva died in AD 1569.

Sankardeva says,

The scholar does not see the straightest path

Nor does the performer of a million sacrifices attain Hari

Both fall down on earth ever and anon.

All rites and rituals,

All pilgrimage to Gaya and Kasi

Made round the years,

All yogas done and rhetoric learnt

Only clouds of vision.

There is no salvation with our Bhakti. (Murthy, 1973, 139).

He advocates an absence of desire and worldliness on the path of Bhakti.

"Worldliness is unhappiness,

Creatures know this.

Yet none forsake it, rather all run after it again.

Like a goat which behaves disgracefully

Even when led to the altar for sacrifice,

Roped by neck.

Or like shameless dog thou uninvited

And vehemently chid.

Comes to partake of the remains of feast" (Murthy, 1973, 143).

To him every one is equal because he says, "God is the soul of the dogs, the donkeys and the outcastes.Knowing this, pay reverence to all living creatures (Murthy, 1973, 197). Caste does not matter and it is only bkakti which is important.

"Why need one be a Brahmana to recite devoutly the name of Krsna? He might be a Chandala, but he is far superior to any man who is not attached to the name of Hari" (Murthy, 1973, 198). Further he says, "In Bhakti there is no distinction of caste. Everybody has equal right to chant Harinama"(Murthy, 1973, 200).

It was in Majuli that Sankar deva in 1546 converted his chief apostle Madhavdeva, who till then was a staunch Sakta by faith.The conversion of Madhav deva had a serious impact upon the belief and behavioural pattern of the people. They got the patronage of the king Malladev (Naranarayan) (1549-1587) and his scholar brother Sukladhvaj (Chilarai), the Commander in Chief. With this kind of a royal support Sankar deva and his disciples felt completely free and secure in Koch Bihar and many of the common people mostly belonging to the Koch tribes became Vaishnav and left their tribal ways and developed a distinct sense of humanism and non-violence. This trait of the people is also mentioned by a medieval English traveler, Ralph Fitch, who states, "....The people .... they be all Gentiles, and they will kill nothing. They have hospitals for sheep, goats, dogs, cats, birds and for all living creatures. When they be old and lame they keep them until they die. If a man catch or buy any quick thing in other places and bring it tither, they will give him money for it or other victuals, and keep it in their hospitals or let it go (Foster, 1921, 25).

However the impact of this movement was limited to only Koch Bihar and the other regions like upper Assam were not effected and continued with their tribal ways of life. After Sankar devas death the Neo Vaisnavite's got divided into four important Samhatis or orders-*Brahma*, *Purusha*, *Nika* and *Kala Samhatis* and among these *Brahma* remained confined mostly to the advanced sections of the society and *Kala* was confined to the downtrodden and outcastes (Sharma, 1966, 68). Some of the monastries established by the Ahom state patronage in the second half of the 17th century like the Auniati Satra, Dakhinpat Satra, Kuruwabahi Satra and Garamur Satra at Majuli also had a lot of impact on the people especially the aristocracy and the advanced castes who used to Bhakti ideology to establish their hold on society. It was the Mayamara Satras in places like Bishnu Balikunchi and Naharita that tried to amalgamate the tribals and downtrodden in their fold.

Diverse eco-zones witnessed many different socio-economic patterns with unique problems. Thus it was the creative genius of the saints who sought to solve the spiritual problems in their socio-economic context while imparting a local flavour the same movement. The connecting eteme of all these Saints was salvation through uhapti and equality of all in the eyes of God.

References

Chatterjee, A.N., *Sri Krsna Chaitanya: A Historical study on Gaudiya Vaishnavism*, Associated Publishing Company, New Delhi.

Foster, William, 1921 (ed), *Travels in India* (1583-1619), Oxford University Press.

Gait, Edward, 1926, *A history of Assam*, 2nd Edition, Calcutta.

Glushkova, Irina, 1996, "The concept of women in the poems of Tukaram" in Anne Feldhaus (ed) *Images of women in Maharashtrian Literature and Religion*, State University of New York Press, Albany.

Glushkova, Irina, 2000" Norms and Values in Varkari Tradition", in Kosambi, Meera (ed), 2000, *Intersections-Socio-Cultural Trends in Maharashtra*, Orient Longman Limited, New Delhi.

Hedoyetullah, Mohammad, 1977, *Kabir: The apostle of Hindu Muslim Unity*, Motilal Banarassidas, Delhi.

Kosambi, Meera (ed), 2000, *Intersections-Socio-Cultural Trends in Maharashtra*, Orient Longman Limited, New Delhi.

Khan, Mohammad Ishaq, 2004, *"The Rishi Movement as a social force in Medieval Kashmir"*, in Lorenzen, David N. (ed), Religious Movements in South Asia, 600-1800, Oxford University Press.

Khan, Mohammad Ishaq, 1986, "The impact of Islam on Kashmir in the Sultanate period, 1320-1586", *The Indian Economic and Social History Review*, XXIII, 2, 187-205.

Murthy, Sreenivasa, H.V. 1973, *Vaisnavism of Samkardeva and Ramanuja* (A comparative study), Motilal Banarsidas, New Delhi.

Neog, R. 1965, *Shankar Deva and his times*, Gauhati University, Gauhati.

Puri, J.R. and Sethi, V.K. 2002, *Sant Namdev* (Hindi), Radha Soami Satsang Beas, Amritsar.

Ranade, R.D. 1933, reprint 1982, *Mysticism in Maharashtra*, Poona.

Rastogi, T.C., 1994, *Assam Vaishnavism*, (Sociological Perspective), Omsons Publications, New Delhi.

Rangarajan, Haripriya, 1990, *Spread of Vaishnavism in Gujarat up to AD 1600* (A study with Special reference to the iconic forms of Visnu), Somaiya Publications, Bombay,.

Rangarajan, Haripriya, 1996, *Ramanuja Sampradaya in Gujarat*-a historical perspective, Somiya Publications, Bombay.

Sharma, S.N. 1966, *The Neo-Vaishnavite Movement and the Satra Institution of Assam*, Gauhati University, Gauhati.

Shukla, Sonal, 1989, "Traditions of teaching-women sant poets of Gujarat", Manushi, *Women Bhaktas*, Delhi.

Tulpule, S.G. 1992, "Tukaram: the making of a saint", in McGregor, R.S. (ed) *Devotional Lietrature in South Asia*, Cambridge University Press. U.K.

Vasu, N.N. 1922, quoting Padma Puran, in *Social History of Kamrup*, Calcutta.

Vadiville, Charlotte, 1999, *Myths, saints and legends in Medieval India*, Oxford. University Press.

Williams, Monier, 1974, reprint, *Religious thought and life in India*, New Delhi.

7

Male Bhakta's Attitude towards Women

Indian society has been patriarchal for most part of recorded history with stages of disabilities against women increasing. Though it has often been stated that the position of women was much better in the Vedic period and things started deteriorating with the coming of Muslims, and the often quoted examples are given of Gargi and Maitreyi who participated in the Sabha and Samitis it cannot be denied that ancient societies were patriarchal on the simple count that the predominant structure and values of society were oriented to giving men a superordinate status, a fact that was reinforced by sacred literature.We can posit the argument that this trend continued in medieval times as we get no evidence of any sharp structural disjuncture that halted patriarchy. In fact one can see continuity in modern times which is one of the reasons that the social reformers and freedom fighters took up this issue as one of the unfinished business of Indian social reform.

In a patriarchal society it is the son who gets highly valued and no such premium is paid on the girl. The *Atharvaveda* has a prayer, Oh, God grant us a son and a daughter elsewhere. The birth of a daughter was less welcome. In the *Atharvaveda* and *Samveda Mantra* we get prayers for a male child. The husband prays along with the wife, "Unto thy womb let a foetus come, a male one as an arrow to a quiver, let a hero be born unto thee......... give birth to a male, a son, after him let a male be born, mayst thou be mother of sons, of those born and who shall bear,etc. (Atharvaveda, Gulati, 1985, 16) A son saves his father from hell, *Put* and hence he is called *Putra* (Protector from Put). A father throws his debt on a son, through a son he conquerors the worlds, through a grandson he obtains immortality and through the sons of the grandson he gains the world of the sun (Visnu Smriti, Charya, 1964, 44-46). According to hindu system of philosophy the purpose of marriage was religious and it is through this institution that a Grihista could discharge his three debts-To Gods, to sages and to ancestors and then he could retire into *Vanaprasthaasram* (Manu, Max Muller, 1985).Hence the son was very central to the hindu way of life. If a woman could not give birth to a son or was barren, the very religious purpose of the family could not be carried out and hence a wife could be superseded if she was barren and gave birth to daughters only (Lakshmidhara, Gulati, 23).

Women have been given a subordinate status in the Brahmanical religion. She is regarded as an untouchable and extremely impure during her menstrual period and during the period of child birth. She is also regarded as polluted during widowhood. She has to purify herself before participating in any religious ceremony. By the time we come to Manu, the Upanayana ceremony became unnecessary for girls and she was debarred from performing religious sacrifices. The Brahmanical law books enjoined that each individual had to live according to Dharma but for women her dharma was only *Stridharma*. By embodying a very critical attitude towards women, their sexuality, their relationship with their bodies and senses, tantricism heralded the process of acculturation of the subordinate and brought women to the focus of things.

According to ancient and later Brahmanical law books it is dharma which governs the religious and social life of an individual. According to these each person has to follow a set of social and religious duties appropriate to that persons individuality (seva-bhav) for each person is a member of a particular community (Jati). Along with Srutis, Smritis, sadachar or accepted good usages constituted an important source of dharma. If each and every one followed their dharma then the results accured would be beneficial. For a woman her dharma was stridharma. Women can function in a socilly sanctioned dharmic way by strictly adhering to her preordained nature and duties. A women thus becomes the mistress of the house and is the custodian of the family dharma and passing it from one generation to another through her children. Due to their fickle nature and the inherent pollution in the female body women are seen as being subordinate to the voice of authority in the family and have to engage in frequent acts of ritual purifications. They had to visit temples with great regularity, perform sacred rites with higher faith and submit to religious fasts. The number of vratas increased and with the passage of time they were spread evenly over the whole year and invested with a moral fervour by associating a number of ethical and moral stories with them. These vratas were meant to purify the body, mind and spirit that was a ritual marker of transition from a state of unclean to cleanliness. In medieval Andhra it was a common practice among women chiefly of royal and noblity to install a deity or keep a *vrata* in the name of their husband, father or son and to donate and make gifts (Padma, 2001, 129-134).

A women is seen by nature *(svabhav)* as not only pollutent but also potentially dangerous because of her sexuality. Therefore in the family her sexuality should always be controlled and she should be subservient to the male authority. Her sexuality is seen as a source of prosperity when it is active but it has to be controlled by her husband in any other situation and she must totally repress it.

Though many of the Bhakti saints were clamourning for change and questioned the existing hierarchies and injustices, women were not a party to this change. They could not rise above the age old prejudice of regarding women as a barrier to the path of salvation. Kabir talks about the fundamental equality of all human beings, irrespective of birth, family status, caste, race and religion because he felt that all human beings are born in the same manner and consist of the same elements (Kabir, Padavali, 1946, 57). He also refused to recognize the distinctions between a ruler, beggar, a high caste man or an untouchable, a hindu, muslim or a Turk (Kabir, Padavalli, 1946, 55, 56) Yet all this did not apply to women and Kabir could not see women as an equal to man. In Kabir's discourse, women find representation only in gender stereo typed roles as mother, wife and Sati. Often Kabir worshipped God representing himself as a woman, a slave of her lover (Tewari, 1989, 10). Yet he is very critical of women, whom he equates with Maya or illusion.

Kabir gives a lot of importance to women's role as a mother. A women's life is worthy if she has given birth to an intellectual and religious son. If a woman cannot give birth to such a son then it was better that she would have become a widow or she would have aborted the child and remained childless all her life (Tewari, 1989, 37). In fact he prefers the dog of a Vaisnava better than the mother who goes to get illgotten wealth through her son (Tewari, 1989, 227). Kabir even reflects on his mother who hides her tears and cries because her son has left weaving and become very involved in bhakti and she does not know how to take care of the financial health of the family (Tewari, 1989, 9). Kabir talks about the economic contributions of the women and regards her as being responsible for building the charater of her children especially sons. The father is never mentioned as being remotely responsible for shaping the character or values of his son (Pande, 1993, 331).

In fact Kabir sees woman only as a Sati. According to him a Pativrata woman would give her mind and body to her husband and enter the pyre as nothing is of any value to her in his absence ((Tewari, 1989, 176). Even after ascending the pyre the pious woman cries out in the grave yard that this is now her only destiny.

The institution of marriage becomes very important to Kabir and he favours strong filial ties.

In the beginning one form

Jiva existed

In the beginning light had

Its manifestation

Desire was made in the

Form of women

To her was given the name Gayatri

To that woman were born three sons

Brahma, Vishnu, Mahesh

Were the names given

Then Brahma asked the mother

Who is they husband and whose wife are thou?

I am thou, thou art I there is no one besides

Thou art my husband and I thy wife

Father and son have the same wife

One mother gave birth to both

Never have I seen a son so

Worthy that he sought out his father (Shah, 1977, 55).

He is very particular about a woman being faith ful to her husband and is very critical of one with loose morals.

She was wife to one

But became the wife of many

The wanton has many mates

Kabir asks, with which will she burn

For she, wife of many husbands (Shah, 1977, 208)

He even mentions adultery and is very critical of it.

I have seen a woman walking

The pitcher below, the water

Carrier above

She was passing on along the highway

The bed was resting upon the sleeper

Dying of cold yet she spares the quilt

She knows not her husband the wife is demented

Evening and morning she lights the lamp

Leaving her husband she dotes upon a lover

Night and day she is

Inebriated with love of him

To her own husband she

Speaks not truth

She left her husband while he slept and went

Now to whom shall I make

Plain this trouble? (Shah, 1977, 87).

Again he says

The wife is called her

Husbands yet she sleeps

With another

Folly abides in her heart. What

Joy can her husband have? (Shah, 1977, 210).

Kabir compares the fact of falling into the clutches of treacherous woman to be worse than that of a snake bite or scorpion bite which at least has some charms for its remedy.

There is charm for the

Snake and the scorpion

And for the poision there are

Antidotes.

If one fall into the clutches

Of treacherous woman

She will tear out his heart

And devour it (Shah, 1977, 198).

While Kabir has many expectations from woman and he wants the woman be a devoted and obedient wife, he also makes fun of men who love woman. In fact woman is another name for Maya, illusion which hinders the path to salvation.He equates woman and gold to poisonous fruits which surely lead us to death. A woman to him is the garbage bin of the world and due to their trap the whole world is liable to be destroyed (Tewari, 1989, 233). Any one who is closely associated with woman can never get salvation because a woman destroys Bhakti, salvation and knowledge (Tewari, 1989, 232).

It is indeed very ironical that while Kabir is very critical of married life and blames the woman as an obstruction to the path of God realization his major imagery is presenting himself as a bhakta and seeking God is with in the parameters of the family and husband wife relationship or of a lover and beloved. In many of his poems Kabir uses the imagery of love between the husband and wife as the relationship that should subsist between the individual soul (atma) and God (parmatma (Padavalli, 1-3). He also compares the atma to the devoted wife who eagerly awaits the return of her husband *(khasam)* and thinks of different ways to meet him. A woman visualizes herself as the slave of her beloved and seeks his grace (Tewari, 1989, 10). She pines to meet her beloved and longingly waits to meet him (Tewari, 1989, 143). In fact her eyes have become like stones waiting for him and her tongue is also full of blisters calling out his name (Tewari, 1989, 146). After this long agony and waiting endlessly her luck turns and she finally meets her beloved and sleeps with him (Tewari, 1989, 6). Kabir equates a woman with maya and she is the biggest obstruction to the path of Bhakti. He equates maya and Bhakti to fire which becomes an obstruction in the path of Bhakti (Tewari, 1989, 235). Kabir constantly mentions many ornaments like bangles, anklet *(payal)*, toerings *(bichwa)*, necklace *(har)* earrings *(kundal)* and many other items of toilet like *kajal, sindur* but the purpose of all this for the woman is to decorate herself and wait for her *swami* (husband). He also states that a good wife must win the affection not only of her husband but that of her mother in law, father in law and elder and younger brothers of her husband.

He also contrasts the devoted wife to the prostitute who sells her ware in the market place and tries to entice the innocent and the unwary. He compares maya to this prostitute and she is equated with a sinful being *(papine)*, destroyer *(dakini)* and enticer *(mohini)* (Kabir, Sakhi, 16/1-

41). Association with such woman robs a man of wisdom (*buddhi*) and sense of discrimination (*vivek*). Hence to Kabir there were only two categories of women, those who were devoted wifes, *Pativrata* and those who were prostitutes, or maya.

Many of the Bhakti saints could not rise from the traditional view of looking upon woman as Maya and an impediment to the path of Bhakti. Tulsi also divides woman in to two categories, *uttam* or woman of high qualities and *Neech* or woman of low qualities. The latter had to be kept under strict control and required surveillance. His expression is well known that a drum, a villager, ashudra, an animal and a woman deserve to be beaten (Manas, 2004, 5/59/3). He states that if woman become independent they break loose like a water channel in flood (Manas, 2004, 4/15/4). He does not find the path of knowledge (gyan) suitable for woman. The only path open to them is service.He also states that a woman can get recognition only through the service rendered to her husband and this is the key to her prosperity. (Manas, 2004, 1/110/1).In fact all the women potrayed by Tulsidas like Kausalya, Mandodari, Tara, who are the high quality women are all very devoted to their husbands. It is the low quality women like Manthara, Taraka and Surpanakha who can have a different standard. Tulsi echoes the traditional view of women as stated by Ravana that woman have eight negative qualities-foolhardiness, falsehood, waywardness, lustfulness, cowardice, lack of discrimination, suspiciousness and cruelty (Manas, 2004, 6/16/2).This is again echoed by Shiva when he warns Parvati of the suspicious nature of women (Manas, 2004, 1/51/3). He finds it very difficult to understasnd the waywardness of women as has been stated in the context of Kaikeyi (Manas, 2004, 2/47/8). To him women had eight negative qualities-foolhardiness, false hood, waywardness, lustfulness, cowardice, lack of discrimination, suspiciousness and cruelty (Manas, 2004, 6/16/2). In fact he states that the waywardness of women is such that it is impossible to understand them (Manas, 2004, 2/47/8). Even the Varkari tradition is very critical of women.

Hence by and large Bhakti Movement created an alternative space for a large mass of people. The dominant discourse of the Bhakti movement was articulated by men and what emerges is that this protest against the prevalent social injustices did not address itself to women. It is interesting to note that, while the majority of the Bhakti saints especially, Nirgun are very critical of all institutions and revolted against idolatry, tyranny of castes' and creeds along with temples and rituals, in.the change which they sought, women were not included. Though clamouring for a change and protesting vocally against the prevalent injustices in society, they conveniently left out the women, relegating her to the domestic sphere and only that women became an ideal who was an obedient wife, a *Pativrata* or a *Sati-Savitri*. By and large women had no place in the change that was being sought. It was a change that was being defined by male parameters. Since the change was being sought with in a given structure it did not attempt at changing the power structure of society vis a vis man and women.The Bhakti saints were but depicting a reality of their times. The saints were living in a patriarchal society and holding patriarchal values, which consider a man superior and a woman subordinate. They could not rise from the traditional view of looking upon woman as Maya and an impediment to the path of Bhakti. A women's status was defined in terms of her role in the family vis a vis her husband and she had no worth outside the institution of marriage through which she must serve her husband. Though this attitude is by and large prevalent among both the Sagun and the Nirgun sants, it is more predominant among the Nirgun sants, who were related to the upcoming non agrarian sectors and being associated with tanning, weaving, trading and tailoring where women were slowly being marginalized and the old prejudice against them still continued. We may thus say that the attitude of the male bhaktas towards the women can be best explained by the fact that the bhakti movement did not articulate any demands for propert rigts to women and thus the production relations were sought to be altered in favour of men and women were given an illusory representation of advancement while the same system continued.

References

Altekar, A.S. 1959, *The position of women in Hindu Civilization*, Motilal, Benarasi Das, New Delhi.

Gulati, Saroj, 1985, *Women and Society Northern India in 11th and 12th centuries*, Chanakya Publications, New Delhi.

Kabir, Padavali, 1946 (ed.), Ram Kumar Verma, 5 Vol. Reprint 2003, Hindi Sahitya Sammelan, Prayag, Allahabad.

Sanjukta Gombrich Gupta, 1991, "Women in the Saiva-Sakta ethos", in Leslie Julia (ed), *Roles and rituals of Hindu women*, Painter, London.

Shah, Ahmad, 1977, *The Bijak*-(or the completer works of Kabir) New Delhi.

Manu Smriti (ed.) Max Mueller (1886), With extracts and from its seven commentaries, *Sacred Books of the East*, Vol. 25, Bombay.

Padma, A., 2001, The socio-cultural world of women in medieval Andhra 11th to 13th centuries A.D. Bhartiya Kala Prakashan, Delhi.

Pande, Rekha, 1993, "Kabir, women, family and roles", Agarwal, C.M. (ed), *Dimensions of Indian womanhood*, Almora Book Depot, Almora.

Manas, Ramcharitra, 2004, Geeta Press, Gorakhpur.

Tewari, Paras Nath (ed), 1989, *Kabir Granthavalli*, Raka Prakashan, Allahabad.

Visnu Smriti, 1964, (ed.) Charya, Pandit V. Krishnama, Madras.

8

Alternative Space for Women in the Bhakti Movement

Through the centuries of patriarchal control, women have negotiated many layers and levels of existence working out forms of resistance that are often unnoticed and subtle, though subliminally and powerfully effective. This is done by creating their own space. Women's need to speak in their own ways, define their own truth in voices that revision society, polity, relationships and religion by creating their own space.

Space is gendered and highly politicized as a social resource in all societies. Through out history certain spaces have been culturally, religiously and politically marked as either,' male' or 'female'. The spaces we refer to as public are assumed to be male and for centuries men have excluded women from these spaces where key decisions related to power are deliberated and implemented. Those spaces that are feminized are considered the least important because these were spaces where women functioned through the benevolence of males, but which they never owned. Notions of family, the household remains fundamentally masculine in terms of all the key institutions of society and women are co-opted into these. Women, thus occupy limited spaces in patriarchal societies in their own right as women or as persons. Space was and continues to be defined by male construct in every way conceivable. Space is thus not a neutral territory, it is highly politicized.

The claim that women's place is in the private, at home, is an old one strategy that mobilizes notions of feminity, locates them in the private and imposes an ideology of domesticity through which female are socialized to believe and accept that the narrow male privileging space called 'home' are the most appropriate space for them to spend all their lives in. There are certain clear cut rules as to how women must behave and act here, and this is what distinguishes a respectable decent woman from the other women. Hence women are a constituency that is effected by patriarchy in uniquely gendered ways. When women become articulate about who they are sexually and caste off old patriarchal myths about what a woman can be and what she is not allowed to become, women become powerful to acquire the ability to say no, demand to dictate life in accordance to their own wishes. They are thus able to transcend a given culture by negotiating it and move into a new one. This is exactly what happened in the Bhakti movement from 12th to 18th centuries.

Religion is one of the areas where there is an avenue open for protest but paradoxically, religion is also the one area which is the last to change though the overall socio-economic context has long changed. Thus change occurs in society at different levels in different contexts. In the context, whatever change occurs tradition cannot be destroyed. Therefore old ideas emerge once again from different angles. In the case of Indian woman, the domestically has been reinforced through insistence on following the family tradition, to maintain the household. Thus historians of religion have seen that patriarchy is rooted in the household and therefore the movement always negated the achievements of women outside the household. Here we may point out to a major disagreement based on two assumptions, one being that the Indian family structure did not change, which is a orientalist reading of Indian history and has been refuted, since many communities like Jats, Nayars, Ahirs, etc. had different familial set up and did not confirm to the ideal textual definition of the family as expounded in the sacred texts. The second assumption is that tradition does not play a positive role. The historical experience of Indian women and in particular the saints shows that tradition can play many positive functions to bring about change, particularly when mediated through religion. This assumption is so deeply entrenched in modern day thinking that tradition is often viewed as an obstacle to development whereas tradition in fact can be considered as the labyrinth of development (Dawa Norbu, 1996). The fact that many radical changes occurred in society because of the Bhakti saints reinterpretation of tradition, which shows that tradition when reinterpreted can bring about changes that are in consonance with the socio-economic aspirations.

Many of the women saints sought to escape patriarchy and the demands of domesticity by creating an autonomous space and also not being termed as wayward loose, by going on long pilgrimages to different holy places. This demonstrates the creative use of tradition as both an element of protest and also to carve out some personal space for themselves.

Another creative use of tradition which was later picked up, was the notion of the sacred hymns. Karaikalammaiyar in a hymn asks God Siva, when her sorrows would end. The creative use of a tradition to paucit a relationship between God and audience borrows from the notion of mantra as a sacred verbal sound (Norman Cutler, 1984, 92). Since the mantra is objectively effective the success of the ritual is ensured. Similarly the Tamil hymns replicate this process which is very similar to the sacrificial view of a devotee and a priest uttering mantras and the God bestowing rewards (Norman, 1984, 92). Since this sacrificial view was supposed to by very powerful and socially accessible to certain castes and Brahmins, who conducted these rituals it was illusive to many others. But this model had a validity with powerful patrons and prosperous clients. This imagery was adopted by the bhakti saints and the women, whose songs became very popular to put forward their views and desires. In these songs of the women we see the reworking of the ritual and the musical traditions to respond creatively to the needs of the time. David Kinsley, finds that in many devotional movements, the theoretical harmony between doing one's duty, *(dharma)* and loving the lord, (bhakti) is called into question. There seems to be a tension between the two. The tension is particularly clear in the lives of several women saints who found it difficult and ultimately impossible to reconcile their traditional marriages with their inherent urge to love the Lord. He gives examples of Mahadevi Akka from Karnataka, Lalleswari from Kashmir, Mirabai from Rajasthan and the whole of Krishna mythology with Radha as its central mode of devotion to show how in the lives of these women, devotion to God becomes an alternative to marriage. Crushed and confined to difficult domestic situations these women found an alternative possibility in their devotion. Renouncing marriage and life in the world generally, they directed their passions to heavenly consorts (Kinsley, 1980).

A product of a new environment, the Bhakti ideology served a purpose. Its saints were not idle philosophers or arm chair reformers. They mostly came from lower sections of society and worked for their living. For the women, Bhakti became an outlet. A glance at the writings of these women Bhaktas show that they negotiated patriarchy through Bhakti which provided a space for them. Most of these women were enclutured into a certain culture which was mostly a closed, patriarchal culture, but through this movement a certain space was created for their freedom and mobility.

As in the case of the male Bhaktas we are to search for the historical figures of the women bhaktas we will hit a wall. There is very little information on them. None of these women have been patronized by any court biographers, nor is any religious hagiography available about them from the time they deemed to have in habited. Much of their history has been reconstructed much later by writes and biographers arising from the emergent middle class. Yet many of these women bhaktas go much beyond the shadowy realms of the past and are very much alive to day in popular culture and the day to day life. We have to hence turn to the collective memories and remembrances which are based on their bhajans and poems. It is from these that we can get few glimpses of the lives of these women in medieval times. Most of these women lived during the period from 12th century to 18th centuries. We need to look into their lives once again to see the role of bhakti in it.

Akka Mahadevi was a contemporary of Basavanna, the founder of Virsaiva movement. She was the daughter of a rich merchant in the village of Udutal. She was a great devotee of Siva and initiated into worship at a very early age by an unknown Guru. She grew up into a beautiful young woman and the chieftain of the land named Kausika fell in love with her. Kausiki was an unbeliever and Mahadevi Akka was forced to marry him much against her wishes. Most probably he used coercion and a show of authority to subjugate Akka Mahadevi. Legend goes that she told him that she would leave him if he touched her thrice against her wishes and when he does so she leaves him (Ramanujan, 1985, 112). When she leaves him she breaks all the marital relations as well as all the taboos and walks about naked and finally finds solace in the company of saints. It was these saints who ultimately helped her consummate her love for Siva by arranging a real marriage to him. This was a marriage of her choice. She died in her early twenties becoming one with Siva at Srisaila. (Ramanujan, 1985, 114). Akka is one of the best known poets of Karnataka. The number of her vachanas which can be culled from various sources is approximnatrely 350. Besides these vachanas some songs and two works titled, The vachanas of creation" and Yogantri are in her name (Dabbe, Manushi, 1989, 42).

Lal Ded lived during the fourteenth centuries in Kashmir. She was born in a Brahmin family and was educated at home in her fathers house. She was married at the age of twelve into another Brahmin family surnamed Nica Bhatt at Pimpore. According to the Kashmiri custom she was renamed Padmavati. We have a number of legends which talk about the cruelty meted out to Lal Ded. She endured this torture for twelve years and finally left home. Again it was Bhakti which provided her a space to renounce her domestic hell. Padmavati is supposed to have danced naked singing in frenzy. She now came to be known as Lal Ded, Lal in Kashmiri referring to the lower part of her belly, which increased in size and hung loose over her pubic region.

Mira bai lived during the end of fifteenth and beginning of sixteenth century. She belonged to the Rajput aristocracy of Rajasthan. She was the daughter of Ratan Singh and his wife, Vir Kunwari of Medtiya of Rathor clan. Mira's paternal grandfather Jodhaji was the founder of Jodhapur. Her paternal grandfather, Dudaji had conquered Medata city and 360 villages around it. He gave Miras father Ratan Singh 12 villages of which the central village was Kudki. Mira was born in this fort. Miras paternal family were Vaishnavas and hence Mira inherited Vaisnava Bhakti as part of her family legacy.

Tradition has it that as a young girl Mira pestered her mother to tell her who was her bridegroom when she saw a marriage procession. To avoid her persistent questioning Mira's mother pointed at a statue of Krishna and told her that this was her bridegroom. Mira hence considered herself wedded to Krishna. When she grew up she was married into the royal family of Sisodia Rajputs of Mewar. The identity of her husband is not well established. Some identify him to be Maharaj Kumbh and others with Bhojraj the son of the famous Rana Sanga. Most probably the marriage was a part of the political alliance between Rators of Jodhpur with the Ranas of Mewar. Here as elsewhere in Rajasthan, the structure of the *Kul* and the *Bhaiyad* (brotherhood) were closely linked to the system of political power and sovereignity. The *kul* included all those related to a common ancestor by ties of male blood. The *Bhaiyad* was composed of the sons and brothers of the rulers who held power over land conquered by them. (Mukta, 1994, 59). Legend has it that when Mira arrived in her inlaws house she was asked to worship godess Shakti for the well being of her husband and his family and she refused. Naturally her husband and inlaws were very angry. Mira even refused to consummate her marriage regarding her self already wedded to Krishna. This was an open defiance and her inlaws could not tolerate this. There were various attempts at her life and finally she left the palace and started staying independently in a temple in the palace compound, but here too she did not find solace because of the disapproval of her Bhakti. She then started wandering around in the company of other saints and visited many temples and palces associated with Krishna. She went to Dakur, then Vrindawan and finally Dwarka. According to legend Akbar and Tansesn travelled to Dwarka to visit her and Tansen sang one of her Bhajans.

Tradition has it that when she was staying at the Ranchhorji temple on the sea coast of Dwarka, her natal and marital families sent a group of priests as emmisarries to persuade her to return. When she refused the Brahmin priests started a fast unto death outside the temple. Mira was now in a delimma and did not want to have Brahmin blood on her hand. She then composed *Hari tum haro jan ke pir* and entered the temple and is said to have absorbed in the statue of Krishna. This is interpreted by many scholars as emerging from the western door of the temple which faces the sea and having leapt into it (Kishwar, Manuhsi, 1989, 85). Mira's Bhakti becomes an escape from the hatred and domination which underlay the Rajput system of marriage. It enunciated the principal of love in an age and a society which was marked by war, vendetta and the rising power of the state.

Mukta Bai of Maharashtra lived during the thirteenth century and was the sister of Nivritti, Jnandev and Sopan who are considered the founders of the Varkari tradition. Their father was a Brahmin and a disciple of Ramanand but he was ostricised by the Brahmin community because after having taken sanyas he reverted back to a householders life. He then committed suicide. Though Mukata Bai according to tradition was a beautiful and intelligent girl she did not marry but lived with her brothers. She is said to have composed over 100 abangs. She died at the young age of eighteen.

Janabai was a contemporary of Muktabai and was a maid servant in the house of Janadev. Not much is known about her except her life as depicted in the abhangs. She talks about her day to day work and how she is helped in this by her God.

The next important saint from Mahàrashtra was Bahina Bai. She lived during he seventh century and is the only woman saint who has written an autobiography. She was born in a poor Brahmin family of Deigoan. When she was three years old she was married to Ratnakar Pathak who was thirty years old and was a priest and an astrologer. For him this was a second marriage. At the age of seven Bahina Bai came to Kolhapur to live with her husband and his parents. Here too she had to suffer a lot due to her Bhakti and she is the only woman saint who remains married through out her life. Her life eases only when her husband gets converted to her way of thinking. She also wrote her *abhangas* in the popular Marathi *ovi* meter, which is used in songs when women go about their daily work like doing the household chores, grinding the corn or husking the grain.

A common theme which runs through out the lives of these women is the restricted spaces in their married homes. Suddenly after marriage they do not have any freedom and come into conflict with their in laws family when they want to lead a life according to their wishes. There are attempts at trying to imprison them, lock them and even poison them. Mahadevi Akka says,

"I have Maya for mother in law

The world for father in law

Three hrothers in law, like tigers.

And the hushands thoughts

Are full of laughing women.

No God this man.

And I cannot cross this sister in law

But I will

Give this wench the slip

And go cuckold my husband with hara my lord

My mind is my maid

By her kindness I join my lord

My utterly heautiful lord

From the mountain peaks

My lord,.white as Jasmine

And I will make him my good hushand (Ramanujan, 1985, 141).

According to Hindu tradition a husband is supposed to be God and irrespective of all his shortcomings a woman is expected to worship him.

Even Lal Ded had a very difficult married life. Many legends talk about the cruel treatment meted out to her by her mother in law. She was scolded on the slighted pretext. She was not allowed to spin yarn on the spinning wheel, though legend has it that she spun yarn as fine as the lotus stalk. She was often ridiculed for not doing anything right and often taunted as to what she had learnt at her fathers house. We have among her sayings,

They may kill a big sheep or a tender lamb,

Lalla will have her lump of stone all right (Kaul, Parimoo, 1978, 10)

She was harassed at her inlaws place, and most probably this was due to her not following the wishes of her in laws family blindly. Another-saying attributed to her states,

I did not give birth to a child nor lay in confinemen (Kaul, Parimoo, 1978, 11).

Since she did not behave in the expected manner, she was tortured. She was served stones in her food and also accused of infidelity to her husband. She however accepts this because,

One has to bear lightning, flashes and thunderbolts

One has to put up with pitch darkness at midday (Kaul, Parimoo, 1978, 13)

Mira's life is better known when compared to the other women Bhaktas. When she got married and came to her in laws family she was accused of not behaving properly like that of a royal woman.

I have lost the honour of the royal family

People say I have gone astray with the sadhus

I constantly rise up.

go to Gods temple and dance

Snapping my fingers

I don't follow the norms

As an oldest daughter in law

I have thrown away the veil (Chaturvedi, 1983, 244)

Her family tries to restrict her movements and they even lock her in.

O friend I cannot live without the delight giver

Mother in law fights, my sister in law teases

The Rana remains angry

They have a watchman sitting at the door

And a lock fastened on it

Why should I give up my first love

My only love

Mira's God is the lifter of mountains

O nothing else pleases me. (Chaturvedi, 1983, 42)

When things get out of hand there is an attempt at her life, because she has brought nothing but disgrace to the Rajput family in which she is wed.

Friends I am completely dyed in this Krishna colour

I drank the cup of immortal bliss

My inebriation never goes away

However many millions of ways I try

Rana sent me a basket with a snake in it

And Mira put it around her neck

Smiling, Mira hugged it, as if it were a

String of new pearls.

Rana took a cup of poison, "Find Mira (he said)

Give it to her

She drank it like charnamrita

Singing the praise of Govinda

I drank the cup of his name nothing else pleases me now. (Chaturvedi, 1983, 40)

Further she states,

Meera danced with ankle bells on her feet

People said Meera was mad

My mother in law said, I had ruined

the family reputation

Rana sent me a cup of poison and

Mira drank it laughing. (Chaturvedi, 1983, 36).

Bahina bai writes in her auto biography,

I was now eleven years of age but I had not had one moments of joy (Abbot, 1929).

Again she states,

I had no independence and my wishes had no effect. I was very depressed in spirits. My daily life was full of troubles. (Abbot, 1929)

She recognises her limitations as a woman.

Possessing a woman's body and myself being subject to others, I was not able to carry out my desire to discard all worldlv things. (Abbot, 1929)

For Bihnas husband this was his second marriage. At the age of seven Bihna Bai left her birthplace and came to Kolhapur along with her husband and parents.

When Bihna was ten years old her parents received a cow and calf as alms and she became very attached to the calf.

If the calf was not at sight, I was troubled. I felt like a fish out of water. Whether I was grinding or pounding grain, or carrying water, I was unhappy, though with others, without the calf. I was the only one to feed it with grass and with out me it was unhappy. (Abbot, 1929, 16)

When Bihna bai and her parents went to attend a *Kirtan* of a well known sant, Jiyaram Swami, she took her calf along with her and when people objected to the calf being in the crowded room, it was driven out. The calf stood outside and cried and Bihna sobbed inside the room. Jiyaram Swami, then had the calf brought inside and blessed both of them. Ratnakar Pathak was very angry when he got to hear about this incident. *He seized me by my hair and beat me to his hearts content.* (Abbot, 1929, 13). Her feet and hand were tied. The calf refused to eat food and died twelve days later. This shocked Bihna and she became unconscious for three days and wished, *I would also accompany the life of my calf* (Abbot, 1929, 8).

In this unconscious state in her dreams she saw Vithoba and accepted Tukaram as her Guru. Naturally her husband did not like this, because Tukaram came from the lower caste and they were Brahmins and custom and sciptures forbade any contact with the lower castes.

My husband began to say vile are Brahmins. We should spend our time in the study of the Vedas. What is all this? The shudra Tuka, seeing him in dreams. My wife is v ruined by all this. (Her husband also gave her bodily suffering on account of this. (Abbot, 1929, 3)

Ratnakar Pathak now started contemplating of leaving his wife,

Who cares for the feeling of bhakti. I will abandon her and go into the forest, for people are going to bow down to her, while she regards me worthless as a straw.

Who will show respect to me in her presence. (Abbot, 1929, 3, 4, 5).

In some of her abhangas she comes across as a rebellious and bold person and her refusal to abandon her Bhakti and her search for truth.

The Vedas cry aloud, the puranas shout

No good comes to woman

I was born with a woman's body

How am I to attain the truth?

They are foolish, seductive, deceptive-

Any connections with a woman is disastrous

Bahina says," If a woman's body is so harmful,

How in this world will I reach the truth?

Hence the common thread that runs through the lives of all these women is the treatment meted out to them in their inlaws house at the hands of husbands, inlwas or sister in laws. Now it is Bhakti which provides them a space and to move out of this house and in the process they get their independence. For all these women bhaktas the rejection of the power of the male figure whom they were tied to in subordinate relationship became the terrain for struggle, self assertion and alternative seeking (Manushi, 1989)

But now bhakt offers a choice and Mahadevi has the courage to state that this husband of hers is no God and she would make her Lord God as a good husband. She also talks about the constant conflict between her duties at home and her Bhakti.

Husband inside

I over outside

I can't manage them hoth

This world and the other

I cant manage them both.

O Lord white as Jasmine

I cannot hold in one hand

Both the round nut

And the long bow (Ramanujan, 1985, 127).

The first and the foremost thing which many of these women do is to cast off all notions of decency and modesty which are the lychpin of the patriarchal society, which neatly divides the respectable family women from the other women, who is not respectable. Akka Mahadevi sheds her clothes and walks naked.

Brother you have come

drawn by the beauty

of these bilklowing breasts, this brimming youth

I am no woman brotheer no whore (Susan Daniel, 1991, 80).

Janabai states,

Let me not be sad because I am born a woman

In this world many saints suffer in this way She further states,

Cast off all shame

And sell yourself

In the market place

Then alone

You can hope to reach the Lord (Vilas Sarang, 1991, 83)

Meera also states,

O my companion there is nothing to be ashamed of now

Since I have been seen dancing openly

In the day I have no hunger

At night I am restless and cannot sleep

Leaving these troubles behind I go to the other side (Keay, 1991, 93)

Akka has a total disdain for the earthly husband, much in contrast to what she has been taught by scriptures and told by tradition because the earthly husband decays and dies.

I love this handsome one

He has no death

Decay or form

No place or side

No end nor birthmark

I love him O mother listen

So the lord white as jasmine is my husband

Take these husbands who die

And decay and feed them

To your kitchen fires (Ramanujan, 1985, 134)

Meera comes out in open defiance.

If Sisodiya is angry, what will he do to me.

I will sing the virtues of Govind my friend

If Rana is angry, he will stay in his own country

If Hari is angry I will wither friend.

I dont care for worldly position (Chaturvedi, 1983, 35).

Meera has no faith in the worldly marriage and prefers being wed to her Hari.

Friends marriage of this world are false

They are wiped out of existence

Wed my indestructible one

The serpent death cannot devour (Chaturvedi, 1983, 194).

Soon Mira became free of her worldly burdens when her husband dies. Now she openly started associating with like-minded people who were involved with bhakti. Her family did not like this, because Mira was breaking tradition and moving out of purdha and by talking and associating with other males, she was bringing shame to the family.

I have found a guru in Raidas

He has given me the pill of knowledge

A women is seen by nature *(svabhav)* as not only pollutent but also potentially dangerous because of her sexuality. Therefore in the family her sexuality should always be controlled and she should be subservient to the male authority. Her sexuality is seen as a source of prosperity when it is active but it has to be controlled by her husband in any other situation and she must totally repress it.

Akka Mahadevi now risen above the body and has no need for any jewels and clothes, which in her earlier life were a very important parameter of her status Vis, a vi her husband.

You can confiscate

Money in hand

Can you confiscate?

The body's glory

To this shameless girl

Where is the need for cover and jewels. (Ramanujan, 1985, 129)

She now has no other ambition except to join her lord.

O Shiva

When shall I

Crush you on my pitcher breasts

O lord white as jasmine

When do I join you

Stripped of body's shame

And my hearts modesty.

She looks upon all men except her lover Shiva as her brothers and dissuades them from coming near proclaiming that she is neither a woman nor a whore.

You have come seeing the beauty

Of rounded breasts and the

Fullness of youth brother

Brother I am not a woman

Brother I am not a whore

Brothers seeing me again and again

For whom have you come?

Look brother any man

Other than the Lord who is white as Jasmine

Is a face I cannot stand (Zydenbos, 1989).

She shows a lot of firmness and courage in her wanderings all alone by herself. There is a hint of being harassed but she remains pure for her lover.

Do not worry

That I am completely alone

What ever they do I will not be afraid

I will eat dried leaves

I will sleep on a sword

O lord white as jasmine

If you want to examine me

I will offer my body and soul to you

And be pure. (Zydenbos, 1989, 42)

It is not that the path of Bhakti is easy. There are lots of dilemmas and struggles. Akka Mahadevi states,

The stream behind the river in front

Tell me which way to go

The pond behind the net infront

Tell me where safety is (Zydenbos, 1989, 42)

However thesc moments of delimma and confusion are very few in comparison to her pain and sufferings

My restless mind has been turned upside down

The whirling wind has become

Scorching

The moonlight has become the heat

For Meera too the pains of home become easy due to her bhakti.

Finally she leaves her home and goes out in search of her real home. There is nothing which can now make her turn back.

Rana to me your slander is sweet

Some praise me, some blame me, I go the other way

On the narrow path, I found God's people

What should I turn back for? (Chaturvedi, 1983, 240)

In her wanderings Mira had to face harassment and disapproval. She has a number of songs which talk about people of the world laughing at her, thinking her to be mad blaming her, even regarding her a destroyer of families. Mira however just ignore these and she is said to have travelled to Dakaur, Vrindavan and Dwarka all place associated with Krishna. Her lover Krishna now becomes the centre of existence.

I go to Giridhar's house

Giridhar is my real lover

I see his beauty and am allured

When nightfall's, I go and when day breaks I come back

Night and day I play with him and

Please him in every way (Tirpathi, 1979, 83).

There is a restlessness in her for her beloved.

Friend the dark ones glance is like love's dagger

It stuck me and

I grew restless

I lost all sense of my body

Pain spreads through my body

My mind is intoxicated

I have found few friends

All of them are mad.......

The chakor loves the moon, the moth by the lamp is burnt

The fish dies without 'water-dear indeed is such love

How can I live without seeing him. My heart is not at rest.
(Manushi, 1989, 89)

Bihna's husband also started thinking of leaving her due to her involment in Bhakti. But then it is discovered that Bihna was three months pregnant and so her husband could not abandon her. Meanwhile Bihna also decided that it was her duty to serve her husband first rather than Vithal or Tukaram, because if her husband left her she would be ruined completely. However, soon her husband became seriously ill and Bihna nursed him very devotedly. He regarded his illness as a punishment for having insulted Vithal and Tukaram. So after he recovered he realized his mistake and came around to Bihnabai's path and they moved to Dehu where Tukaram lived and accepted him as their guru. It was only after her husband came around to her path of bhakti did Bahina's life become easy.

Hence it is Bhakti which gives these women the moral courage to stand against patriarchal political authority and create an alternate space for themselves. They defy patriarchal norms of marriage and walk out (except in the case of Bahina bai). In Hinduism devotion of the wife to her husband and her complete merger in him is the highest aim.

even if the husband was a fiend. The women in Bhakti found the courage to defy this and either walked out of their houses and the restricted spaces of patriarchal control or changed their husbands to their way of thinking. It is interesting to note that, while the majority of the Bhakti saints especially, Nirgun are very critical of all institutions and revolted against idolatry, tyranny of castes' and creeds along with temples and rituals, in the change which they sought, women were not included. At this time many of the women saints were leading non-traditional, non-conformist lives and talking of individual freedom. Many of the Bhakti saints, though clamoring for a change and protesting vocally against the prevalent injustice in society, conveniently left but the women, relegating her to the background. She had no place in the change that was being sought. It was a change that was being defined by male parameters. Since the change was being sought within a given structure, it did not attempt at changing the power structure vis a vis the family. The Bhakti saints did not attempt at reorganisation of social relationships within the family. There was every attempt at marginalising the women and pushing them back into the domestic sphere and only that women became an ideal who was an obedient wife, a Pativrata or a Sati-Savitri. At this time the women Bhakta negotiated patriarchy and created an alternative space for them selves.

References

Abbot, Justin E. 1929, *Bihna Bai*, A translation of her autobiography and verses, New Jersey, USA.

Altekar, A.S. 1959, *The position of women in Hindu Civilization*, Motilal, Benarasi Das, New Delhi.

Chaturvedi, Parshuram, 1983, *Mira Bai ki Padavalli*, Hindi Sahitya Sammelan, Allahabad.

Dabbe, Vijaya and Roberyt Zydenbos, 1989, Akka Mahadevi, *The women Bhaktas*, Manushi, New Delhi.

Dawa Norbu, 1996, "Cultural Pre-conditions for Development", in Baidyanath Saraswati (ed.) *Interface of cultural identity development,* IGNCA & D.K. Print World, Delhi.

Gulati, Saroj 1985, *Women and Society Northern India in 11th and 12th centuries,* Chanakya Publications, New Delhi.

Kaul, Jayalal, 1978, *Lal Ded,* Sahitya Academy, New Delhi.

Kinsley, David, 1980, Devotion as an alternative to marriage in the lives of some Hindu women devotees, *Journal of Asian and African Studies,* Vol. XV, No. 1-2.

Kishwar, Madhu and Ruth Vanita, 1989, Poison to Nectar, the life and work of Meera Bai *The women Bhaktas,* Manushi, New Delhi.

Manu Smriti ed. Max Mueller, 1886, With extracts and from its seven commentaries, *Sacred Books of the East,* Vol. 25, Bombay.

Mukta, Parita, 1994, reprint, 1997, *Upholding the common life-The community of Mirabai,* Oxford University Press, New Delhi.

Norman, Cutler, 1984, "The devotees experience of religion-the sacred Tamil Hymns", *History of religoins,* Vol. 24, No. 2, University of Chicago Press, USA.

Parimoo, B.N., 1978, *The assent of self,* Motilal Banarsidas, Delhi.

Ramanujan, A.K. 1985, *Speaking of Siva,* Hamondsworth.

Thapar, Romila, 1973, *The Past and Prejudice,* Publication Division, Government of India.

Vionu Smriti, 1961, (ed.) Charya, Pandit V. Krishnama, Madras.

Zydenbos, Robert, 1989, Translation of Akka Mahadevi *The Women Bhaktas,* Manushi, New Delhi.

9

Conclusions

Through out the course of Indian history there have been a large number of religious reform movements which have brought in many new issues to the forefront and questioned the existing hierarchy. Bhakti Movement was one such movement that brought the creative wisdom of a wide variety of marginalized men and women as an attempt to create an alternative space. It would be an understatement to overlook the impact of this movement on the religious doctrines, rituals and values, popular beliefs and culture of the people in medieval times. It is a truism that great upheaveals and diversities in addition to the intellectual fervour that they create, like the bhakti movement are relevant even today. This movement is a very good example of the unity in diversity in Indian religion in the sense that we see so much of borrowings and adaptations from different regions, fusion of Sanskritic and folk religions and many streams of thought.

It was only in 19th century that a monolith definition of Hinduism was put forward. In the confrontation between the Colonizer and the Colonized it was the western standards and Christianity which became the basis to evaluate Hinduism. There was an inability to view Hinduism on its own terms and conditions. Attempts were made to find notions of monotheism, a salvation and notions of after life of Christianity in Hinduism. Hinduism to the Colonial administration became an imagined religion of a vast majority of the population. This was something which never existed in the consciousness of the Indian people them selves. We also see here that a literal reading reduced many movements to philosophical excercises like Buddhism was talked of in terms of a philosophy of the six systems and later scholars have viewed Buddhism as a social movement. Similarly in the case of bhakti, it would be puerile to debate whether bhakti was just a social movement as there were philosophical redefinitions of all relationships and beyond. Thus to reduce bhakti either as a purely socio-religious movement or to study it under the domain of history of ideas would be a reductionist exercise out of which we have to come out.

The transition from the Company's commercial activities to direct rule in the late 18th century also marked a period of colonial self questioning, with in the British society. It was in this long process that it made various political and ideological adjustments to justify its rescue of India. Many of the texts of this period represented India as a site of eastern decadence and despotism breeding corruption. It was also during this time that the first generation of British Civil servants of India like Sir William Jones, and H.T. Colebrooke discovered an Indian classical past as a Hindu golden age or a pristine Aryan society which had fallen into decline and decadence. The goals of both these visions of India were to lead the way to the 19th century civilizing mission as the corner stone of British Empire. The first narratives built up certain generalizations and subsequent generalizations followed in this direction and are only now begining to be deconstructed.

These scholars went at great length to show that the religion practiced by the Hindus was a highly evolved and questioned the colonial assumption that all cultures outside the Christian pale were primitive, tribalistic and animistic. Many of these scholars did not try to understand what

Hinduism meant to millions of Indians. They invariably made a distinction between the popular Hinduism which they did not deem worthy of study and the philosophical Hinduism which they tried to define as a set of hard and fast doctrinal propositions and to place in current theories about the nature of history of religions. In the process they created Hinduism in their own image. These scholars brought in a new concept of the Hindu golden age as a legacy for the rising Indian intelligentsia along with the evolution of a new historical consciousness among Indian for recovering their forgotten past. This western attribution of unity to Hinduism strategically helped the anti colonial Indians create a national identity in religion. Even for the Indian intellectuals intent on purifying Hinduism, this newly defined religion gave them an identity of modernity and yet retaining their roots in indigenous traditions. Hence none questioned the creation of Hinduism and this became an entrenched category which could be used to buttress contradictory statements.

Hinduism can never be viewed as one monolith tradition on account of the various accretions, practices and diversities. Hinduism is polytheistic, monotheistic and monistic. Many Gods and Goddesses are worshipped. Visnu, Shiva and Devi are the principal deities but they have many forms and there are many more deities. A historical gaze at Hinduism shows that there have been various independent reform movements which questioned the authority of the Vedas and created alternative spaces. The Bhakti movement was one such movement in Medieval India which is under emphasied in Indian history as the informants to the Company were mainly the Pandits from Benares who were not favourably disposed to bhakti.

India witnessed significant socio-economic changes during the medieval times brought about by interrelated processes like large scale agrarian expansion and emergence of strong regional kingdoms which gave rise to new social groups which could not fit into traditional hierarchy. The newly emerging social groups attempted to redefine their position and status with in the given traditional hierarchy and spearheaded a movement articulating their demands for restructuring the existing order. By declaring that God dwells in each individual and one could attain God through faith these saints brought religion to the downtrodden and henceforth marginalized sections of society. This movement is referred to as the Bhakti movement.

Bhakti is a religious concept and means devotion and surrender to a personal God, a God who is conceived as a supreme God for salvation. Though this doctrine is traced to the Brahmanical tradition, in the religious scripture of Geeta, it was in the south that between the seventh and tenth centuries that this movement became broad based and acquired a huge social support. This was primarily due to the efforts of the Alwars and Nayanars, the two sects in south India who transformed bhakti into a popular religion and in the process incorporated the core ideas and forms from a popular base. After them it was the Acharyas who provided a philosophical basis for this movement. The Bhakti movement is a very good example of unity in diversity in Indian culture because though this movement occurred in many parts of India and there was much regional difference among the various movements, yet there was a common thread running through out this movement because all the saints in their own ways questioning the existing system of religion and promoted religious egalitarianism. The Bhakti saints wanted the religious space to open up and provide an alternative space to the existing one. This task was carried forward by the Acharyas in South India and they provided a philosophical base to the doctrine of Bhakti. Ramanuja was the first of the Acharyas who widened the social base of the movement. Ramananda and Vallabha charya also widened the base of the Bhakti movement.

Though Bhakti as a concept was very ancient in India it could not take roots in Northern India earlier because prior to the Turkish conquest in India the socio-religious milieu was dominated by the Rajput Brahmin alliance which was hostile to any heterodox movement. The Turkish conquest brought this supremacy to an end and paved the way for the rise of a large number of hetrodox movements.

The coming of the Turks saw feudal oppression being intensifies much more because now there was a clear mechanism to extract the surplus and pass it on to the ruling elite through the Iqta system. Though the Turkish ruling class lived in the towns the extraction of the surplus from the rural areas brought in enormous resources in their hands. This along with a spread of feelings of regionalism prepared the base for the Bhakti movement.

The medieval period is charaterised by the rise of a large number of regional states which is a political expression of the emergence of regional elites. The period between thirteenth to sixteenth century was that of the decline of an all powerful state and the rise of a number of provincial and regional states. In north India the dominant features of the period between 7th to 12th centuries have been identified as the growing weakness of the state, the growth of the power of the local landed elites and their decentralizing authority by acquiring greater administrative, economic and political roles, the decline of towns, the setback to trade, especially long distance trade and allocation of land to the Brahmins in larger proportion than before. This was also a period in Northern India of the rise of Rajputs. The Rajputs accepted the support of the Brahmins and accepted their claims to superiority by a tacit alliance with those who controlled land and possessed political authority. In fact the Rajputs paid the price of their elevation from barbarianism to civilization by accepting and confirming their claims of superiority. A large number of land grants were also given for the building and maintenance of temples. The growth of magnificent temples all over India is an index not only of a resurgence of Hinduism but even more of the newly acquired power and wealth of the Brahmins.Incidentally the sacred geography of the temples leads us to some broad generalizations like the concentration of temples in the favourable, well watered ecozones with a high density of population characterized by larges scale land grants, dense population and a Brahmin presence. The Brahmins enjoyed many other powers and privileges. They were appointed as Raj-Purohits and often asked to advice on various matters of dharma and polity.The advent of Islam in north India and the overthrow of the powerful Rajput states by the Turks towards the end of 12th century paved the way for the growth of Bhakti as a popular movement, for it ended the Rajput Brahmin alliance which was a big obstacle in the growth of popular hetrodox movements. The economic forces unleashed through this change gave a further impetus to this movement.

On the economic front the Delhi Sultanate witnessed a number of changes like a superior economic organization characterized by large scale urbanization, increase in craft production and alternations in agrarian conditions. The technological co-relates of this process can be see in in Seri culture, carpet weaving on the verticle loom, introduction of the spinning wheel (charkha) in the cotton textile sector, the Persian wheel, the introduction of paper, the appearance of magnetic compass as an aid to navigation and the invention of accurate time keeping devices for the regulation of economic activity

In this changed context which unleashed these forces there were opposing trends seen in the nature of denying space to the newly emergent artisanal class by the Brahmans. In order to maintain their status quo, complex rites and rituals were practiced and those that did not fit into the traditional four castes were degraded and devoid of any social prestige and all the privileges which were the exclusive domain of the Brahmin such as recitation of the Vedas, offering of sacrifices to the fire. This was a period when Jainism and Buddhism had practically disappeared and saw the revival of the orthodox Brahmins who emerged supreme. They alone understood Sanskrit in which the ancient religious texts were produced and this made the performance of various rites and rituals their monopoly.

One can see a similar kind of material base in the Southern region also which gave an impetus to the Bhakti movement.This region in the medieval period witnessed many transformations in the politico-economic and socio-cultural spheres. Politically, the state gradually transformed into a multi-centered power structure, fragmented and segmented at different levels, owing to the extensive growth of socio-religious, philanthropic and service tenures, which operated with in the matrix of tax-tribute–plunder. The dharmic kingship of ancient times transcended into ritual kingship, further legitimized by the performance of *Dana*, *dakshina*, *titha*, *darshana* etc. Deforestation and land reclamation during the Kakatiyan and Vijaynagara times contributed to the growth of brahminical institutions, *brahmadeyas* and *devabhogas* on the one hand and the growth of artisanal activity and agricultural expansion on the other. This resulted in the consolidation of the peasant and non-peasant groups like the merchants and artisans into guilds; the caste cum professional organizations, but also the temple as an institution that controlled the power structure of state and society.

Increasing external and internal trade during this period coincided with urban growth and establishment of an alliance between the peasant farmer and the trader. Bulk assignments of paddy, sugar and a variety of grains and spices came to the towns under the aegis of both the peasant farmer and the trader. Trade brought in wealth which was redeployed into urban centers and into the temples.

Many of the donations made by the rich merchants covered the cost of the temple ritual and food. The oil or ghee used in the rituals as well as flowers and aromatics were supplied by the merchants, as well as textile and clothing.Hence the sacred and the economic geography coincided and as a result of patronage the nearness to the temple increased the social mobility of the merchants while also setting them above the other artisans and farmers.

Tracing the beginnings of Bhakti Movement to the 7th century, Tamil country, we see a great religious revival in every part of South India with the two-fold intention of eradicating the influence of popular creeds of Buddhism and Jainism on the one hand and to popularize the new mode of salvation against the monopoly of Brahmins. The emphasis now shifted to the devotion and the use of mantras for purification from a purely sacrificial religion with a narrow social base. It was emphasized that these two aspects were accessible to all and could be used even by the lowly and unlearned to gain salvation. This new concept of Bhakti brought religion closer to the masses by engaging them and making them as active participants both ritually and also in socio-economic terms. The separation of the Vaisnava cult from Saivism and its development as a distinct sect was greatly due to Vaishnava saints or Alwars is another development of the Bhakti movement after the downfall of Jainism.

With the coming of the Acharyas there is a new epoch in the history of Sri-Vaisnavism. The Acharya parampara seems to have begun in the first half of the 9th century A.D. The Acharyas were learned in Sanskrit as well as Tamil and they tried to interpret the essence of Vedas and Upanishads in terms of Tamil Prabandhams. They combined the gyan and karma with bhakti for realizing god. All the Acharyas were orthodox Brahmins who discharged their duties strictly. They encouraged the study of Vedas, performance of rituals and other temple festivals, strictly according to Vaisnava Agamas but at the same time they also introduced the study of the recitation of *Prabandhams* (the hymns of the Alwars) in public and private worship.In the ebbs and flows of the Bhakti movement, Ramanuja's actions saw an effort to regain the vigor of Vaisnavism by giving it a solid philosophical grounding on the one hand and also restoring certain moral and spiritual practices of earlier times to avoid the grossly erotic and sensuous practices under the garb of mysticism. It was this blending of the ritual form and the philosophical content that revitalized the Vaishnava Bhakti under the ageis of Ramanuja.

Ramanuja's limited attempt at integrating different castes under SriVisnavism could not continue for long due to the brahmanical control of temples and temple lands. Entry of the lower castes was not conceded though they were provided with certain occupations in the lower level administration.

By the later half of the 13th century Sri Vaisnavism split into two subsects namely the Vadagalai or the northern school and Tengalai the southern school or parabandhic subsect. This was a reflection of the tensions on the subject of primacy over Tamil and Sanskrit and the Vadagalai sect that was more brahmanical subscribed to a Sanskritic pattern. Reflecting the primacy of the Tamil language was the Tengalai sect a that was more revolutionary and willing to accommodate the new changes. It made its doctrine easily accesible to all people including the lower castes. This sect developed to a great extent under the Vijaynagara rulers.

In the Tamil country, the supremacy of the Saivaites was unquestioned as we see the rise of the nayanars and their subsequent flowering under the patronage of the Cholas.The 63 nayanars drawn from all castes and mainly from the Brahmana and Vellala castes inaugurated a spree of temple building in the Chola dominions which became the institutional base for the dissemination of Bhakti and was also an organization that oversaw the reordering of society

A branch of the Saivism which became very popular in North western parts of Karnataka and was opposed to the temple was Vir Saivism under the leadership of Basavvana around 12th century. This movement assumes a lot of significance because it created an alternate space against the then hierarchical social structures of brahmanical superiority.In Karnataka the support of the urban moneyed class was particularly relevant to the Vir saivas, who rejected public worship of images, discouraging there by the large-scale employment of professional religious priests. The absence of landgrants to the Vir Saiva monks would also suggest their greater dependence on moneyed elite. Even in the 1980's most of the Lingayat came from the three commercial districts of Karnataka, Dharwar, Bijapur and Belgaum.

Inspite of its zeal and philosophy to bring about a social change, the Virsaiva sect did not make much headway in Andhra. The influence of this sect was limited more to the Telengana region,as there was no social base of artisans in Andhra as large as in the neighbouring regions. Vir Saivism had declined in Karnataka and it was no longer as radical in its ideology as the earlier phase and had become very divided and exclusive. Though the literature of the Vir Saiva faith appears to be revolutionary, the propagators of this faith were unable to put forth their ideals into practice. Infact Mallikarjuna Pandita continued to wear his sacred thread. Thus their revolutionary ideology was mostly confined to literature. This faith in Andhra took a very mild form of Aradhya sect and in no time merged with the Vedic religion.

Bhakti had originated in south India and it had then spread to different parts of India. There was a philosophical and ideological link between the southern school of Bhakti and Bhakti as it spread to different parts of India. In north India one can see this movement in two streams, the monotheistic movement and the Vaisnava movement. The two main proponets of the monotheistic movement in North were Kabir and Nanak. Kabir was a follower of Ramananda, who was a disciple of Ramanuja and hence one can see an ideological and philosophical connection between south and North India.

The 14th century was a period of regeneration. Under the Khiljis and Tughluqs, the narrow Turkish domination was replaced by a ruling class which had a broader social base among the muslims. However the 15th century was again a period of political disintegration. The invasion of Timur in 1399, had laid a heavy blow to the stability of the

Delhi sultanate. The Sayyids came to power for a short interval and then the Lodi's who were Afghans took over the reigns of the kingdom ending the long rule of the Turks. Sufism was very popular during this period and Kabir was very much influenced by this as well as by the Nathpanthis who believed in Yogic practices.

It was in 15th century that Kabir established a seperate identity of the Nirgun stream of Bhakti as against the Sagun stream led by Chaitanya, Tulsidas, Meera and Surdas. Kabir a deciple of Ramananda, can rightly be called the originator of the medieval school of nirgun Bhakti of a formless God.The beginnings made by Kabir were carried further by Nank, Raidas and Dadu.

After North, the north western part of the country also witnessed the influence of Bhakti tradition resulting in the emergence of Sikhism in Punjab due to the spread of the teachings of Guru Nanak. The main principles of Sikhism evolved out of the contemporary heterodox tradition in the background of Hindu cultural context.

In Bengal Vaishnavism began to get popularity due to the effort of Sri Chaitanya. He popularised bhakti through the Gandiya Vaisnava school and broadened its base to include social reforms.

In Maharashtra it was Bhagavat Puran which was the basic inspiration behind the movement. It was the Varkari tradition that was popular here. The Bhakti movement in Maharashtra has to be viewed against the background of the lack of an indigenous mercantile community and the traditional base of its chiefly agrarian economy. The village economy was largely self sufficient with a variant of the Jajmani system, known as *balutedari*. The saints of the Varkari movement were drawn from different sections of the society. Jnaneswar and Eknath were Brahmins, Tukaram and Namdev came from peasant and artisan classes and Cokhamela was a Mahar. Hence the Bhakti philosophy which provided them an alternative space for egalitarian devotional, away from the harsh realities of caste had a powerful appeal. However many of these saint poets were not very vocal about the Varna-dharma. In fact many of them compromised and accepted their existing status instead seeking an egalitarian world in the realm of the sacred.

In Kashmir it was Saiva Bhakti which flourished and it was made popular by a women saint Lalded. Lal Ded lived during the fourteenth centuries in Kashmir. Her place in the Bhakti pantheon is largely on account of her rational approach on many topics that are handed down to us in the form of songs.

In Gujarat Bhakti was preached by Vallabha sect which owed its philosophical origins to Vallabhacharya. It was Narsimha Mehta who popularized this, and he found a large number of following among the merchant class. The wave of Bhakti gave way for the growth of outstanding literature related to Vaishnavism. This wave swept Gujarat somewhere around the end of fourteenth and beginning of fifteenth century as a highly developed bhakti in which the concept attained a new dimension. The two important personalities who led the growth of bhakti cult in Gujarat were Meerabai and Narasimh Mehta.

Shankardeva's Neo-Vaishnavite movement was the first organized attempt in Assam at breaking down the age old bondage to the restrictions of caste, superstitions, ignorance, poverty and uncleanliness through the medium of Bhakti. Under the Ahom rulers there was a constant integration of tribals into the Hindu fold, but the pattern of society was very different on account of ethnic and historical influences.Due to a confused admixture of different Hindu and Buddhist tantrik cults a mysterious atmosphere was created and this region came to be known to the outside world as a land of mysticism and sorcery. However, the impact of the movement was limited to only Koch Bihar and other regions like upper Assam were not effected and continued with their tribal ways of life.

We posit that, the Bhakti movement did not translate to women, though there were a large number of women who were part and parcel of this movement. There was a duality to the whole character of the movement. At one level there was talk of freedom and to do as one wishes, whereas at another level we see features of co-option and contestation that ultimately reveals facets of progress and conservatism. By and large Bhakti Movement created an alternative space for a large mass of people. Analysing the threads one comes across the dominant discourse of the Bhakti movement that was articulated by men and what finally emerges is that this protest against the prevalent social injustices did not address itself to women. Though clamouring for a change and protesting vocally against the prevalent injustices in society, they conveniently left out the women, relegating her to the domestic sphere and only those women were deemed as an ideal, one who was an obedient wife, a *Pativrata* or a *Sati-Savitri*. It was a change authored by a male vocubalry and defined and redefined after readjustments by male parameters. Since the change was being sought with in a given structure it did not attempt at changing the power structure of society vis a vis man and women and also did not alter the production and property relations.Thus it was a movement which could not rise from the traditional view of looking upon woman as Maya and an impediment to the path of Bhakti.

On the other hand, this movement also released forces that enabled many women to create their own alternative space through Bhakti. By stating that Bhakti is available to everyone the Brahman, the upper castes and the lower castes and the women, this movement opened up the religious space. For the women Bhakti became an outlet and they negotiated patriarchy, sometimes very effectively, through it. Hence many women could walk out of married and domestic life and remain childless. Going a step further, some could even renounce the tyranny imposed by crippling notions of respectable feminine behaviour by either walking naked, wearing anklet bells or dancing in public. Women could also decide on their own individual path and follow it as a matter of choice, though this feature cannot be generalized wholly. Tradition played a positive function to bring about change when mediated through religion. In going on pilgrimage, using songs we see a reworking of ritual and the musical traditions to respond creatively to the needs of the time. For some women bhaktas, the rejection of the power of the male figure that they were tied to in subordinate relationship became the terrain for struggle, self assertion and seeking alternative paths. In traditional scriptures devotion to her husband and complete merger in him is the highest goal for a woman both in this life and the other. At a considerable remove from this view, we see women in Bhakti who found the courage to defy this normative order and either walked out of their houses and the restricted spaces of patriarchal control or changed their husbands to their way of thinking. Bhakti gives these women the moral courage to stand against patriarchal authority and create an alternate space for themselves.

To sum up we may say that the process of analyzing Bhakti starts from the premise of deconstructing categories imposed on Indian historiography by the Europen Orientalists. Proceeding from the above to use contemporary texts and read them in their context we see the large scale socio-economic changes released many forces leading to a social churning. Since religion was one of the dominant features of life in medieval India, all these tensions were articulated through the voice of religions by the saints and in this process created many alternative spaces. Proceeding from the Tamil country in the 7th century AD throughout the length and breadth of the subcontinent the singular aim of Bhakti in its regional incarnations was the quest for union with the almighty that was denied to large section of the population on the basis of caste, gender and status. In their vibrant outpourings, the saints and mystics created a number of alternate spaces for many groups over a vast temporal and spatial landscape and also negotiating the process of co-option whose constant interplay is dealt with in this book. We end by saying that there can be multiple readings including a gendered reading that reveals in contrast to the textual version of an imagined freedom at one level there were invisible forces that set the clock back. The gains of the Bhakti movement were large and they propelled many classes and castes to create and articulate their visions which also included many women. After some centuries changed conditions in different historical context saw the Bhakti movement slowly moving into various directions in different regions either by being co-opted, accommodated while some movements still thronged to return to the original message and revive the momentum. None can deny the prevalence of the Bhakti movement in all its vibrancy in everyday life of contemporary India, where the wisdom of the Bhakti saints has once again emerged on the centre stage of historical enquiry. Inspite of the passage of time and the erasure of many aspects by the colonial encounters, the popularity of the Bhakti movement of 7th to 18th centuries, even today is a pointer to its universality and continuity as a living tradition and the multi vocality and ecelecticism of Indian cultural ethos.

Appendices

Appendix 1 (The Alwars)

Sr. No.	Name	Place of Birth	Caste	Works
1.	Poygai	Kanchipuram	Brahmin	The songs of these three are called Ilarpa-Tiruvandadi and form part of Nalyira Divya Prabandham
2.	Bhuttalwar	Kadamalai Mahabalipuram	-do-	
3.	Peyalwar	Mayilai, Mylapur	-do-	
4.	Tirumalaisaiyalwar	Tiruvalukani	Sudra	Tiruccanda-Viruttam Nanmugan Tiruvandadi
5.	Nammanlwar	Tirunagari	Vellala	Tiruviruttam Tiruvasiriyam,Periya Tiruvandadi, Tiruvaim oli
6.	Madhurkavi	Tirukkalur	Brahmin	Kanninum Siruttamu
7.	Kulasekharalwar	Kollinagar	Kshatriya	Perumal Tirumoli
8.	Periyalwar	Srivilliputtur	Brahmin	Periyalwar Tirumoli
9.	Andal	-do-	-do-	Nacciyar Tirumoli Tirruppalli Eluchchi
10.	Tondaradippodiyalwa	Mandangudi	Soliya Brahmin	Tirumalai, Tiruppalli eluchchi
11.	Uraiyur	Pariah	Pariah	Amalanadi Piran
12.	Tirumangaialwar	Tanjore	Vellala	Periya Tirumoli, Tirukkurandandakam,Tiruvedun dandakam, Seriya Tirumandal, Periya Tirumadalkai.

Sources:

Gopinath Rau, T.A. 1923, Sri Subrahmanya Ayyar Lectures on the History of Sri Vaisnavism, University of Madtras, pp.1-7.

V. Rangacharya, 1975, 'Historical evolution of Sri Vaishnavism in South India", Cultural Heritage of India, Vol. IV, Calcutta.

Appendix 2

The Acharyas

Nathmuni (A.D.824-924)

|

Pundarikaksha

|

Sri Ram Misra

|

Yamunacharya (A.D.916-1040)

|

Ramanujacharya (A.D. 1016-1137)

|

Kurukesa

|

-Visnuchitta

-Vardacharya

|

Aitreya Ramanuja

(split of Vasisnavism)

Vadagalai Tradition—Vedantadasika (A.D. 1269-1369)

Tengalai Tradition-Pillailokacharya (A.D. 1213-1327)

Source:

Hemchandra Roy Choudhuri, 1920, Materials for the study of early History of Vaisnava sect, Calcutta.

V. Rangacharya, 1975, "Historical evolution of Sri Vaisnavism in South India", Cultural Heritage of India, Vol. IV, Calcutta.

Appendix 3

Vaisnavite women Saints (12th to 17th century)

Sr. No.	*Name*	*Period*	*Caste/Occupation*	*Region*	*Remarks*
1.	Tirupati Srikaryam seyyum ammai	12th		Tamilnadu	
2.	Tirunaraiyur ammai	12th		Tamilnadu	
3.	Tirukkanappurattu Ammai	12th		Tamilnadu	
4.	Manyar Koyil Porreru ammai	12th		Tamilnadu	
5.	Tiruvaparisaratha	12th		Tamilnadu	
6.	Tiruvanantu Ammai	12th		Tamilnadu	
7.	TiruvanantuPurattu Ammai	12th		Tamilnadu	
8.	Andal ammai	12th		Tamilnadu	Wife of Kurattazhvar
9.	Nayaka Deviyar	12th		Tamilnadu	
10.	Tuyya Perundeviyar	12th		Tamilnadu	Mother of Govinda Embar, initiated in Sanyas by Ramanuja
11.	Sairiya Andal	12th		Tamilnadu	Wife of Govinda Embar,initiated in Sanyas by Ramanuja
12.	Kantimati or Bhumi piratti	12th		Tamilnadu	Daughter of Sri Sala Purna, mother of Ramanuja
13.	Ponnchiya or Hemembal	12th	Malla (Professional wrestlers)	Tamilnadu	Wife of Pillai Uranga Dasar
14.	Akkachchi	12th		Tamilnadu	Wife of Parashar Bhattar

Contd.

Sr. No.	Name	Period	Caste/Occupation	Region	Remarks
15.	Lakshmi Devi or Paritikolla Nachchiyar	12th		Tamilnadu	Of Varadacharya Karpasaranna. She is said to have fed Ramanuja and his disciples by selling herself to a merchant and was transformed through Gurus grace.
16.	Muktabai	13th			
17.	JahanaBai	13th	Shudra	Sevant maid	Servant in the house of Namdev
18.	Kanhopatra	13th	Devadasi		
19.	Rajai	13th	Shudra		Wife of Namdev
20.	Gonai	13th	Shudra		Daughter of Namdev
21.	Mahadamba	13th			
22.	SoryaBai	14th	Mahar untouchable		Wife of Chokkamela
23.	Nirmala	14th	Mahar untouchable		Sister of Chokkamela
24.	Bahina Bai	17th			
25.	VeenaBai	17th			
26.	AkkaBai	17th			
27.	BayaBai	17th			Disciple of Ramdas
28.	Karuramma	17th			
29.	Nagapennu	17th			

Source: Vijay Ramaswamy, 2001, Women saints in medieval Indian society, A. Rahman (ed.), *History of Indian Science, Technology and Culture*, Vol. III, Part I, Oxford.

N. Jagadeesan, 1977, History of Sri Vaishnavism—post Ramanuja, Koodal Publishers, Madurai.

Appendix 4

The Nayanars

1. Sundaramurthy Nayanar
   8th C. One of the four Tamil Samaya Acharyas (four Tamil religious Teachers)

2. Thiru Neelakanta Nayanar
   Lived in Chidambaram. Potter by caste.

3. Iyarpahai Nayanar
   native of Kaveripoompattinam. Vaisya by caste.

4. Ilayangudi Mara Nayanar
   A farmer who lived in a village called Ilayangudi.

5. Maiporul Nayanar
   A pious King who ruled over the hill tribes of Sethi.

6. Viralminda Nayanar
   Vellala by caste. Lived in the hill town of Sengunru.

7. Eirpatha Nayanar
   born in Kaaruvur, on the banks of the river Ambiravathi.

8. Enadinatha Nayanar
   A Shanar (toddy topper) born in Eyinanur in Chola Kingdom.

9. Kannappa Nayanar
Tinnanar, son of a hunters' King Nagan.

10. Kungiliya Kalaya Nayanar
A brahmin born in Thirukadavur in Chola Kingdom; got the name because he always holding a pot (an incense pot)in his hand.

11. Manakanchara Nayanar
Lived in Kancharur in Chola Kingdom. A vellala by caste, a hereditary Senathipathi. A contemporary of Sundaramurthy Nayanar.

12. Arivattaya Nayanar
Lived in Kannamangalam in Chola Kingdom.

13. Anaya Nayanar
A cowherd in Mazhanad (Trich district).

14. Murthy Nayanar
A vaisya king born in Madura of Pandya King. To adore Lord Shiva with sandalwood paste, smearing it all over the Lingam is regarded as a great form of worship by him.

15. Muruga Nayanar
Born in Tirupukalur. Contemporary of Gnana Sambandar.

16. Rudra Pasupathi Nayanar

17. Thiru Nalai Povar Nayanar

18. Thiru Kurippu Thonda Nayanar

19. Chandeswara Nayanar

20. Thirunavukkarasar Nayanar (Appar)

21. Kulichirai Nayanar

22. Perumizhalai Kurumba Nayanar

23. Karaikal Ammaiyar
24. Thiru Nalai Povar Nayanar
25. Appuddi Nayanar
26. Thiruneelanakka Nayanar
27. Nami nandi adigal
28. Thiru Gnana Sambandar
29. Eyorkon Kalikama Nayanar
30. Dandi Adigal Nayanar
31. Ripathi Nayanar'
32. Enathi nayanar
33. Kanappa Nayanare
34. Murga Nayanar
35. Somasira Nayanar
36. Sakkiya Nayanar
37. Siruppuli Nayanar
38. Siruthonda Nayanar
39. Cheraman Perumal Nayanar
40. Gananatha Nayanar
41. Kootruva Nayanar
42. Pugal chola Nayanar
43. Narasinga Muniyaraiyar
44. Adipattha Nayanar
45. Kalikampa Nayanar

46. Kaliya Nayanar
47. Satti Nayanar
48. Kanampulla Nayanar
49. Kari Nayanar
50. Ninra Seer Nedumara Nayanar
51. Mangayairkaraciyar
52. Vayilar Nayanar
53. Munaiyadavur Nayanar
54. Idangazhi Nayanar
55. Pugaz thunai Nayanar
56. Kotpuli Nayanar
57. Pusalar Nayanar
58. Nesa Nayanar
59. Kochangat Chola Nayanar
60. Thiru Neelakanta Yazhpanar
61. Sadaya Nayanar
62. Isaignaniyar
63. Manickavacagar.

Appendix 5

Saivite and Vir Saivite women saints (12th to 17th centuries)

Sr. No	*Name*	*Period*	*Caste/Occupation*	*Region*	*Remarks*
1.	Akka Mahadevi	12th	Traders	Tamilnadu	
2.	Gangambike	12th		Tamilnadu	
3.	Nilamma	12th	Dancing girl	Tamilnadu	Wife of Basavva
4.	Akka Nagamma	12th		Tamilnadu	Sister of Basavva
5.	Kalavve	12th	Shudra carpenter	Tamilnadu	Wife of saint Balche, author of Vachanas
6.	Lakshamma	12th		Tamilnadu	Wife of saint Kondeyya Manchanna, the chief Officer of Bijjala
7.	Mahadevi	12th		Tamilnadu	Wife of saint Molige Marayya
8.	Lakkhamma	12th	Agricultural landless labourer	Tamilnadu	Wife of saint Ayadakki Marayya
9.	Kadire Kayakkala Remmave	12th	Weaver spinner	Tamilnadu	

Contd.

Sr. No.	*Name*	*Period*	*Caste/Occupation*	*Region*	*Remarks*
10.	Bontaladevi			Tamilnadu	
11.	Kalavve		Spinner	Tamilnadu	Wife of Siddha Buddhayya
12.	Viramma	12th	Jedara weaver	Tamilnadu	Wife of Dasarayya
13.	Rechchave			Tamilnadu	Wife of Kata Kuttayya
14.	Auviaiyar	12th and 13th	Low caste, Anuloma	Tamilnadu	Saivite daughter of a Pulaya women
15.	Vasukiyar	14th	Vellala	Tamilnadu	Wife of Tiruvalluvar
16.	Uttiranallur Nangai	15th	Paraiya shepherdess	Tamilnadu	Author of Paichalur Padikam
17.	Guddave	15th	Chandala	Tamilnadu	Wife of Battaleshvara, Lame but believed to have got her legs through Shiva's grace

Source: Vijay Ramaswamy, 2001, "Women saints in Medieval Indian Society, A. Rahman (ed.), History of Indian Science, Technology and Culture, Vol. III, Part I, Oxford.

N. Jagadeesan, 1977, *History of Srivaishnavism-post Ramanuja*, Koodal Publishers, Madurai.

Appendix 6

Bhakti Saints in the Northern Regions (13th to 17th centuries)

I. Nirgun School

A. Gyan marg

1. Ramananda (End of 13th and Beginning of 14th centuries)
2. Kabir-1398-1449 A.D.
3. Rai Das
4. Dharma Das
5. Guru Nanak-1469-
6. Dadu Dayal-1601-1660 A.D.
7. Sundas Das-1653-1660 A.D.
8. Maluka Das-1639 1739 A.D.
9. Rajjab
10. Jambhanath
11. Singha Jee
12. Hari Das Niranjani.

B. Prem margi

1. Mulla Daud
2. Qutban
3. Malik Muhammad Jayasi
4. Manjhan.

II. Sagun School

A. Krishna Bhakti

1. Vallabha Charya-1479-1531 A.D.
2. Surd as-1540-1620 A.D.
3. Nand Das-dt. 1625 A.D.
4. Krishna Das
5. Parmanand Das
6. Khumban Das
7. ChaturBhuj Das
8. Chitti Swamy
9. Govind Swamy
10. Hit Hari Vansh
11. Gada Dhar Bhatt
12. Meera Bai-1498-1546 A.D.
13. Swami Hari Das
14. Surdas Madan mohan
15. Shri Bhatt-Birth 1515-

16. Vyas Ji
17. Ras Khan
18. Rahim
19. Dhruva Das

B. Ram Bhakti

1. Tulsi Das-1554-1680 A.D.
2. Swami Agra Das
3. Nabha Das
4. Pranchand Chauhan
5. Hriday Ram

Source: Ram Chandra Shukla, 1994, (Hindi), *Hindi Sahitya Ka Itihas*, Nagari Pracharini Sabha, Varanasi.

Verma, Ram Kumar, 1948, (Hindi) *Hindi Sahitya Ka Alochanatmak Ithihas*, 4th edition, Ram Narayan Lal, Prayag.

Appendix 7

Vaisnava temple

1. Srirangam (Thiruvarangam)
2. Thiru Arimeya Vinnagaram
3. Thiru Anbil
4. Thiru Aadhanur
5. Thiru Indhallur
6. Thiru Kandiyur
7. Thirukkannangudi
8. Thirukkannappuram
9. Thirukkannamangai
10. Thirukkovalur
11. Thirukkarambanur
12. Thirukkavithalam
13. Thirukkaavalambadi
14. Thirukkkaazhicheeraama Vinnagaram (Sirgazhi)
15. Thirukkudandhai (Kumbakonam)
16. Thirukkoodalur
17. Thirukkozhi

18. Thiruchitrakoodam (Chidambaram)
19. Thiruchirupuliyur
20. Thiruchembonsei Koil
21. Thiruchaerai
22. Thiru Thanjai Maamanikkoil
23. Thiruthalaichanga Naanmadhiyam (Thalaichangadu)
24. Thiruthetriyambalam
25. Thiruthevanaar Thogai
26. Thiru Nandipura Vinnagaram
27. Thiru Naraiyur
28. Thiru Naagai (Naagapatinam)
29. Thiru Paarthanpalli
30. Thiruppullamboodhangudi
31. Thiruppaer Nagar
32. Thirumanikkoodam
33. Thirumanimaadakkoil
34. Thiruvannpurudothamam (Thiru Nangur)
35. ThiruVazhundhur (Thaerezhundhur)
36. Thiru Vaaliyum Thiru Nagariyum
37. Thiru Vinnagar (Uppiliyappan Koil)
38. Thiru Vellakkulam
39. Thiru Vellarai

40. Thiru Velliyangudi
41. Thiru Vaigundha Vinnagaram
42. Thiruvaheendrapuram
43. Thiru Ashtapuyagaram (Kancheepuram)
44. Thiru Idavendhai (Thiruvadandhai)
45. Thiru Ooragam (Kancheepuram)
46. Thiru Evvull (Thiruvallur)
47. Thirukkachi-Atthigiri (Kancheepuram)
48. Thirukkadalmallai (Mahabalipuram)
49. Thirukkadigai
50. Thirukkallvanur (Kancheepuram)
51. Thirukkaragam (Kancheepuram)
52. Thirukkaarvanam (Kancheepuram)
53. Thiruthankaa (Thoopul-Kancheepuram)
54. Thirunilaathingal Thundam (Kancheepuram)
55. Thiru Ninravur (Thinnanur)
56. Thiru Neeragam (Kancheepuram)
57. Thiruneermalai
58. Thiru Parameshwara Vinnagaram (Kancheepuram)
59. Thiru Pavala Vannam (Kancheepuram)
60. Thiruppadagam (Kancheepuram)
61. Thirupputkuzhi
62. Thiruvallikeni

63. Thiruvekha (Kancheepuram)
64. Thiruvaelukkai (Kancheepuram)
65. Thirukkandamennum Kadinagar (Devapprayaagai)
66. Thirusaalakraamam
67. Thirusingavel Kundram
68. Thirudwarakai
69. Thiru Naimisaaranyam
70. Thirupirudhi (Joshi Mutt)
71. Thiruvadamadurai (Mathura)
72. Thiruvadhariyaashramam (Badrinath)
73. Thiruvayodhi (Ayodhya)
74. Thiruvaayppadi (Gokulam)
75. Thiruvengadam
76. Thirukkadithaanam
77. Thirukaatkarai
78. Thiruchenkundrur
79. Thiru Naavaai
80. Thirupuliyur (Kuttanaadu)
81. Thirumoozhikkalam
82. Thiruvannparisaaram
83. Thiruvanvandur (Thiruvamundur)
84. Thiruvallavazh (Thiruvalla)
85. Thiruvananthapuram

86. Thiruvattaru

87. Thiruvaaranvilai (Aarammula)

88. Thiruvittuhvakkodu

89. Thirukurugur (Alwar Thirunagari)

90. Thirukulandhai (Perungulam)

91. Thirukurungudi

92. Thirukoodal (Madurai)

93. Thirukkotiyur

94. Thirukkolur

95. Thiruchirivaramangai

96. Thiruthankaal

97. Thirutholaivilimangalam

98. Thiruppullani

99. Thiruppulingudi

100. Thirupaerai

101. Thirumaaliruncholai

102. Thirumeyyam

103. Thirumogur

104. Thiruvilliputhur (Sri Villiputhur)

105. Thiru Vaigundam (Sri Vaigundam)

106. Thiruchirivaramangai

107. Thiruthankaal

108. Thirutholaivilimangalam

Appendex: 8

Saiva Temples

1. Koyil (Chidambaram)
2. Tiruvetkalam
3. Tirunelvayil
4. Tirukkazhippalai
5. Tirunallurpperumanam
6. Mahendrapalli
7. Ten Tirumullaivayil
8. Kalikkaamoor
9. Tiruchaaikaadu
10. Pallavaneeswaram
11. Tiruvenkadu
12. Tirukkattuppalli
13. Tirukkurukaavur
14. Sirkali
15. Tirukkolakka
16. Pullirukkuvelur (Vaidee-swaran Koyil)
17. Kannaar Kovil
18. Tirukkadaimudi
19. Tiruninriyur
20. Tiruppunkur
21. Tiruneedur
22. Anniyur
23. Tiruvelvikudi
24. Edirkolpaadi
25. Tirumanancheri
26. Tirukkurukkai
27. Karuppariyalur
28. Kurakkukka
29. Tiruvaalkoliputrur
30. Tirumannippadikkarai
31. Omampuliyur
32. Tirukkaanaattumulloor
33. Tirunaarayur

34. Kadambur
35. Pandanainallur
36. Kanjanoor
37. Tirukkodikka
38. Tirumangalakkudi
39. Tiruppanantaal
40. Tiruvaappaadi
41. Tirucheignalur
42. Tirundudevankudi
43. Tiruviyalur
44. Kottaiyur
45. Innambar
46. Tiruppurampayam
47. Vijayamangai
48. Tiruvaikavur
49. Kurangaaduturai
50. Tiruppazhanam
51. Tiruvaiyaru
52. Tiruneittanam
53. Tirupperumpuliyur
54. Tirumazhapadi
55. Tiruppazhuvur (Aalanturai)
56. Tirukkaanoor
57. Anbilalanturai
58. Tirumaanturai
59. Tiruppaatrurai
60. Tiru Aanaikkaa
61. Tiruppainneeli
62. Tiruppaachilasramam
63. Tiruveengoimalai

Other Siva Temples

1. Vaatpokki
2. Kadambar Kovil
3. Tirupparaaitturai
4. Tirukkarkudi (Uyyakkondan Malai)
5. Uraiyur
6. Tiruchirappalli
7. Tiruverumbur
8. Nedunkalam
9. Melaittirukkattuppalli
10. Tiruvalampozhil
11. Tiruppoonturutti
12. Tirukkandiyur
13. Tiruchotrutturai
14. Tiruvedikkudi

15. Tenkudittittai
16. Tiruppullamangai
17. Tiruchakrapalli
18. Tirukkarukaavoor
19. Tiruppaalaitturai
20. Tirunallur
21. Aavoor Pasupateeswaram
22. Satthi Mutram
23. Patteeswaram
24. Pazhaiyarai Vadatali
25. Tiruvalanchuzhi
26. Tirukkudamookku
27. Tirukkudandai Keezhkottam
28. Kudandaikkaaronam
29. Tirunageswaram
30. Tiruvidaimarudur
31. Ten Kurangaaduturai
32. Tiruneelakkudi
33. Vaikanmaadakkovil
34. Tirunallam
35. Tirukkozhambam
36. Tiruvavaduturai
37. Tirutturutti
38. Tiruvazhundur
39. Mayiladuturai
40. Viilanagar
41. Tiruppariyalur
42. Tiruchemponpalli
43. Tirunanipalli
44. Tiruvalampuram
45. Tiruttalaichankadu
46. Aakkoor
47. Tirukkadavur
48. Tirukkadavur Mayaanam
49. Tiruvettakkudi
50. Tiruttelicheri
51. Dharumapuram
52. Tirunallar
53. Tirukkottaru
54. Ambar
55. Ambar Maakaalam
56. Tirumeeyachur
57. Tirumeeyachur Ilamkovil
58. Thilatalpati
59. Tiruppaampuram

60. Sirukudi
61. Tiruveezhimizhalai
62. Tiruvanniyur
63. Karuvili Kottittai
64. Penu Perunturai
65. Naraiyur
66. Arisirkaraiputtur
67. Sivapuram
68. Kalayanallur
69. Tirukkarukkudi
70. Tiruvanchiyam
71. Nannilam
72. Tirukkondeeswaram
73. Tiruppanaiyur
74. Virkudi
75. Tiruppugalur
76. Tiruppugalur Vardhamaneswaram
77. Ramanadeeswaram
78. Tiruppayatrankudi
79. Tiruchenkattankudi
80. Tirumarugal
81. Tiruchaattamangai
82. Nagaikkaronam
83. Sikkal
84. Keevalur
85. Tiruttevur
86. Palliyin Mukkoodal
87. Achaleswaram
88. Tiruvarur
89. Arurparavaiumandali
90. Vilamar
91. Karaveeram
92. Peruvelur
93. Talaiyalankadu
94. Tirukkudavaayil
95. Tirucherai
96. Tirunalurmayaanam
97. Kaduvaaikaaraiputhur
98. Tiruvirumpoolai
99. Aradaipperumpazhi
100. Avalivanallur
101. Paridiniyamam
102. Tiruvenniyur (Koyil venni)
103. Tiruppoovanur

104. Paadaaleeswaram
105. Tirukkalar
106. Tiruchitremam
107. Tiru Usaattaanam
108. Tiruidumbavanam
109. Kadikkulam
110. Tandalaineeneri
111. Kottur
112. Vanduturai
113. Tirukkollampudur
114. Pereyil
115. Tirukkollikkadu
116. Tenkoor
118. Tirunatyattankudi
119. Tirukkarayil
120. Kanraappur
121. Valivalam
122. Kaichinam
123. Tirukkolili
124. Tiruvaimur
125. Tirumaraikkadu
126. Tiru Agathiyan Palli
127. Kodikkarai
128. Tiruvidaivai
129. Tirukkonamalai
130. Tirukketheeswaram
131. Aalavaai (Madurai)
132. Aappudaiyaar Kovil
133. Tirupparankunram
134. Tiruvedakam
135. Tirukkodunkunram
136. Tirupputhur
137. Tiruppunavayil
138. Rameswaram
139. Tiruvaadaanai
140. Tirukkaanapper
141. Tiruppoovanam
142. Tiruchuzhial
143. Kutralam
144. Tirunelveli
145. Tiruvanjaikkalam
146. Avinaasi
147. Tirumuruganpoondi
148. Tiru Nana
149. Kodimadachenkunroor (Tiruchengode)

150. Venchamaakoodal
151. Paandikkodumudi
152. Karuvoor Aanilai
153. Tirunelvayil Aratturai
154. Pennaagadam
155. Goodalaiyatrur
156. Erukkattampuliyur
157. Tiruttinai Nagar
158. Tiruchopuram
159. Tiruvatikai
160. Tirunaavalur
161. Tirumudukunram
162. Tirunelvennei
163. Tirukkovalur Veerattam
164. Arankandanallur
165. Tiruvidaiyaru
166. Tiruvennainallur
167. Tirutturaiyur
168. Vatukur
169. Tirumaanikkuzhi
170. Tiruppaatirippuliyur
171. Tirumundeeswaram
172. Puravaar Panankattur
173. Tiru Aamaathur
174. Tiruvannamalai
175. Kachi Ekambam
176. Kachi Metrali
177. Onakanthan Tali
178. Tirunellikka Kachi Anekatangapadam
179. Kachi Nerikkaaraikkadu
180. Kuranganilmuttam
181. Tirumaagaral
182. Tiruvothur
183 Panankattur
184. Tiruvallam
185. Tirumalper
186. Tiruvooral
187. Ilambayankottur
188. Tiruvirkolam
189. Tiruvalankadu
190. Tiruppaasur
191. Tiruvenpakkam
192. Tirukkallil
193. Sree Kaalahasti
194. Tiruvotriyur

195. Tiruvalithaayam

196. Tirumullaivayil

197. Tiruverkadu

198. Tirumayilai (Mylapore)

199. Tiruvanmyur

200. Tirukkachoor

201. Tiruvidaichuram

202. Tirukkalunkunram

203. Tiru Acharapakkam

204. Tiruvakkarai

205. Arasili

206. Irumbai Maakalam

207. Gokarnam

208. Tirupparuppatham (Sree Sailam-Andhra Pradesh)

209. Indraneelaparvatam (Nepal)

210. Anekatangavadam (Gowrikund)

211. Tirukkedaram (Kedar-nath)

212. Tirukkayilaayam (Mount Kailash)

Appendix 9

Temples in Andhra

1. Agastheeswara Temple at Chadiparla near Kamalapuram (Cuddapah)
2. Agastheeswara Temple at Gopalapuram near Kolhapur (Mahbubnagar)
3. Agastheeswarar Temple at Yaganti near Kurnool
4. Agastheeswarar Temple at Tondavada near Tirupati
5. Ahobala Narasimha Temple at Ahoblam near Kurnool
6. Alampur Navabhrama Temples at Alampur near Kurnool
7. Amaravati Amareswara Temple at Amaravati near Vijayawada
8. Annavaram Satyanarayana Swami Temple at Annavaram near Kakinada
9. Basar Saraswathi Temple at Basar near Nizamabad
10. Bekkeswara Temple at Bekkam near Mahbubnagar
11. Bhadrachalam Rama Temple at Bhadrachalam near Khammam
12. Bhadrakali Temple at Warangal
13. Bhairavaswamy Temple at Gopalapuram near Kolhapur (Mahbubnagar)

14. Bhavanarayanaswamy Temple at Pattisam near Polavaram (West Godavari)

15. Bhimeswara Temple at Gopalapuram near Kolhapur (Mahbubnagar)

16. Bhimeswara Temple at Samalkot (Bhimaramam, Somaramam) near Samalkot

17. Bhimeswara Temple at Draksharama near Kakinada

18. Bhogeswara Temple at Pamidi near Gooty (Anantapur)

19. Birla Mandir at Hyderabad

20. Chandrasekhara Temple at Bikkavolu near Ramachandrapuram (E. Godavari)

21. Chenna Kesava Temple at Pushpagiri near Cuddapah

22. Chintalarayaswamy Temple at Tadpatri near Gooty (Anantapur)

23. Doddeswara Temple at Hemavati near Madakasira (Anantapur)

24. Ekaratri Mallikarjuna Temple at Sreekakulam

25. Endala Mallikarjunaswamy Temple at Ravivalasa near Tekkali (Srikakulam)

26. Gangadhareswara Temple at Gopalapuram near Kolhapur (Mahbubnagar)

27. Gangeswara Temple at Tadikalapudi near Eluru (West Godavari)

28. Ghanpur Temples at Ghanpur near Warangal

29. Golingeswara Temple at Nidadavole near Kovvuru (West Godavari)

30. Golingeswara Temple at Bikkavolu near Ramachandrapuram (E Godavari)

31. Govindarajaswami Temple at Tirupati

32. Guntimalleswara Temple at Khammam

33. Hanumakonda Thousand Pillared Temple at Warangal

34. Indranatheswara Temple at Pushpagiri near Cuddapah

35. Jaladheeswara Temple at Ghantasala (Krishna)

36. Jateswara Temple at Gopalapuram near Kolhapur (Mahbubnagar

37. Kaleswara Temple at Gopalapuram near Kolhapur (Mahbubnagar)

38. Kamalasambhaveswara Temple at Pushpagiri near Cuddapah

39. Kanakadurga Temple at Vijayawada

40. Kanyaka Parameswari Temple at Proddatur (Cuddapah)

41. Kapileswarar Temple at Tirupati

42. Kapoteeswara Temple at Chejerla near Narasaraopet (Guntur)

43. Kapoteswara Temple at Kadali near Razole (East Godavari)

44. Kasi Viswanatha Temple at Pushpagiri near Cuddapah

45. Kesavaswami Temple at Ryali near Rajamundry

46. Koppulingeswaraswamy Temple at Palivela near Kottapeta (East Godavari)

47. Koteeswara Temple at Kaluvakolanu near Mahbubnagar

48. Kotilingam Temple at Panchadarla near Anakapallee

49. Ksheerarameswaraswamy Temple at Palakollu (Ksheeraramam) near Narasapur (West Godavari)

50. Kukkuteswara Temple at Pithapuram near Kakinada

51. Lakshmi Narasimha Temple at Yadagirigutta near Hyderabad

52. Madanagopala Temple at Gopalapuram near Kolhapur (Mahbubnagar)

53. Mahanadi Temple at Thimmapuram near Kurnool

54. Mahanandi Temple at Nandyal near Kurnool

55. Mahavishnu Temple at Sreekakulam

56. Mallanna Temple at Komaravelu near Jangaon (Warangal)

57. Malleswaraswami Temple at Hemavati near Madakasira (Anantapur)

58. Malleswaraswami Temple at Vijayawada

59. Malleswaraswami Temple at Mangalagiri near Vijayawada

60. Malleswaraswami Temple at Gopalapuram near Kolhapur (Mahbubnagar)

61. Mallikarjunaswamy Temple at Jonnavada near Nellore

62. Mallikarjunaswamy Temple at Ayinavolu near Warangal

63. Mangalagiri Narasimhaswami Temple at Mangalagiri near Vijayawada

64. Manikanteswara Temple at Kanipakkam near Chittoor

65. Manthani Temple at Manthani near Karimnagar

66. Mogileeswara Temple at Mogili near Bangarupalem (Chitoor)

67. Mukhalingam Temple at Mukhalingam near Sreekakulam

68. Mukteeswara Temple at Kaleswaram (Manthani) near Karimnagar

69. Muktirameswara Temple at Proddatur (Cuddapah)

70. Nageswaraswamy Temple at Duvva near Tanaku (West Godavari)

71. Nageswaraswamy Temple at Chebrolu

72. Navanandikotkur Malleswaraswami Temple at Nandikotkur near Kurnool

73. Nignur Shiva Temple at Nignur near Karimnagar

74. Nilakanteswara Temple at Nizamabad

75. Nilakanteswara Temple at Gudlur near Kandukur (Prakasam)

76. Padmanathaswamy Temple at Gopalapuram near Kolhapur (Mahbubnagar)

77. Pallikonda Sivaperuman Temple at Suruttuppalli near Nagalapuram

78. Panduranga Swamy Temple at Chilakalapudi near Machilipatnam

79. Papanaseswarar Temple at Alampur near Kurnool

80. Parasareswara Temple at Yogimallavaram near Tirupati

81. Parasurameswara Temple at Gudimallam near Tirupati

82. Parusavedeeswara Temple at Meenambaram near Mahbubnagar

83. Peravali Ranganatha Temple at Peravali near Kurnool

84. Polasteeswara Temple at Polasa near Jagtial (Karimnagar)

85. Raghavendraswamy Temple at Mantralayam

86. Rajarajeswara Temple at Bikkavolu near Ramachandrapuram (E. Godavari)

87. Rama Temple at Kondapaka near Siddhipet (Medak)

88. Ramalingeswara Temple at Tadparti near Anantapur

89. Ramalingeswara Temple at Kaudur near Mahbubnagar

90. Ramalingeswara Temple at Nandikandi near Sangareddi (Medak)

91. Ramalingeswara Temple at Gopalapuram near Kolhapur (Mahbubnagar)

92. Ramalingeswaraswamy Temple at Achanta (West Godavari)

93. Ramappa Temple at Palampet near Warangal

94. Rameswaraswamy Temple at Tadpatri near Gooty (Anantapur)

95. Rudreswara Temple at Palampet near Warangal

96. Sambasiveswara Temple at Gopalapuram near Kolhapur (Mahbubnagar)

97. Sambu Lingeswara Temple at Warangal

98. Saneeswara Temple at Mandapalli near Rajamundry

99. Sangameswara Temple at Kudali (Alampur) near Kurnool

101. Sangameswara Temple at Sangam Jagarlamudi near Tenali

102. Santana Malleswaraswamy Temple at Pushpagiri near Cuddapah

103. Shiva Temple at Kailasakona near Puttur (Chittoor)

104. Shiva Temple at Talakona near Piler (Chitoor)

105. Shiva Temple at Penukonda (Anantapur)

106. Shiva Temple at Pedakkani near Vijayawada

107. Sidhdheshwaraswamy Temple at Tallapakam near Rajampet (Cuddapah)

108. Sidhdheshwaraswamy Temple at Muttayikota near Medak

109. Sidhdheshwaraswamy Temple at Hemavati near Madakasira (Anantapur)

110. Simhachalam VarahaLakshminarasimha Temple at Simhachalam near Vishakapatnam

111. Skandagiri Temple at Secundrabad

112. Someswara Temple at Devunigumpa near Parvatipuram (Srikakulam)

113. Someswara Temple at Mandapaka near Tanuku (West Godavari)

114. Someswara Temple at Kotipalli near Draksharama

115. Someswara Temple at Bhimavaram (Somaramam) near Bhimavaram

116. Sree Kalahasteeswarar Temple at Sri Kalahasti near Tirupati

117. Sree Sailam Mallikarjuna Temple at Sreesailam near Kurnool

118. Suryanarayanaswamy Temple at Arasavalli near Srikakulam

119. Tiruchanur Padmavati Temple at Tiruchanur near Tirupati

120. Tirupati Venkateswara Temple at Tirumala-Tirupati

121. Trikoteswara Temple at Pushpagiri near Cuddapah

122. Tripurantakeswara Temple at Tripurantantakam near Kurnool

123. Ugra Narasimha Temple at Vedadri near Vijayawada

124. Uma Maheswara Temple at Gopalapuram near Kolhapur (Mahbubnagar)

125. Uma Maheswara Temple at Pushpagiri near Cuddapah

126. Umakamandaleswarar Temple at Ryali near Rajamundry

127. Umamaheswara Temple at Rajahmundry

128. Vaidyanatha Temple at Pushpagiri near Cuddapah

129. Vedanarayana Swamy Temple at Nagalapuram near Tirupati

130. Veerabhadraswami Temple at Lepakshi near Anantapur

131. Veerabhadreswaraswamy Temple at Pattisam near Polavaram (West Godavari)

132. Vemulawada Shiva Temple at Vemulawada near Karimnagar

133. Venkatramana Temple at Tadpatri near Gooty (Anantapur)

134. Venugopalaswamy Temple at Bobbili near Vizianagaram

135. Vijayeswara Swami Temple at Vijayawada

136. Virabhadra Temple at Gopalapuram near Kolhapur (Mahbubnagar)

137. Virupaksheswara Temple at Hemavati near Madakasira (Anantapur)

138. Visweswara Temple at Kolanupaka near Bhuvanagiri (Nalgonda)

Appendix 10

Temples in Karnataka

1. Adi Narayana Temple at Dodballpur near Bangalore
2. Adikesava Temple at Kaginelli (Haveri) near Dharwar
3. Agastyeswara Temple at Tirumukkoodal near Mysore
4. Ahobala Narasimha Temple at Niratadi near Davangere
5. Aihole Temples near Dharwar
6. Akkanna Basti at Sravanabelagola near Hassan
7. Allanatha (Varadaraja) Temple at Maddur
8. Amaranarayana Temple at Kaivara near Kolar
9. Amritalingamanikeshwara Temple at Nanditavare (Malebennur) near Chitradurga
10. Amriteshwara Temple at Amritapura near Tarikere
11. Amriteshwara Temple at Annigeri near Hubli
12. Anantapadmanabha Temple at Hosa Budanur near Mandya
13. Ananteshwara Temple at Udupi near Mangalore
14. Anjaneya Temple at Tekal near Kolar
15. Annapoorani Temple at Kalasa near Chikmagalur

16. Aprameya Temple at Malur near Kolar
17. Arkeshwara Templ at Talakad near Mysore
18. Arkeshwara Temple at Hale Arur (Chamrajnagar) near Mysore
19. Avimukteshwara Temple at Hoskote near Bangalore
20. Badami Temples near Dharwar
21. Badri Narayana Temple at Melkote near Krishnarajpet (Mandya)
22. Bagandeshwar Temple at Baagamandala near Madikeri
23. Balakrishna Temple at Udupi near Mangalore
24. Balarama Temple at Pandeshwar (Udupi) near Mangalore
25. Banashankari Temple at Annigeri near Hubli
26. Basappa Temple at Annigeri near Hubli
27. Basavanna Temple at Haveri near Dharwar
28. Bhandari Basti at Sravanabelagola near Hassan
29. Bharateshwara Temple at Avani (Mulbagal) near Kolar
30. Bhimeshwara Temple at Kaivara near Kolar
31. Bhrama Jinalaya at Kuppattur near Shimoga
32. Bhrama Jinalaya at Lakkundi (Gadag) near Dharwar
33. Bhrammeshwara Temple at Kikkeri (Krishnarajpet) near Mysore
34. Bucheshwara Temple at Koramangala near Hassan
35. Chamundeswari Temple at Chamundi Hill near Mysore

36. Chandeshwari Temple at Srinivaspur near Kolar

37. Chandeswari Temple at Vogata (Hosakote) near Bangalore

38. Chandramoulishwara Temple at Udupi near Mangalore

39. Chandramoulishwara Temple at Chintamani near Kolar

40. Channakesava Temple at Chikballapur near Kolar

41. Chatteshwara Temple at Chat Chattanahalli (Halebidu) near Hassan

42. Chennakesava Temple at Haranhalli (Arsikere) near Hassan

43. Chennakesava Temple at Aralaguppe near Tiptur

44. Chennakesava Temple at Belur near Hassan

45. Dattatreya Temple at Koormagadde (Naradagadde) near Raichur

46. Dharmeshwara Temple at Kondarahalli (Hosakote) near Bangalore

47. Dineshwara Temple at Hale Arur (Chamrajnagar) near Mysore

48. Dodda Basappa Temple at Dambala (Gadag) near Dharwar

49. Durga Temple at Agara (Yelandur) near Mysore

50. Eshwara Temple at A

51. Gajina Basappa Temple at Annigeri near Hubli

52. Galageshwara Temple at Heggare near Chitradurga

53. Gangadhareshwara Temple at Srirangapattana near Mysore

54. Gangadhareshwara Temple at Shivaganga near Tumkur
55. Gangadhareshwara Temple at Turuvekere near Tumkur
56. Gangeshwara Temple at Madhugangur near Shimoga
57. Gavi Gangadhareshwara Temple at Bangalore
58. Gopalakrishna Temple at Tonnur (Melkote) near Krishnarajpet (Mandya)
59. Gopalakrishna Temple at Krishnaraja Sagar near Mysore
60. Gopalakrishna Temple at Patrenahalli near Kolar
61. Govindeshwara Temple at Near Hassan
62. Gowreeshwara Temple at Yelandur near Mysore
63. Harihareshwara Temple at Harihar (Davangere) near Chitradurga
64. Hire Hanuman Temple at Annigeri near Hubli
65. Hoysala Temple at Mosale near Hassan
66. Hoysaleswara Temple at Halebidu near Hassan
67. Ishwara Temple at Arsikere near Hassan
68. Ishwara Temple at Nandigudi near Male Bennur, Chitaladrug
69. Ishwara Temple at Arsikere near Hassan
70. Ishwara Temple at Nanditavare (Malebennur) near Chitradurga
71. Jagadeka Malleshwara Temple at Belagami near Shikarpur
72. Jain Temple at Bannikere near Shimoga

73. Jambunatha Swamy Hill Temple at Hospet
74. Jwalamukhi Tripurasundari Temple at Uddanahalli (Nanjangud) near Mysore
75. Jwarahareswara Temple at Kandavara near Kolar
76. Kalabhairava Temple at Seethi near Kolar
77. Kalahasteshwara Temple at Kaginelli (Haveri) near Dharwar
78. Kalaseshwara Temple at Kalasa near Chikmagalur
79. Kalleshwara Temple at Heggare near Chitradurga
80. Kanakachalapathi Temple at Kanakagiri near Hospet
81. Kappe Chennigaraya Temple at Belur near Hassan
82. Kasi Visweswara Temple at Lakkundi (Gadag) near Dharwar
83. Kasi Visweswara Temple at Hosa Budanur near Mandya
84. Kattale Basti (Adinatha Jinalaya) at Chandragiri Hill near Hassan
85. Kedareshwara Templ at Halebidu near Hassan
86. Kesava Temple at Somnathapura near Mysore
87. Kirti Narayana Temple at Talakad near Mysore
88. Kodandaramaswamy Temple at Kanchankatte (Saligram) near Krishnarajpet (Mandya)
89. Kolaramma Temple at Kolar
90. Kumaraswamy Saila Temple at Bangalore
91. Lakshmaneshwara Temple at Avani (Mulbagal) near Kolar

92. Lakshmi Devi Temple at Dodda-gaddavalli near Hassan
93. Lakshmi Narasimha Temple at Hole Narasipur near Sravanabelagola
94. Lakshmi Narayana Temple at Chamundi Hill near Mysore
95. Lakshmi Temple at Kaginelli (Haveri) near Dharwar
96. Lakshminarasimha Temple at Nuggihalli near Tiptur
97. Maha Ganapati Temple at Kurudumale near Kolar
98. Mahabaleshwar Temple at Chamundi Hill near Mysore
99. Mahabaleshwar Temple at Gokarna near Karwar
100. Mahadeva Temple at Itgi near Raichur
101. Mallari Temple at Gudda Guddaapura near Ranebennur (Dharwar)
102. Mallikarjuna Hill Temple at Near Talakkad near Mysore
103. Mallikarjuna Temple at Basaralu near Mandya
104. Mangayi Basti at Sravanabelagola near Hassan
105. Markandeshwara Temple at Vokkalery Hill near Kolar
106. Markandeshwara Temple at Kallur near Raichur
107. Markandeshwara Temple at Kallur near Raichur
108. Maruleshwara Temple at Talakad near Mysore
109. Mookambika Temple at Kollur near Mangalore
110. Murdeshwar Temple at Murdeshwar (Bhatkal) near Karwar
111. Nagara Jinalaya at Hatna near Tiptur

112. Nakeshwara Temple at Near Hassan
113. Nambi Narayana Temple at Tonnur (Melkote) near Krishnarajpet (Mandya)
114. Nandi Temples at Nandi Hills near Bangalore
115. Narada Temple at Naradagadde near Raichur
116. Narasimha Temple at Devaraya Durga Hill near Tumkur
117. Narasimha Temple at Kaginelli (Haveri) near Dharwar
118. Narasimha Temple at Kunigal (Tumkur) near Bangalore
119. Narasimha Temple at Maddur
120. Narasimha Temple at Savandrurga near Bangalore
121. Narasimha Temple at Agara (Yelandur) near Mysore
122. Navalinga Temples at Kuknur near Hospet
123. Omkareshwara Temple at Madikeri
124. Paataleswara Temple at Talakad near Mysore
125. Pakshi Ranganatha Temple at Kumsi near Shimoga
126. Pancha Basadi at Humcha near Nagar Taluk
127. Para Vasudeva Temple at Gundlupet near Mysore
128. Parsvanatha Basti at Chamrajanagar near Mysore
129. Parsvanatha Basti at Heggere near Chitradurga
130. Pattabhirama Temple at Hampi near Hospet
131. Pattabhirama Temple at Ramanathapura near Krishna-rajpet (Mandya)
132. Pattadakal Temples at Pattadakal near Dharwar

133. Ramalinga Swamy Temple at Avani (Mulbagal) near Kolar

134. Ramanatheshwar Temple at Ramanathapura near Krishnarajpet (Mandya)

135. Rameswara Temple at Agara (Yelandur) near Mysore

136. Ranganatha Nagareshwara Temple at Bankapura near Hubli

137. Ranganatha Temple at Anegondi near Hospet

138. Ranganatha Temple at Srirangapattana near Mysore

139. Ranganna Temple at Biligiri Rangan Hills near Mysore

140. Sadasiva Temple at Nuggihalli near Tiptur

141. Sangameshwara Temple at Kaginelli (Haveri) near Dharwar

142. Sangameshwara Temple at Mekedatu near Bangalore

143. Sankareshwara Temple at Near Belur near Hassan

144. Santemallappa Temple at Oderhalli near Chiknayakan-halli

145. Savati Ghandavarana Basti at Chandragiri Hill near Hassan

146. Shankaranarayana Temple at Shankaranarayana (Agumbe) near Shimoga

147. Shantinatha Basti at Sravanabelagola near Hassan

148. Shantinatha Jinalaya at Jinanathapura near Hassan

149. Shatrughneshwara Temple at Avani (Mulbagal) near Kolar

150. Shiva Temple at Paparajanhalli near Kolar

151. Siddhadeva Temple at Haveri near Dharwar

152. Siddheshwara Temple at Bankapura near Hubli

153. Someshwara Temple at Suttur (Nanjangud) near Mysore

154. Someshwara Temple at Lakshmeshwar near Hubli

155. Someshwara Temple at Gadag near Dharwar

156. Someshwara Temple at Hale Budanur near Mandya

157. Someshwara Temple at Kurudumale near Kolar

158. Someshwara Temple at Kunigal (Tumkur) near Bangalore

159. Someshwara Temple at Magadi near Bangalore

160. Someshwara Temple at Husigala (Hosakote) near

161. Someshwara Temple at Kaginelli (Haveri) near Dharwar

162. Someshwara Temple at Kolar

163. Someshwara Temple at Haranhalli (Arsikere) near Hassan

164. Soumyakesava Temple at Nagamangala near Mandya

165. Gomateswara Temple at Sravanabelagola near Mysore

166. Srikanteswara Temple at Nanjangud near Mysore

167. Sripathishwara Temple at Seethi near Kolar

168. Subramanya Temple at Subramanya near Mangalore

169. Suryanarayana Temple at Lakkundi (Gadag) near Dharwar

170. Talakad Vaidyeswara Temple at Talakad near Mysore

171. Terina Basti Jinalaya at Sravanabelagola near Hassan

172. The Bull Temple at Bangalore

173. Tiru Narayana Temple at Melkote near Krishnarajpet (Mandya)

174. Tirumulasthanam Udayar Templ at Hale Arur (Chamrajnagar) near Mysore

175. Trikuteshwara Temple at Gadag near Dharwar

176. Trinishwara Temple at Mysore

177. Vaidyeswara Temple at Mambali (Yelandur) near Mysore

178. Varahaswamy Temple at Mysore

179. Veeraanjaneya Swamy Temple at Mulbagal near Kolar

180. Veerabhadra Temple at Chikballapur near Kolar

181. Venkataramanaswamy Temple at Guttahalli near Kolar

182. Venkatramana Temple at Chiknayakanhalli near Tumkur

183. Venugopalaswamy Temple at Devanhalli near Bangalore

184. Vidyashankara Temple at Sringeri near Mangalore

185. Vijayendra Temple at Bethamangala (Mulbagal) near Kolar

186. Vira Narayana Temple at Gadag near Dharwar

187. Vira Narayana Temple at Belur near Hassan

188. Virabhadra Temple at Kaginelli (Haveri) near Dharwar

189. Virabhadra Temple at Halebidu near Hassan

190. Virabhadra Temple at Savandrurga near Bangalore

191. Virupaksha Temple at Virupakshipura (Mulbagal) near Kolar

192. Virupaksha Temple at Hampi near Hospet

193. Vithala Temple at Hampi near Hospet

194. Yoga Narasimha Temple at Tonnur (Melkote) near Krishnarajpet (Mandya)

195. Yoga Narasimha Temple at Melkote near Krishnarajpet (Mandya)

196. Yoga Narasimha Temple at Mudgere near Chikmagalur

Appendix 11

Temples in Indo Gangetic Plains

1. Amarnath Cave Temple at Pahalgam near Srinagar in Jammu & Kashmir: A long and arduous trek takes thousands of pilgrims to this ancient shrine each year where Shiva is worshipped as a natural lingam of ice

2. Anjana Devi Temple at Haridwar in Uttar Pradesh: Located on top of a hill near Haridwar

3. Annapurna Temple at Uttar Kashi in Uttar Pradesh

4. Annapurna Temple at Haridwar in Uttar Pradesh

5. Ardhanari Temple at Mandi in Himachal Pradesh: A modern temple with a rare Ardhanari image with carvings of high order

6. Badrinarayan Temple at Badrinath in Uttar Pradesh: One of the most revered shrines in the country, Badrinath is a well visited Himalayan shrine on the banks of the river Alkananda at a height of 11, 400 ft above sea level.

7. Baijnath Temple at Baijnath near Dharmshala in Himachal Pradesh: A very ancient stone temple with intricate sculptural work-dedicated to Shiva.

8. Bajreswari Temple at Kangra near Dharmsala in Himachal Pradesh: Large temple with lofty towers dedicated to Devi worshipped as a lingam. The Guptganga ghats are a km away from the temple.

9. Balaji Temple at Rishikesh in Uttar Pradesh: Modern temple built in the South Indian style.

10. Bharat Mata Temple at Shanti Kunj near Haridwar in Uttar Pradesh: A modern temple housing images of several deities, religious leaders and national heros portraying unity in diversity inaugurated by the late Prime Minister Indira Gandhi.

11. Bharatji Mandir at Rishikesh in Uttar Pradesh: Oldest temple in Rishikesh dedicated to MahaVishnu.

12. Bijli Mahadev Temple at Bijli Mahadev near Kullu in Himachal Pradesh: Ancient Shiva temple accessible only by foot 11 km away from Kullu. Known for its lightning conducting flag staff.

13. Bisheshar Mahadev Temple at Kullu in Himachal Pradesh: A large stone monument with beautiful icons and carvings.

14. Chandi Devi Temple at Chandi Parvat near Haridwar in Uttar Pradesh: Located on a hill near Haridwar.

15. Chandra Mowliswara Temple at Rishikesh in Uttar Pradesh: Modern temple built in the South Indian style.

16. Chintpurni Temple at Chintpurni near Jwalamukhi in Himachal Pradesh: A revered Shakti shrine where the Goddess is worshipped in the form of a stone lingam.

17. Daksh Mahadev Temple at Kangal near Haridwar in Uttar Pradesh: A temple said to be the site of a yagna conducted by Daksha according to Hindu mythology.

18. Ganga Mata Temple at Gangotri in Uttar Pradesh

19. Gaurishankar Temple at Jagatsukh near Manali in Himachal Pradesh: A small shikhara temple excavated and discovered in this century.

20. Gayatri Temple at Jagatsukh near Manali in Himachal Pradesh: Ancient temple with intricate woodwork with modern marble image of Gayatri.

21. Gayatri Temple at Shanti Kunj near Haridwar in Uttar Pradesh: 24 images of Gayatri near the Saptarishi Ashram, with yantras-on the banks of the Ganges.

22. Gurdwara Guru Gobind Singh at Mandi in Himachal Pradesh: A gurdwara constructed by the side of a rock where Guru Gobind Singh meditated.

23. Hidimba Devi Temple at Manali in Himachal Pradesh: Ancient cave temple celebrating Hidimba of Mahabharata with intricately carved wooden doors and a wooden shikhara.

24. Jwalamukhi Temple at Jwalamukhi in Himachal Pradesh: One of the revered Shakthi Peeths in India, where the mother Goddess is worshipped in the form of an undying flame.

25. Kalbhairav Temple at Haridwar in Uttar Pradesh

26. Kamleshwar Mahadeo Temple at Srinagar inUttar Pradesh

27. Karna Temple at Karna Prayag near Joshi Math in Uttar Pradesh: A temple dedicated to Karna one of the heroes of the epic Mahabharata.

28. Kedarnath Temple at Kedarnath in Uttar Pradesh: One of the 12 Jyotirlingams in India and an important center for pilgrms all over India in the lofty Himalayas, it is accessed only after a long trek. Kedarnath, Madhya Maheshwar, Rudranath, Tunganath and Kalpeswar constitute the Panch (5) Kedar shrines.

29. Khir Bhavani Temple at Tulamulla near Srinagar in Jammu & Kashmir: Bhavani is worshipped here in the form of a stone lingam, in a small shrine in the middle of a tank.

30. Krishna Mandir at Mandi in Himachal Pradesh: A 17th century temple with a silver idol of Krishna.

31. Maansa Devi Temple at Haridwar in Uttar Pradesh: A white temple with a spire on the Vilvparvat hill accessible by a motor winch.

32. Maha Saraswathi Temple at Krall near Ramban in Jammu & Kashmir: Modern temple in the Dravidian style commemorating the time immemorial shrine to Saraswathi in the Kashmir area, now in ruins.

33. Manikaran temple at Manikaran near Kulu in Himachal Pradesh: This town known for its hot springs houses a very ancient temple dedicated to Shiva

34. Mata Maheshwar Temple at Gupt Kashi in Uttar Pradesh: A temple dedicated to Ardhnarishwar.

35. Nandikeshwar Temple at Chamunda near Dharmsala in Himachal Pradesh: A center for Shakti worship housing Chamunda and Nandikeshwar, on the banks of the river Banganga.

36. Narasimhaswami Temple at Joshi Math in Uttar Pradesh: Narasimha worshipped as a Saligrama stone, said to be installed by the religious leader Adi Sankara in the past millennium.

37. Neelkanth Mahadeo Temple at Nilkanth Mahadeo near Rishikesh in Uttar Pradesh: Shiva temple at a height of 5000 ft above sea leve.

38. Raghunath Temple at Jammu in Jammu & Kashmir: This is one of the most important of the several temples in Jammu. The walls around the central shrine are adorned with the incarnations of Vishnu.

39. Raghunathji Temple at Vasishta near Manali in Himachal Pradesh: Located on the banks of the Beas river with adjoining hot springs.

40. Triyugi Narayan Temple at Triyugi Narayan near Gupt Kashi in Uttar Pradesh: Temple dedicated to Shiva,

Parvati and Narayan where an undying flame is the object of interest and worship.

41. Vaishnao Devi Temple at Vaishnao Devi in Jammu & Kashmir: Scores of pilgrims undertake a trek to this temple located 55 km away from Jammu.

42. Vasisht Temple at Vasishta near Manali in Himachal Pradesh: Located on the banks of the Beas river with adjoining hot springs.

43. Vishwanath Temple at Uttar Kashi in Uttar Pradesh

44. Vishwanath Temple at Gupt Kashi near Gupt Kashi inUttar Pradesh

Appendix 12

Temples in Western India

1. Achaleshwar Mahadeo Temple at Achalgarh near Mt. Abu in Rajasthan: Shiva temple featuring an image of the toe of Shiva and a brass Nandi.

2. Achalgarh Jain Temples at Achalgarh near Mt. Abu in Rajasthan: Colorful Jain temples with great views.

3. Adbudji Jain Temple at Nagada near Udaipur in Rajasthan: Ruined temple with interesting architectural features, a black marble statue of Shanti Nath dating back to the 15th century.

4. Adhar Devi Temple at Mt. Abu in Rajasthan: Durga temple in rock cleft near Mt. Abu.

5. Adinath (Jain Temple) at Rikhabdeo near Udaipur in Rajasthan: Ancient temple (15th century) with elegant architecture.

6. Adiswara temple at Palitana in Gujarat: Most notable temple in the Shatrunjaya Jain Temple complex of 863 temples on a hill.

7. Amar Sagar Jain Temple at Amar Sagar near Jaisalmer in Rajasthan: Beautifully carved temple under renvoation.

8. Amba Mata Temple at Junagadh in Gujarat: Located on top of the 600 meter high Girnar Hill.

9. Ambika Mata Temple at Jagat near Udaipur in Rajasthan: 10th century temple dedicated to Ambika.

10. Arbada Mata Temple at Eklingji near Udaipur in Rajasthan: Located in Eklingji home to the famous Eklingji temple.

11. Atri Rishi Temple at Guru Shikhar near Mt. Abu in Rajasthan: On top of the 5300 ft high hill the Guru Shikhar the loftiest point in Rajasthan.

12. Balaji Temple at Bharatpur near Jaipur in Rajasthan

13. Baroli Temples at Baroli near Kota in Rajasthan: One of the oldest temple complexes (9th century AD) in Rajasthan.

14. Bhand Sagar Jain Temples at Bikaner in Rajasthan: 16th century temples dedicated to Adinath and Parasvanath.

15. Bhrama Temple at Pushkar near Ajmer in Rajasthan: Only one of its kind Bhrama temple with a red spire.

16. Bhrigu Rishi Temple at Broach in Gujarat: City name Bharuch derived from Bhrigukachba after this temple.

17. Bijolia Temples at Bijolia near Bundi in Rajasthan: A complex of ancient temples once numbering 100, now just 3.

18. Chamunda Temple at Jodhpur in Rajasthan: Durga temple located in the Meherangarh Fort in Jodhpur.

19. Chaumukh Temple at Palitana in Gujarat: Adinath temple in the Shatrunjaya Jain Temple complex of 863 temples on a hill.

20. Chaumukha Temple at Ranakpur near Udaipur in Rajasthan: Huge marble 15th century Jain temple with 29 halls, 1444 pillars, no two alike. Temple is located in the Ranakpur Temple complex.

21. Chintamani Temple at Bikaner in Rajasthan: Part of the Bhand Sagar Temple complex.

22. Durgiana Temple at Amritsar in Punjab: 16th century Durga Temple.

23. Dwarakadish Temple at Kankroli near Udaipur in Rajasthan: Similar to the Nathdwara temple at Nathdwara.

24. Dwarkanath Temple at Dwarka in Gujarat: One of the holiest Hindu temples dedicated to Krishna with a 5 storey spire and 60 columns.

25. Eklingji Temple at Eklingji near Udaipur in Rajasthan: Ornate 8th century Shiva temple with beautiful pillars.

26. Gaumukh Temple at Gaumukh Temple near Mt. Abu in Rajasthan: Associated with the mythological sage Vasishta.

27. Gopinath Temple at Bhangarh near Alwar in Rajasthan: Abandoned beautiful yellow stone carved temple on a 14 ft high platform, with intricate sculptural work.

28. Hanuman Temple at Bhangarh near Alwar in Rajasthan

29. Har Mandir Shiva Temple at Bikaner in Rajasthan: Located in the Junagarh Fort at Bikaner.

30. Harshat Mata Temple at Abhaneri near Jaipur in Rajasthan: Known for sculptural remains of the post Gupta period monuments of the 9th century AD.

31. Hathee Singh Temple at Ahmedabad in Gujarat: 19th century marble Jain temple dedicated to Dharamanath.

32. Jagdish Temple at Udaipur in Rajasthan: Grand 17th century temple to Vishnu located near Udaipur city palace.

33. Jain Temples at Jaisalmer in Rajasthan: 12th-15th century Jain temples dedicated to Rikhabdevji and Sambhavanthji.

34. Jaisalmer Shiva Temple at Jaisalmer in Rajasthan: Located in the Jaisalmer fort along with a Ganesh Temple.

35. Kailashpuri Temple Ruins at Eklingji near Udaipur in Rajasthan: Ruins of Shiva and Vishnu temples in Eklingji known for the Eklingji temple.

36. Kali Temple at Amber near Jaipur in Rajasthan: Temple located in the fortress palace in Ambar (16th century AD).

37. Kalika Mata Temple at Chittorgarh in Rajasthan: An 8th century Sun temple converted to Kali temple in the Chittorgarh Fort near the Padmini palace.

38. Karni Mata Temple at Deshnok near Bikaner in Rajasthan: Marble carvings and a silver door adorn this temple where rats are cared for.

39. Kiradu Temples at Kiradu near Barmer in Rajasthan: 11th century Kathiawar style temples with Gupta elements.

40. Krishna Temple at Jaisalmer in Rajasthan: Temple near the arched gateway to the Gadi Sagar Water Tank.

41. Krishna Temples at Bet Island near Dwarka in Gujarat: Modern Krishna Temples in this island near Dwarka.

42. Kumar Shah Temple at Palitana in Gujarat: One of the temples in the Shatrunjaya Jain Temple complex of 863 temples on a hill.

43. Kumbha Shyam Temple at Chittorgarh in Rajasthan: Large temple in the Chittorgarh Fort.

44. Laxmi Narayan Temple at Amritsar in Punjab: Laxmi and Narayan temple built in the middle of a lake.

45. Lodruva Jain Temples at Lodruva near Jaisalmer in Rajasthan: Ornate temples with arches in the ruins of an ancient capital.

46. Mahamandir Shiva Temple at Mahamandir near Jodhpur in Rajasthan: A 100 pillared Shiva Temple.

47. Mallinath Temple at Junagadh in Gujarat: Marble temple on Girnar Hill along with 4 other Jain temples dating back to the 12th century.

48. Mat Bhavani Temple at Ahmedabad in Gujarat: Associated with the Mat Bhavani step well.

49. Meera Temple at Chittorgarh in Rajasthan: Ornate temple located in the Chittorgarh fort.

50. Menal Shiva Temples at Menal near Bundi in Rajasthan: A complex of Shiva temples from the Gupta period.

51. Nasiyan Temple (Red Temple) at Ajmer in Rajasthan: Century old Jain temple with wooden figures.

52. Nathdwara at Nathdwara near Udaipur in Rajasthan: 19th century temple bearing image of Vishnu brought from Mathura in the 17th century.

53. Neelkanth Mahadev Temple at Chittorgarh in Rajasthan: Temple located near Padmini's palace of the Chittorgarh fort.

54. Neminath Temple at Ranakpur near Udaipur in Rajasthan: Jain Temple located in the Ranakpur Temple complex.

55. Nemintah Temple at Junagadh in Gujarat: 12th century marble Jain temple along with 4 other Jain temples on Girnar hill.

56. Osian Temples at Osian near Jodhpur in Rajasthan: Ruins of 16 Hindu and Jain temples from the 8th to 11th centuries in this town inhabited by hundreds of peacocks.

57. Parasnath Temple at Ranakpur near Udaipur in Rajasthan: Jain Temple located in the Ranakpur Temple complex.

58. Ramgarh Temples at Ramgarh near Kota in Rajasthan: Accessed by jeep.

59. Ranchodrai Temple at Dakor near Baroda in Gujarat: Krishna temple famous for the Shard Purnima festival in Oct-Nov.

60. Rangji Temple at Pushkar near Ajmer in Rajasthan: An important temple in the temple town of Pushkar.

61. Rathasan Devi Temple at Eklingji near Udaipur in Rajasthan: Rashtrasena Devi temple in Eklingji known for the famous Eklingji temple.

62. Sammidheshwar Temple at Chittorgarh in Rajasthan: Temple located in the Rana Kumbha palace of the Chittorgarh fort.

63. Sampriti Raj Temple at Palitana in Gujarat: One of the temples in the Shatrunjaya Jain Temple complex of 863 temples on a hill.

64. Sanganer Jain Temples at Sanganer near Jaipur in Rajasthan: A group of Jain temples with fine carvings.

65. Sas Bahu Temple at Eklingji near Udaipur in Rajasthan: A complex of temples with fine carvings, dating back to the 11th century.

66. Sharda Pith Temple at Pilani in Rajasthan: Modern marble temple of learning at the Birla Institute of Technology and Science.

67. Shatrunjaya Temple Complex at Palitana near Bhavnagar in Gujarat: Jain Temple Complex of over 863 temples on a 600 meter high hill built over 900 years.

68. Shiva Temple at Chittorgarh in Rajasthan: Temple located in the Rana Kumbha palace of the Chittorgarh fort.

69. Sidhpur Temple Ruins at Sidhpur near Ahmedabad in Gujarat: Near the Mehsana the drop off point for Modhera.

70. Sila Devi (White Marble) Temple at Amber near Jaipur in Rajasthan: Temple located in the fortress palace in Ambar (16th century AD).

71. Singa Chowri Jain Temple at Chittorgarh in Rajasthan: Located in the Chittorgarh Fort.

72. Sirsa Mata Temple at Bhangarh near Alwar in Rajasthan

73. Someshwar Mahadev Temple at Bhangarh near Alwar in Rajasthan: Shiva temple with a grand lingam (marble) in the abandoned Rajput settlement.

74. Somnath Temple at Somnath Patan near Veraval in Gujarat: One of the 12 Jyotirlingams in India, and an ancient temple, current structure belongs to this century.

75. Soyalla Shiva Temple at Soyala near Jodhpur in Rajasthan: 75 km from Jodhpur on the Nagaur Road.

76. Sun Temple at Ranakpur near Udaipur in Rajasthan: Temple is located in the Ranakpur Temple complex.

77. Sun Temple at Galta near Jaipur in Rajasthan: A temple built on a hill dedicated to Surya.

78. Sun Temple at Modhera near Ahmedabad in Gujarat: Ruins of well known 11th century temple intricately sculpted.

79. Sun Temple at Somnath Patan near Veraval in Gujarat: Ancient temple with interesting sculpture. dating back to the period of the Somnath temple, near a rebuilt Somnath temple of the Ahilyabai Holkar period.

80. Surya (Sun) Temple at Jhaira Patan near Kota in Rajasthan: Ruins of an ancient temple.

81. Swami Narayan Temple at Ahmedabad in Gujarat: 19th century temple enclosed in a large courtyard.

82. Takteshwar Temple at Bhavnagar in Gujarat: Hill top temple with great views.

83. Talaja Jain Temples at Talaja near Bhavnagar in Gujarat: Complex of Jain temples on a hill

84. Tejpal (Dilwara) Temple at Mt. Abu in Rajasthan: Jain Temple (Neminath) with intricate marble carvings in the Dilwara Temple group.

85. The Golden Temple at Amritsar in Punjab: The holiest Sikh shrine in India housing the original Granth Sahib.

86. Vimal Shah Temple at Palitana in Gujarat: One of the temples in the Shatrunjaya Jain Temple complex of 863 temples on a hill.

87. Vimal Vasahi (Dilwara) Temple at Mt. Abu in Rajasthan: Jain temple dedicated to Adhinath-Finest specimen of Jain architecture-in the Dilwara temple group.

88. Vindhyavasani Devi Temple at Eklingji near Udaipur in Rajasthan: Located in Eklingji known for its famous Eklingji temple.

Appendix 13

Temples in the North East

1. Asvakranta Temple at Guwahati in Assam: Temple with interesting carvings enshrines a reclining image of Vishnu of great workmanship.

2. Barpeta Satra at Barpeta near Guwahati in Assam: This Vaishnavite congregational site is decorated with finely engraved and painted wooden panels and ceilings.

3. Dah Parbatiya Temple at Tezpur in Assam: Ruins of the oldest and finest piece of architectural work in Assam.

4. Devi Dol Temple at Gaurisagar near Golaghat in Assam: This is a temple dedicated to Devi with interesting architectural and sculptural features.

5. Devi Temple at Shibsagar in Assam: A large temple dedicated to Devi on the banks of the Shibsagar tank.

6. Govindaji Temple at Imphal in Manipur

7. Hatimura Temple at Silghat in Assam: Mahisamardini temple, an important center of Sakti worship, a brick temple built over old stone temple ruins (17th century).

8. Hayagriva Mahadeva Temple at Hajo near Guwahati in Assam: An imposing temple with a shikhara and interesting sculptural work where the presiding deitiy is worshipped as the Man Lion incarnation of Vishnu by the Hindus and as Budha by Budhists. (Ancient temple rebuilt in the 16th century)

9. Kamakhya Temple at Guwahati in Assam: A center for Shakti worship (a Peetha), rebuilt in the 16th century-on Neelachal Hill and is a good specimen of Assamese sculptural work.

10. Kedareswara Temple at Hajo near Guwahati in Assam

11. Navagraha Temple at Guwahati in Assam: Located on Chitrachal hill and once a center for the study of astrology this temple dates back to the 17th century.

12. Negriting Temple at Shibsagar in Assam: Shiva temple dating back to the 17th century rebuilt on a hill in the 18th century. A grand temple with beautiful sculptural work.

13. Sib Dol Temple at Shibsagar in Assam: This Shiva temple on the banks of the Shibsagar Tank is an important landmark in the artistic history of Assam.

14. Sukreswara Temple at Guwahati in Assam: Said to be worshipped by Sage Sukra, this 18th century temple is said to have the largest lingam in India.

15. Sun Temple at Goalpara in Assam: A relatively modern temple enshrines a circular stone tablet with 12 Adityas with Kasyapa in the center. The Surya Pahar hill is virtually a picture gallery of archeological remains.

16. Tamresvari Temple at Sadiya in Assam: Ruins of this temple represent one of the oldest and important temples in the region-a center of tantric worship.

17. Ugra Tara Temple at Guwahati in Assam: This important Sakta shrine dates back to the 18th century.

18. Umananda Temple at Guwahati in Assam: Located on peacock island in the middle of a river accessible by ferry this 17th century temple (later rebuilt) has some fine rock cut figures.

19. Vasishtashrama Temple at Guwahati in Assam: The Shiva temple in Vasishtashrama is the last Ahom monument in the Guwahati region. (18th century)

20. Vishnu Temple at Shibsagar in Assam: A three acre temple dedicated to Vishnu on the banks of the Shibsagar tank.

Appendix 14

Temples in the East

1. Ekteshwar enshrines a temple to Shiva, in the village of Ekteshwar near Bankura.

2. Dakshineshwar in Hooghly district is known for its Kaali temple, made famous through its association with Ramakrishna Paramahamsa, the spiritual Guru of the religious leader Swami Vivekananda. Located in Calcutta, nearby is the well known Kalighat temple also dedicated to Kaali.

3. Tarakeshwar is one of the prominent pilgrimage centers in Bengal. Tarakeshwar is located near Serampore near Calcutta in Bengal.

4. Kalighat is located in the city of Calcutta on the banks of the river Hooghly (Bhagirathi). The name Calcutta is said to have been derived from the word Kalighat.

5. Syamaleshwar is located in Dantan, south of Kharagpur, on the south bound railroad to Orissa. It is located very close to the border and the temple displays a profound Oriyan Influence.

6. The Kapila muni temple at this site is a center of worship at Ganga sagar. The river Ganga which originates in the Gangotri glacier in the snow clad Himalayas, descends down the mountains, reaches the plains at Haridwar, flows through ancient

pilgrimage sites such as Benaras and Prayag, and drains into the Bay of Bengal. Sagar Island, at the mouth of the river Hooghly in Bengal (accessed from Diamond Harbor), where the Ganga breaks up into hundreds of streams, and drains into the sea, is honored as a pilgrimage site, signifying the spot where the ashes of the ancestors of Bhagiratha were purified by the waters of the Ganga. The origins of this temple are obscured in antiquity-the current structure being a recent one, housing a stone block considered to be a representation of Kapila Muni; there are are also images of Bhagiratha, Rama and Sita.

Bibliography

Inscriptions

Epigraphia Indica, 1979, Vol. III and IV, (ed) E. Hultzsch, Government of India Press, Janpath, New Delhi.

Nellore Inscription Ongole, 850-1350 A.D.in Inscriptional Glossary of Andhra Pradesh, Hyderabad, 1967, entry under, Veeramushtulu.

South Indian Inscriptions, Vol. IV, 1986, (ed) Rao Bahadur H., Krishna Sastry, Government Press, Madras, 1923. Reprint 1886, Mysore.

South Indian Inscriptions, Vol. VI, 1986, (ed) Subrahmanya Aiyyer, K.V. Government Press, Madras, 1925, Reprint 1986, Delhi.

South Indian Inscriptions, Vol. IX, (ed) Shyamsastry, R. Government Press, Madras, 1939.

South Indian Inscriptions, Vol. X, 1986, (ed) Ramayya Pantulu J. Government Press, Madras, 1948, Reprint 1986, Mysore.

South Indian Inscriptions, Vol. XIII, 1986, Chola Inscription, Delhi.

Tirumala Tirupati Devsthanam Inscriptions, Vol. II, 1933, Inscriptions of Saluva Narsimha's Time–1445-1504 (ed.)

V. Vijay Raghavacharya Mahant Devsthanam Press, Madras.

Tirumala Tirupati Devsthanam Inscriptions, Vol. III, 1935, Inscriptions of Krishna Kayas Time–1509-1531 A.D. (ed.) V. Vijay Raghavacharya Mahant Devsthanam Press, Madras.

Tirumala Tirupati Devsthanam Inscriptions, Vol. IV, 1936, Inscriptions of Achyuta Rayas Time–1530-1542 A.D., T.T.D. Press, Madras.

Temple Inscriptions of Andhra Pradesh, Vol. I, 1980, Srikakulam District, (eds.) Dr. N. Ramesan and N. Mukunda Row, Government of A.P., Hyderabad.

Tirumala Tirupati Devsthanam Epigraphical Series, Vol. II, 1998, (ed.) Sadhu Subrahmanya Sastri, T.T.D. Publication, Tirupati.

Modern Works

Aiyangar, S. Krishnaswami, 1981, *Contributions of south India to Indian culture*, New Delhi.

Ashraf, K.M. 1970, *Life and conditions of the people of Hindustan*, Munshiram Manoharlal, New Delhi.

Ashin Das Gupta, M. N. Pearson (ed), 1987, *India and the Indian Ocean* (1500-1800), Oxford University Press.

Alston, A.J. 1980, *The devotional poems of Mirabai*, Motilal Banarsidas, Delhi.

Aziz Ahmad, 1964, *Studies of Islamic culture in Indian environment*, Clarendon Press, Oxford.

Arasaratnam, Sinappa, 1994, *Maritime India in the 17th Century*, O.U.P.Delhi.

Ashin Das Gupta, Pearson, M.N. (ed), 1987, *India and the Indian Ocean* (1500-1800 A.D.), O.U.P. New Delhi.

Appadorai, A. 1936, *Economic conditions in south India* (1000-1500 A.D.) Madras University, Madras.

Appar Tevaram, 1964, Vol. 4, 5 (Tamil) Tirumurai Tarumapuram Atinam, Tarumapuram.

Basham, A.L. 1995, *The Wonder that was India*, Rupa, New Delhi.

Bandaru, Tammaiah (ed), 1962, *Palakurki Somanatha, Basavpuranam*, (Telugu), ed. Madras.

Bhattacharya, Chandra (Ed), 1995, *Vaisnavism in eastern India*, Firma K.L.M. Pvt. Ltd. Calcutta.

Bhatt, S.R. 1980, *The philosophy of Pancharatra*, Butala and Company, New Delhi.

Bhandarkar, R.G., 1913, reprt. 1983, *Vaisnavism Saivism, and minor religious systems*, Strassburg, Trukner.

Barz, Richard Keith, 1976, *The Bhakti Sect of Vallabhacarya*, Thomson Press, Faridabad.

Bhattacharya, N.N. (ed), 1988, *Medieval Bhakti Movement in India*, Munshi Manoharram, Delhi.

Bailey, C.A. 1983, *Rulers, Townsmen and Bazaars*, North Indian Society in the age of British Expansion, 1700-1879, Cambridge.

Banerjee, A.C. 1988, *The State and Society in Northern India* (1206-1526 A.D.), Bag chi and Company, Calcutta.

Bharatiya Vidya Bhawan, 1980, *"The Delhi Sultanate"*, The succession states of the Delhi Sultanate, pp.155-286. New Delhi.

Cole, W.Owen, 1984, *Sikhism and its Indian Context*, 1469-1708, D.K. Agencies, New Delhi,

Coomaraswamy, Ananda, 1997, *Hinduism and Buddhism*, Munshilal Manoharlal Publications, New Delhi.

Charlotte, Vandeville, 1974, *Kabir*, Vol. I, Oxford and Clarendon Press,

Chandra Satish, 1982, *Medieval India*, (Society, the Jagirdari crisis and the village), Munshiram Manoharlal, New Delhi.

Chandra Satish, 1988, *The 18th Century in India* (its economy, the role of the Marathas, the Jats, the Sikhs and the Afghans), K.P. Bagchi and Company, Calcutta.

Chatterjee, A.N., 1983, Sri Krsna Chaitanya: *A Historical study on Gaudiya Vaishnavism*, Associated Publishing Company, New Delhi.

Clooney, Francis X, 1994, *The art and theology of Sri vaisnava thinkers*, T.R.Publication for Satya Nilayam Publication, Madras.

Das Gupta, S.N. 1940, *A History of Indian Philosophy*, Vol. III, Cambridge Univeristy Press.

Das Gupta, S.N, 1950, *A History of Indian Philosophy*, Vol. IV. Vols, Cambridge University Press.

Das Gupta, S.N. 1955, *A History of Indian Philosophy*, Vol. V. Cambridge University Press.

Devahuti (ed), 1980, *Problems of Indian Historiography*, D.K. Publications, Delhi.

Devahuti (ed), 1980, *Bias in Indian Historiography*, D.K. Publications, Delhi.

Dabbe Vijaya and Robert Zydenbose, 1989, *"Akka Mahadevi"*, in Madhu Kishwar (ed), *Women Bhakta poets*, New Delhi.

Dehejia, Vidya, 1998, *Slaves of The lord-The Path of the Tamil saints*, Delhi.

DaYâlan, D, 1992, *Early Temples of Tamilnadu*, Delhi.

Dhavamony, Maraisusai, 1971, *Love of God according to Saiva Siddhanta*, Oxford University Press, U.K.

Embree, Ainslie, T. 1958, reprint, 1991, *Sources of Indian Tradition*, Vol. 1, From the Beginning to 1800, 2nd Edition, Viking, Penguin Books, USA.

Foster, William, 1921 (ed), *Travels in India* (1583-1619), Oxford University Press.

Gait, Edward, 1926, *A history of Assam*, 2nd Edition, Calcutta.

Ganguly, K.K. 1983, *Cultural History of Rajasthan*, Sundeep Prakashan, New Delhi.

Gopalakrishnan, R.1990, *Religion and Mysticism in the Periyapuranam*, Madras.

Gandhi, Surjit Singh, 1978, *History of the Sikh Gurus-A comparative Study*, Gurdas Kapur & Sons, Delhi.

Gavinn Flood (ed), 2003, *The Blackwell Companion to Hinduism*, Blackwell Publishing, U.K.

Gupta, Kamala, 1987, *Status of Hindu women in Northern India*, (1206-1707), Inter India Publication, New Delhi.

Grewal, J.S. and Indu Banga (ed), 1981, *Studies in Urban history*, Guru Nanak Dev University, Amritsar.

Gonda, J.1976, *Visnuism and Sivaism-a comparison*, Munshiram, Manoharlal Publishers, New Delhi.

Gupta, S.N. Das, 1955, *A History of Indian Philosophy*, Vol.V, Cambridge.

Hardy, Friedhelm, 1983, *Viraha bhakti*-the early history of Krsna devotion in south India, Oxford University Press, New Delhi.

Harendradayal, T. 1981, *Ancient cultures of India*, Delhi.

Hedoyetullah, Mohammad, 1977, *Kabir: The apostle of Hindu Muslim Unity*, Motilal Banarasidas, Delhi.

Hopkins, T. J. 1971, *The Hindu religious tradition*, California.

Habib, Mohammad, 1974, *Politics and Society in early medieval period*, Vol. I, Aligarh Muslim University.

Habib, Mohammad, 1981, *Politics and Society in early medieval period*, Aligarh Muslim University, Vol. II.

Habib, Irfan, 1963, *The agrarian system of Mughal India*, (1556-1707), Bombay.

Handoo, Chandra Kumari, 1964, *Tulsidas* (poet, saint and philosopher of 16th century, Orient longmans, London.

Hasan, S. Nurul, 1973, *Thoughts on agrarian relations in Mughal India*, People's Publishing House, New Delhi.

Ishwaran, 1983, *Religion and society among the Lingayats in South India*, Vikas, New Delhi.

Jackson J. William, 1998, *Songs of three great south Indian saints*, Oxford University Press, Delhi.

Jaffar, S.M. 1972, *Education in Muslim India*, Idarah-I-Adabiyat-I-Delhi, Delhi,

Jagadeesan, N. 1977, *History of Sri Vaishnavism in Tamil Country* (Post Ramanuja), Koodal Publishers, Madurai.

Jaggi, O.P. 1983, *Science and Technology in medieval India*, D.K.Publishers, New Delhi.

Jaggi, O.P. 1983, *Medicine in Medieval India*, D.K. Publishers, New Delhi.

Jain, Simmy, 2003, *Encyclopaedia of Women through the Ages*, (Vol. 2), Kalpaz Publications, Delhi.

Krishna Kumari, 1985, *The rule of the Chalukya Cholas in Andhra Desa*, Delhi.

Kohli, S.S. 1990, *Sikhism and Guru Granth Sahib*, National Book Shop, Delhi.

Kosambi, Damodar Dharmanand, 1962, reprint, 1998, *Myth and reality*, Popular Prakashan, Mumbai.

Kosambi, Meera (ed), 2000, *Intersections-Socio-Cultural Trends in Maharashtra*, Orient Longman Limited, New Delhi.

Krishnamoorthy, Vaidehi, 1970, *Social and economic conditions in eastern Deccan*, (1000-1250 A.D), Hyderabad.

Karmarkar A.P. and N.B. Kalamdani, 1989, *Mystic teachings of the Haridasas of Karnataka*, Dharwar.

Kamble, J.R. 1985, *Pursuit of equality in Indian history*, National Publishing house, New Delhi.

Kaul, Jayalal, 1973, *Lal Ded*, Sahitya Academy, New Delhi.

Keay, F.E, 1931, *Kabir and his followers*, Associated Press, Calcutta.

Kinsley, David, R. 1979, *The Divine Player A study of Krsna Lila*, Delhi.

Kohli, Surinder Singh, 1976, *Critical Study of the Adi Granth*, Motilal Banarsidas.

Law, Narendra Nath, 1973, *Promotion of learning in India*, (during Mohammadan rule by Mohammadans), Idarah-I-Adabiyat-I-Delhi, Delhi.

Lakshmikantam, P. (Ed), 1991, *Srinathas's, Palanati vira Charitra*, (Telugu), Hyderabad.

Lalitamba, K. 1976, *Vir Saivism in Andhra*, Guntur.

Lorenzen, David, N. (ed) (1996), *Bhakti religion in North India–* Community, Identity and Political action, (1995, State University of New York Press, Albany), reprnt. Manohar Publishers and distributers, New Delhi.

Maculiffe, Max.Arthur, 1989, *The Sikhs-Their Religion, Gurus, Sacred writings and Authors*, Cosmo Publication, New Delhi.

Macauliffe, Max.Arthur, 1909, *The Sikh Religion*, Oxford University Press.

Mulati, Leela, 1989, *The Bhakti movement and the status of woman*-The case of Virsaivism, Abhinav Publications, New Delhi.

Mc Leod, W.H, 1968, *Nanak and the Sikh Religion*, Oxford University Press. Delhi.

Mc Leod, W.H., 1976, *The Evolution of the Sikh Community*, Claredon Press, Oxford.

Mafatia, Mrudula, I, 1967, *The philosophy of Vallabhacarya*, Munshiram Manohar Lal, New Delhi.

Moreland, W.H. 1929, *Agrarian systems of Moslem India*, Cambridge University Press

Murthy, Sreenivasa, H.V.1973, *Vaisnavism of Samkardeva and Ramanuja* (A comparative study), Motilal Banarsidas, New Delhi.

Murthy, M. Chidananda 1980, "Basava and Vir Saivism in Karnataka", in S.P. Sen (ed), *Social Content of Indian Religious reforms*, Calcutta.

Misra, Rekha, 1967, *Women in Mughal India*, (1526-1748), Munshi Ram, Manohar Lal, New Delhi.

Manushi, 1989, *Women bhakti poets*, No.50, 51, 52, Manushi Trust.

Malik, S.C. (ed), 1977, *Dissent, Protest and Reform in Indian civilization*, Indian Institute of advanced Study, Simla.

Mukta, Parita, 1994, 1997, *Upholding the common Life:* The community of Meerabai, Oxford University press, Delhi.

Nandimath, S.C. 1979, *A handbook of Virsaivism*, Delhi.

Nirmala, T, 1989, *Nannechoda Kumarsambhava Pariseelamu* (Telugu), Vijaywada.

Naidu, Gopal Krishna, G.T.1979, *Lord Venkateswar and Alwars*, S.C. 1979, A handbook of Vir Saivism, Delhi.

Naqvi, H.K. 1968, *Urban Centers and industries in upper India* (1556-1803), Asia Publishing House, New York.

Narayan Das, Swami (ed) 1959, *Shri Dadu Vani*, Varanasi.

Neog, R.1965, *Shankar Deva and his times*, Gauhati University, Gauhati.

Nizami, K.A. 1956, *Studics in medieval Indian History*, Cosmopolitan Publishers, Aligarh.

Nizami, K.A.1961, reprint, 2002, *Religion and politics in India during the 13th century*, Oxford University Press, New York.

Padma, A., 2001, *The socio-cultural World of women in medieval Andhra* 11th to 13th century, Bharatiya Kala Prakashan, New Delhi.

Paul, Younger (ed), 1978, *Hinduism*, Argus communications, Niles, 1978.

Prentiss, Karen Pechilis, 1999, *The embodiment of Bhakti*, Oxford University Press, New York

Pande, Rekha, 1990, *Succession in the Delhi Sultanate*, Commonwealth Publications, New Delhi.

Pande, Susmita, 1989, *Medieval Bhakti movement*, Kusumanjali Prakashan, Meerut.

Pande, Susmita, 1982, *Birth of Bhakthi in Indian Religion and Art*, Books and Books Publishers, New Delhi.

Pal, H.B. Capt. 1974, *Historic Rajasthan*, Sagar Publications, New Delhi.

Peterson, Indira, Viswanathan, 1991, *Poems to Siva:* The Hymns of the Tamil Saints, Delhi.

Parvathamma, C., 1972, *Sociological essays on Vir Saivism*, Popular Prakashan, Bombay.

Pillai, Vaiyapuri, S. 1956, *History of Tamil Language and Literature*, Madras.

Qaisar, Ahsan Jan, 1982, *The Indian response to European Technology and Culture*, (1498-1707), Oxford University Press.

Rangaswamy, Dorai, 1958, *The Religion and Philosophy of the Tevaram*, Madras.

Rangarajan, Haripriya, 1990, *Spread of Vaishnavism in Gujarat up to AD 1600* (A study with Special reference to the iconic forms of Visnu), Somaiya Publications, Bombay.

Rangarajan, Haripriya, 1996, *Ramanuja Sampradaya in Gujarat-a historical perspective*, Somiya Publications, Bombay.

Ramaswamy, Vijaya, 1996, *Divinity and Divine, Women in Virsaivism*, Oxford Univerdity Press. Delhi.

Ranade, R.D. (1933), *Mysticism in Maharashtra*, Poona.

Rao, Hanumanth, B.S.L reprint, 1973, original 1913, *Religion in Andhra*, Guntur, Andhra Pradesh.

Rao, Hanumanth B.S.L., 1983, (Telugu), *Andhrula Charitra*, Guntur.

Ram Chandra Rao, C.V. 1985, *Administration and society of Medieval Andhra* (1038-1536 A.D.) Hyderabad.

Reddy, Soma, 1984, *History of Religious Institutions in Andhra Desa* (1300-1600 A.D.), New Era Publications, Madras.

Reddy, R. Narasimha, 1967, *Corporate life in medieval Andhradesa*, University Grants Commission, New Delhi.

Reddy, S. Pratap (Telugu), 1982, *Andhrula Sanghika Charitra*, Hyderabad, 1982.

Ray Chaudhuri and Irfan Habib, 1982, *The Cambridge economic history of India*, Vol. I (1200-1750), Orient Longman, and Cambridge Univ. Press.

Rao Venkat, Nidadavolu, 1956, *Lives of Telugu Poets*, Madras.

Rao, Gopinath T. A. 1923, *Sri Subrahmanya Ayyar: Lectures on the history of Sri Vaishnavas*, Madras.

Rangacharya, V. 1975, *Historical evolution of Sri Vaisnavismin south India*, Vol. IV (The Religions), Calcutta.

Raghavcharya, T.K.T.Vira, 1977, *History of Tirupati*, Vol.I, Tirumala Tirupati Devastanam, Tirupati.

Rastogi, T.C., 1994, *Assam Vaishnavism*, (Sociological Perspective), Omsons Publications, New Delhi.

Sastri, K. A. N. 1991, *History of South India*, Madras.

Sambandar, Tevaram, 1964, Vol. 1, 2, 3 (Tamil), Tirumurai, Tarumpuram, Atinam, Tarumapur.

Salatore, R.N, 1989, *Encyclopedia of Indian Culture*, Vol. IV, Sterling Publishers Pvt Ltd, Delhi.

Sinha, S.K. 1964, *Medieval history of the Deccan Bahmanids*, The Government of A.P. Archeological Series, Hyderabad.

Sivanand Swami, 2003, *The Bhagvat Gita*-The word to word meaning, translation and commentary, Divine Life society, Uttranchal, Himalayas.

Sachau, reprint, 1983, *Alberunis India*, Vol. 1, Chapter, II, New Delhi.

Scott, G.H, 1985, *Kabir and the Kabir Panth*, New Delhi.

Sharma, R.S. 1965, *Indian Feudalism*, c.300-1200, Calcutta.

Sharma, R.S. 1969, *Social change in early medieval India* (A.D. 500-1200), Delhi.

Shrama, R.S. 1974, *Historical Probings*, New Delhi.

Sharma, S.N. 1966, *The Neo-Vaishnavite Movement and the Satra Institution of Assam*, Gauhati University, Gauhati.

Shah, Ahmad, 1977, *The Bijak*-(or the completer works of Kabir) New Delhi.

Shulman, David Dean, 1980, *Tamil Temple Myths*, Princeton, USA.

Sivathamby, K, 1986, *Literary History in Tamil*, Thanjavur.

Shobha, Savitri Chandra, 1983, *Social life and concepts in Medieval Hindi Bhakti poetry*-A socio-cultural study, Chandrayan Publications, New Delhi.

Sastri, P.V.Parabrahma, 1978, *The Kakatiyas of Warangal*, Government of Andhra Pradesh, Hyderabad.

Saskia C. Kersen boom-Story, 1987, *Nityasumangali*, Motilal Banarsidas Delhi.

Satyanarayana, K. 1983, *A study of the history and culture of Andhra Desa*, Vol. II, New Delhi.

Sundaram, K 1968, *Studies in Social and economic conditions in Medieval Andhra Desa* (1000-1600 AD) Machilipatnam.

Surya Narayana, K. 1986, *History of minor Chalukya families in Andhra Desa*, Delhi, 1986

Sarojini Devi, Konduri, 1990, *Religion in the Vijaynagara Empire*, Sterling Publishers, New Delhi.

Sharma, B.N.K., 1960, *A history of the dvaita school of Vedanta and its literature*, Vol. 1, Bombay.

Subramanyam (ed) 1968, *Basavapuranam*, (Telugu), A.P. Sahitya Academy, Hyderabad,

Subbaiah Venkata (Ed), 1985, *Sahitya Prabandhamu*, (Telugu), Hyderabad.

Sastri, Nilkanth, K.A. 1963, *Development of religion in South India*, Madras.

Sontheimer, G.D. and Kulke (ed), 1997, *Hinduism Reconsidered*, Manohar, New Delhi.

Said, Edward, W., 1978, *Orientalism*, Routledge and Kegan Paul, London.

Sharma, Krishna, 1987, *Bhakti and the Bhakti movement*, Munshi Ram Manohar Lal, New Delhi.

Tagore, Ravindranath, 1945, *One hundred poems of Kabir*, assisted by Evelyn Underwill, India edition, Macmillan and Co. Ltd. St. Martins Street, London.

Thapar, Romila, 1973, *The Past and Prejudice*, Publication Division, Government of India, New Delhi.

Thapar, Romila, 1978, *Ancient Indian social History:* Some Interpretations, Delhi.

Thapar, Romila, 1993, *Interpreting Early India*, Oxford University Press.

Thoru, Susie, Lalitha K. (ed.) 1991, *Women writing in India*, Vol. I, Oxford University Press.

Trimingham, J. Spencer, 1971, *The Sufi orders in Islam*, Oxford University press, New York,

Tyagi, I. C. 1982, *Saivism in ancient India*, Meerut.

Tarachand, 1936, *Influence of Islam on Indian Culture*, Allahabad.

Vasu, N.N. 1922, *Social History of Kamrup*, Calcutta.

Vaidehi, Krishna Moorthy, 1970, *Social and Economic Conditions in Eastern Deccan*, (1000-1250 A.D.), Hyderabad.

Varadachari, V. 1982, *Agamas and South Indian Vaisnavism*, Prof. M.Rangacharya Memorial Trust, Madras.

Vudiville, Charlotte, 1999, *Myths, saints and legends in Medieval India*, Oxford University Press.

Vaudeville, Charlotte, 1974, *Kabir*, Vol. I, Oxford Press.

Vyas, A.U. Ramnarayan, 1977, *The Bhagavata bhakti cult and three Advaita acaryas, Sankara, Ramanuja, and Vallabha*, Nag Publishers Delhi

Vyas, Ramnarayan, 1983, *Melody of bhakti and enlightenment*, Cosmo Publications, New Delhi.

Westcott, G.H., 1953, *Kabir and Kabir Panth*, Sushil Gupta (India) Limited, Calcutta.

Weber, Max, 1958, reprint, 1967, *The Religion of India*-The sociology of Hinduism and Buddhism, tr,.by Hans H. Garth and Don Martindale, The Free Press, Macmillan Publishing House, London.

Weber, Max, 1922, reprint, 1963, *"Religion of the non-privileged classes"*, The Sociology of Religion, Beacon Press, Boston.

Yasin, Mohammad, 1958, *A social History of Islamic India*, 1605-1748 A.D. Upper India Publishing House Ltd. Lucknow.

Yazdani, G. (ed.) 1960, *Early History of the Deccan*, Oxford University Press.

Articles

Bhidwani, Bhanwar, 1975, "Economic conditions in Pargana Merta (Rajasthan) (A.D. 1658-63) in *Proceedings of Indian History Congress*, Aligarh.

Chattopadhyay, B.D. 1976, "Origin of the Rajput: The political, economic and social processes in early Medieval Rajasthan", in *Indian Historical Review*, Vol. III, No. 1, July.

Champaklaxmi, R, 2004, "From devotion and Dissent to Dominance-The Bhakti of the Tamil Alvars and Nayanars" in Lorenzen, David N. (ed), *Religious Movements in South Asia* 600-1800, Oxford University PressNew York.

Dirks, Nicholas, 1979, "Political authority and structural change in early south Indian history", *Indian Economic and Social History Review.*

Glushkova, Irina, 1996, "The concept of women in the poems of Tukaram" in Anne Feldhaus (ed) *Images of women in Maharashtrian Literature and Religion*, State University of New York Press, Albany.

Glushkova, Irina, 2000, "Norms and Values in Varkari Tradition", in Kosambi, Meera (ed), 2000, *Intersections-Socio-Cultural Trends in Maharashtra*, Orient Longman Limited, New Delhi.

Habib, Irfan, 1969, Presidential Address, Section II, "Technological change and society, 13th and 14th centuries, Varanasi Session, *Proceedings of Indian History Congress.*

Habib, Irfan, 1978, "Economic History of India", *Indian Historical Review*, Vol. IV, No. 2, Jan. pp. 289-291.

Habib, Irfan, 1980, "The economic History of Delhi Sultanate" in Devahuti (ed), *Bias in Indian Historiography*, D.K. Publication, New Delhi.

Hart, George L. 1960, "The Theory of reincarnation among the Tamils" in Wendy Doinger O'Flaherty, (ed) *Karma and Rebirth in Classical Indian Tradition*, California.

Kopf, David, 1980, "Henumeeutics versus history", *Journal of Asian Studies*, 39, 3, pp. 495-505.

Kundan, Dhar, T.N. 2004, "Saints and sages of Kashmir', in M.N. Kaw (ed), *Kashmir and its people*, A.P.H. Publishing Corporation, New Delhi.

Khan, Mohammad Ishaq, 2004, "The Rishi Movement as a social force in Medieval Kashmir", in Lorenzen, David N. (ed), *Religious Movements in South Asia*, 600-1800, Oxford University Press.

Khan, Mohammad Ishaq, 1986, "The impact of Islam on Kashmir in the Sultanate period, 1320-1586", *The Indian Economic and Social History Review*, XXIII, 2, 187-205.

Nandi, R.N. 1975, "Origin of the Vir Saiva movement", in *The Indian Historical Review*, Vol. II, No. 1.

Nandi, R.N. 1976, "Origin and nature of Saivaite Monasticism: The case of Kalamukhas" in R.S. Sharma (ed) *Indian Society: Historical probings*, Delhi.

Nagaswamy, R., 1965, "South Indian Temple as an Employer" *Indian Economic and Social History Review.*

Nagabhushanam, A., 1978, Agricultural guilds in medieval Deccan, *Proceedings of A.P. History Congress*, Vijaywada.

Pandita, K.N. 2004, "Some fallacies of Medieval Kashmir History", in, M.N. Kaw (ed), *Kashmir and its people*, A.P.H. Publishing Corporation, New Delhi.

Pande, Rekha. 1985, "The Social Context of the Bhakti movement - a study in Kabir" *Proceedings of Indian History Congress*, Amritsar.

Pande, Rekha, 1987, "The Bhakti Movement - an Interpretation" *Proceedings of Indian History Congress*, Goa.

Pande, Rekha, 1990, The socio-economic context of Sri Vaishnavism in 11th and 12th century Andhra, *Itihas*, Vol. XVI, No.1, Hyderabad.

Pande, Rekha, 1990, "The Bhakti Movement in Medieval Andhra - Problems and Perspectives" *Proceedings A.P. History Congress*, Guntur.

Pande Rekha, 1991, The bhakti movement and the status of women in 14th and 15th century, in J.P.Mishra (Ed) *Aspects of Indian history*, New Delhi.

Pande Rekha, 1992, Ramanuja and Sri Vaishnavism-some observations on its social content, in G.Kamalakar (Ed), *Vishnu in art, thought and literature*, Hyderabad.

Pande Rekha, 1993, Kabir, women, family and roles, in C.M.Agarwal (Ed), *Dimensions of Indian Womanhood*, Vol. II, Almora.

Pande, Rekha, 1998, Transition and the recreation of Patriarchal Ideology, *Journal of Historical Research*, Vol.VIII, Assam.

Pande, Rekha, 1999, Bringing in the invisible women back into history, *Adhyayan*, Vol. IX, No. 1-2.

Pande Rekha, 1999, "Women's History", in *Encyclopedia of Historians and Historical Writing*, in Fitzroy Dearborn Publishers, London.

Pande, Rekha, 2000, The Bhakti Movement-A historiographical Critique, *Journal of Historical Research*, Vol. X.

Pande, Rekha, 2000, "Women and empowerment-the issue of family", in C.M.Agarwal (Ed), *Nari-Facets of Indian womanhood*, Vol. I, Indian Publishers and Distributors, New Delhi.

Pande Rekha and A. Padma, 2000, "Property rights of women in early medieval Andhra", in C.M.Agarwal (Ed) *Nari-Facets of Indian womanhood*, Vol. II, Indian Publishers and Distributors, New Delhi.

Pande Rekha and K. Sri Lakshmi, 2000, "Temple economy, Land grants and women in 16th century Vijaynagara", in C.M.Agarwal (Ed), *Nari-Facets of Indian womanhood*, Vol. I, Indian Publishers and Distributors, New Delhi.

Pande Rekha, 2001, "The status of women in the past-some historical memories", in M.Ramakrishnayya (ed), *Historical Memories and Nation Building in India*, Book Links Corporation, Hyderabad.

Rekha, Pande, 2004, "Sir-Vaisnavism in Medieval Andhra", in Prof. V. Kishan Rao (ed), *Glimpses of our Past-Historical Researches*, in Honour of Prof. M. Radha Krishna Sarma, Published by, Felicitation committee and Department of History,Osmania University, Hyderabad.

Pande, Rekha, 2004, "At the service of the Lord-Temple Girls in Medieval deccan (11th to 17th century), *Deccan Studies*, Vol. II, No. 2, July-December.

Pande, Rekha, 2005, "Some facets of Vir Saivism aand aspects of social dynamism in Medieval Andhra Deas", in Satyanarayana And Chenna Reddy (ed), *Recent Trends in Historical Studies*, Pathak Research India Press, New Delhi.

Reddy, P. Chenna, 1986, "Privileges of guilds in medieval Andhra desa–India" *Past and Present*, Vol. III, No. 2.

Soma Reddy, 1993, Medieval Presidential Address, Proceedings of *Andhra Pradesh History Congress*, Tirupati.

Shobha, Savitri Chandra, 1976, "Two aspects of Hindu social life and thought as reflected in the works of Tulsidas", *Journal of the Economic and Social History of the Orient*, xix, pt. 1, pp.48-60.

Spencer, George.W, 1969, "Religious Networks and Royal influences in 11th century south India" *Journal of the Economic and Social History of the Orient*, Vol. XII.

Stein, Burton, 1984, "The State, The temple and Agricultural Development", in Burton Stein (Ed), *All the Kings Mana:* Papers in medieval South Indian History, New Era Publication, Madras.

Stein, Burton, 1984, "Social Mobility and Medieval South Indian Hindu Sects", in Burton Stein (Ed), *All the Kings Mana:* Papers in medieval South Indian History, New Era Publication, Madras.

Stein, Burton 1984, "The economic functions of medieval South Indian Temple", in *All the kings Mana,* Papers in medieval South Indian History, New Era Publication, Madras, 1984,

Tulpule, S.G.1992, "Tukaram: the making of a saint", in McGregor, R.S. (ed) *Devotional Lietrature in South Asia,* Cambridge University Press. U.K.

Thapar, Romila, 2004, "Imagined religious communities- Ancient history and the modern search for a hindu identity" in Lorenzen, N.David (ed), *Religious Movements in South Asia* 600-1800, Oxford University Press, New York.

Vijay Ramaswamy, Anklets on the feet: women saints in Medieval Indian Society, *Indian Historical Review,* Vol. vii.

Venkatasubramanian, T.K. 1984, "Social Roots of Tamilian Religious Ideology", *Proceedings of Indian History Congress,* Annamalai.

Yasodadevi, V., 1978, "Ramanuja and the Bhakti movement in Andhradesa,", in S.P. Sen (Ed), *The social context of Indian religious reform movement,* Calcutta.

Zvelebil, Kamil Veith, 1974, *A History of Indian Literature–* Tamil Literature, (ed) Jan Gonda, Otto Harrasowig Weisbaden, vol X.

Books in Hindi

Badathval, Pitambar Dutt, 1950, (Hindi), *Ramananda ki Hindi Racnayen,* Nagari prachar Sabha, Kasi.

Bhatti, Dev Raj Singh, 1985, *Meerabai aur unki Padavalli,* Ashok Prakashan, New Delhi.

Chaturvedi, Parshuram, 1984, *Bharatiya sahitya me bhakti-dhara*, Bharati Bhandara, Allahabad.

Dayal, Rameshwar, 1975, *Madhyayugina Krshna-bhakti parampara aura loka-samskrti*, Pandulipi Prakasana, Dilli.

Dixit, Chhote Lal, 1698, *Ramakrshna kavyetara Hindi saguna bhakti-kavya*, Bharata Prakasana Mandira, Aligarh.

Gopeswar Singh (ed), 2002, *Bhakti Aandolan Ke Samajik Aadhar*, Bharatiya Prakasan Sansthan, New Delhi.

Gupta, Asha, 1984, *Bhakti siddhanta*, Lokabharati Prakasana, Allahabad.

Kabir, Padavalli, 1946 (ed.) Ram Kumar Verma, 5 Vol., Reprint 2003, Hindi Sahitya Sammelan, Prayag, Allahabad.

Lalitavati, 1989, *Uttara Bharata mem bhakti parampara ka itihasa*, Pratika Prakasana, Agara.

Manas, Ramcharitra, 2004, Geeta Press, Gorakhpur.

Murthy, Kesav, S. 1996, *Mirabai, Akka Mahadevi aivam Andal Ka Tulnatmak Adhyan*, Annapurna Prakashan, Kanpur.

Pandey, Manage, 1993, (Hindi), *Bhakti Andolan aur Surdas Ka kavya*, Vani prakashan, New Delhi.

Pandey, Rajakisora, 1994, *Bhakti sahitya sodha prabandha vivaranika*, Bhakti Sahitya Sodha Samsthana, Haidarabad.

Puri, J.R. and Sethi, V.K.2002, *Sant Namdev*, Radha Soami Satsang Beas, Amritsar.

Raina, Krshna, 1977, *Hindi nirguna santa-kavya: darsana aura Bhakti*, Sarada Prakasana, Nai Dilli.

Raina, Krshna, 1977, *Kasmiri nirguna santa-kavya: darsham aur bhakti*, Sharda Prakshan, New Delhi.

Sharma, Suman, 1974, *Madhyakalina bhakti-andolana ka samajika vivecana*, Visvavidyalaya Prakasana, Varanasi.

Sharma, Nityanand, 1975, *Uttaramadhyakalina Hindi kavya mem bhakti ka svarupa*, Asa Prakasana Grha, Nai Dilli.

Sharma, Munshi Ram, 1979, *Bhakti ka vikasa:* Vaidika bhakti evam Bhagavata bhakti tatha Hindi ke bhaktikalina kavya mem usaki abhivyakti, Caukhamba Vidyabhavana, Varanasi.

Surdas, 1969, *Sursagar*, Kashi Nagari Pracharini Sabha, 4th edition, Kashi.

Sundar Das, Shyam (ed), 1959, *Kabir Granthavali*, Nagari Prachar Sabha, 7th edition. Kasi.

Shastri, Hans Das and Prasad, Mahabir, 1950, *Kabir Saheb Ke Bijak*, Kabir Granth Prakashan Samiti, Harak, Barabanki District, Uttar Pradesh.

Shukla, Ram Chandra, 1994, *Hindi Sahitya Ka Itihas*, Nagari Pracharini Sabha, Varanasi.

Shukla, Ramchandra, 1999, *Jayasi Granthawali-Atharth Padmavat, Akharavat aur Akhiri Kalam*, Nagiri Pracharini Sabha, Varanasi.

Verma, Ram Kumar, 1948, (Hindi) *Hindi Sahitya Ka Alochanatmak Ithihas*, 4th edition, Ram Narayan Lal, Prayag.

Vajpei, Narain Prasad, 1978, *Bhakti Kavya ki darsanika cetana*, Raja Publising House, Delhi.

Vajapeyi, Nandadulare, 1976, *Mahakavi Suradasa: Suradasa ke kavya, jivana, aura bhakti ka antaranga vivecana*, Rajakamala Prakasana, Nayi Dilli.

Yadava, Cauthirama, 1974, *Madhyakalina bhakti-kavya mem virahanubhuti ki vyanjana*, Racana Prakasana, Allahabad.

Index

C

D

E

S

T

Y